Puritans Behaving Badly

Tracing the first three generations in Puritan New England, this book explores changes in language, gender expectations, and religious identities for men and women. The book argues that laypeople shaped gender conventions by challenging the ideas of ministers and rectifying more traditional ideas of masculinity and femininity. Although the Puritans' emphasis on spiritual equality had the opportunity to radically alter gender roles, in daily practice laymen censured men and women differently – punishing men for public behavior that threatened the peace of their communities and women for private sins that allegedly revealed their spiritual corruption. In order to retain their public masculine identity, men altered the original mission of Puritanism, infusing gender into the construction of religious ideas about public service, the creation of the individual, and the gendering of separate spheres. With these practices, Puritans transformed their *errand into the wilderness* and the normative Puritan became female.

Monica D. Fitzgerald is a professor in the Justice, Community, and Leadership program at Saint Mary's College of California.

Puritans Behaving Badly

Gender, Punishment, and Religion in Early America

MONICA D. FITZGERALD

Saint Mary's College of California

CAMBRIDGE
UNIVERSITY PRESS

CAMBRIDGE
UNIVERSITY PRESS

University Printing House, Cambridge CB2 8BS, United Kingdom

One Liberty Plaza, 20th Floor, New York, NY 10006, USA

477 Williamstown Road, Port Melbourne, VIC 3207, Australia

314–321, 3rd Floor, Plot 3, Splendor Forum, Jasola District Centre, New Delhi – 110025, India

79 Anson Road, #06-04/06, Singapore 079906

Cambridge University Press is part of the University of Cambridge.

It furthers the University's mission by disseminating knowledge in the pursuit of education, learning, and research at the highest international levels of excellence.

www.cambridge.org
Information on this title: www.cambridge.org/9781108478786
DOI: 10.1017/9781108778817

First published 2020

Printed in the United Kingdom by TJ International Ltd, Padstow Cornwall

A catalogue record for this publication is available from the British Library.

ISBN 978-1-108-47878-6 Hardback

To Frank, Megan, and Matt
(my Fab Fitzs)

Contents

Figures

Tables

Acknowledgments

However much the phrase is overused, it really did "take a village" to complete this book. I am most thankful to the many librarians who assisted and guided me through this project. I am especially indebted to the librarians at the Massachusetts Historical Society; the New England Genealogical and Historical Society; the Connecticut State Library; the Congregational Library; the Boston Public Library; the Shields Library at the University of California, Davis; and Saint Mary's College of California Library. Generous grants provided by UC Davis, the Massachusetts Historical Society, and Saint Mary's College of California made my research possible. The Massachusetts Historical Society's Summer Fellowship, UC Davis Graduate Student Grant, and a Saint Mary's Provost Grant made my research possible. Through conferences, my project improved greatly, and I especially acknowledge the Western Association of Women Historians, the Front Range Early American Consortium, the Berkshire Conference of Women Historians, the Society of Early Americanists, the Omohundro Institute of Early American History and Culture, the Pacific Coast Branch of the American Historical Association, and the Colonial Society of Massachusetts. Then there are the mentors and colleagues who read conference papers and provided feedback, encouragement, and writing time – Samantha Francois, Erika Gasser, Mary Irwin, Ann Little, R. Todd Romero, Sandra Slater, John Smolenski, Jennifer Stevens, Clarence Walker, Jessica Weiss, and Marilyn Westerkamp – thank you. Many thanks to Dee Andrews, who first introduced me to the field of early American history and has continued to champion my path for the past twenty years. And so much gratitude to Alan Taylor, who took a chance on me – and that made all the difference. Thanks to my Saint Mary's village – Manisha Anantharaman, Shawny Anderson, Jennifer Heung, Molly Metherd, María Luisa Ruiz, Myrna Santiago, Tammy Spencer, Frances Sweeney, Michael Viola, and Denise Witzig – you got me through this in more ways than you can ever know. I am grateful to my publisher Deborah Gershenowitz, who patiently supported this project and to Cambridge

University Press and its team: Lisa Carter, Rachel Blaifeder and Preethi Sekar who worked diligently to get this to press.

Starting this path with young children in tow, my village of friends truly made this happen. Without Kathy, Leslie, Laurie, and Mary – first helping with the kids and, as the kids grew, being my support network, I could not have completed this project. But to Sydney Austin there are not enough thank-yous or accolades to extend. She first helped me by keeping me on track – literally sitting down with me to make sure I worked on my book – but as the project grew, so did her involvement. From storyboarding my entire book on butcher paper in her living room to becoming my line editor (she has read every version of every chapter since my dissertation days), she has been a true gift and collaborator. Thank you to my mom, who paid all my library fines as a child, who gushed with pride at whatever I did, and from whom I inherited my commitment to leave the world a better place. I wanted to write a book my mom would enjoy reading; I hope I have succeeded.

I started graduate school as a young mother, at a time when it did not feel normal, or entirely accepted, in the academy. A professor once told me I was just a "middle-class housewife exercising her brain." While there *should* be nothing wrong with middle-class housewives exercising their brains, I wanted to be a professor and a scholar of history, and that comment was meant to convey to me that I was not a "real" or "serious" scholar. I hope my book plays some small part in continuing to break down expectations based on gender. However, being in higher education for two decades, I can say that women (and mothers), especially women of color, continue to face too many barriers and challenges. We need to look seriously at how we as historians and academics can deconstruct some of the formal and informal infrastructures that impede women. The path I chose to do this as a mom was a slower road, but my children grounded me and never let me forget what was important – living by your values and principles. Thank you to my amazing children, Megan and Matt. This book grew up with them (but they matured much faster). They always had patience with my weird history stuff and (almost) always allowed us to stop at historical points of interest on road trips. As young adults forging their own paths, they give me hope, and I am proud that they are solid feminists who can call out gender bias – even in Happy Meal toys.

Most of all, I am grateful for the patience, love, encouragement, and support of my husband, Frank. On a hot August evening in 1995, after a long day of running my own daycare, I turned to him and said, "I have to go to grad school." He has never wavered in his support of my goals and dreams. We really are "Tougher than the Rest," Frankie; I love you.

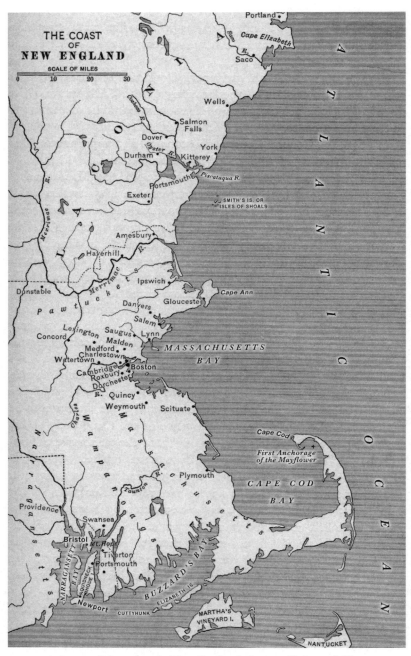

FIGURE 0.1. Map of early New England. *Source:* Universal History
Archive/Universal Images Group Editorial/Getty Images.

Introduction

Disciplining the Sinful: A Gendered Lived Religion

The gossip surrounding Content Mason and Peter Wood had circulated for years. Many thought the young widow Mason would quickly remarry. Instead, she found company with the already-married Mr. Wood. Juicy gossip surrounding their relationship turned into serious accusations once Peter's wife conspicuously left town after the birth of Content's second illegitimate child. Content realized that they had to get away. So she packed what she could from her father's house, pocketed some money, and fled with Peter. Along with all of her hurried thoughts on abandoning her home, she must have conceded that life could take unexpected turns. Thirteen years prior, in 1679, the twenty-year-old Content was just beginning her married life and settling in as a goodwife in the Massachusetts Bay town of Dorchester. Unfortunately, her husband died after only three years of marriage, leaving Content a young widow with two little children. She must have had suitors over the years, but no single man could win her hand in marriage. Rumors started to spread about exactly where her heart wandered. Things got worse when Content and Peter's wife, Abigail, both delivered sons only ten days apart, in the spring of 1688. Not until a few years later, though, with the birth of Content's second illegitimate baby, did things come to a head. That's when Abigail Wood finally left Peter and moved out of Dorchester. While mere town gossip was insufficient to mount church disciplinary procedures, this turn of events was all the evidence needed. It was part of the responsibility of Puritan congregations to reprimand their members for their sins. And so, on a hot summer Sabbath in 1692, the Dorchester

3

congregation at Meeting House Hill excommunicated the widow Mason for her "great wickedness."[1]

Content's story exemplifies the many complications of daily lived experience in Puritan New England and how Puritans created a disciplinary process to correct wayward members. This book examines church disciplinary cases such as Content's to explore how these practices impacted men, women, and Puritanism itself. If Dorchester did not excommunicate the widow Mason, who knew what could happen to its community? Excommunicating the sinful Mason would protect the community from jeopardizing the good fortune God bestowed upon it. The people could not risk God's wrath; after all, they were supposed to be a model of godly society. Puritans believed that if the church did not recover or "purge out" the sinners, the sinner could "infect" the whole community, whereupon God could send down his wrath on the town in judgment.[2] Sin had to be eradicated.

Church discipline was key to maintaining godliness. Laymen, the male members of the congregation, were charged with enforcing church discipline instead of putting it in the hands of ministers. Puritans were skeptical of allowing ministers too much control, for fear of corruption or abuse of power. As part of the Protestant revolution, Puritans did not support hierarchy and were suspicious of centralized authority. Throughout the seventeenth and early eighteenth centuries, even though each congregation had local control, most churches in Massachusetts Bay followed similar standards for censuring their members.

Congregations censured men and women for a wide variety of sinful behaviors, including dishonoring the Sabbath, child or spousal abuse, lack of deference, immodesty, absence from church, stealing, false witness, cursing, contempt for church, idleness, witchcraft, entertaining sin, lying, slander, blasphemy, fraud, fornication, and drunkenness. Censure represented the only judgment or punishment a congregation could mete out to maintain the social order; they could not fine, jail, or execute a sinner. An accused sinner could be forgiven, found innocent, admonished, suspended from the Lord's Supper, or excommunicated. An admonishment, suspension, or excommunication would hang over the sinner until the congregation determined that the sinner had adequately confessed and repented.

---

[1] *Records of the First Church at Dorchester in New England, 1636–1734 (Boston: George Ellis, 1981), 15.*

[2] For a discussion of the roots of church discipline in European Puritanism, see Amy Nelson Burnett, "Church Discipline and Moral Reformation in the Thought of Martin Bucer," *Sixteenth Century Journal* XXII (Fall 1991): 439–56; and Robert Isaac Wilberforce, *Church Courts and Church Disciplines* (London: John Murray, 1843).

Church discipline was the ecclesiastical process of monitoring behavior but also worked in conjunction with secular authorities. The church and the courts could charge an offender for the same sin, as Puritans believed civil authorities should also protect the godly way. Religious and civil leaders in New England shared ideals about Christian watchfulness, a civil government based on the word of God, and a system of censures and punishments for those who transgressed.[3] Being a "city on a hill" required vigilance.[4]

Americans have long been fascinated by the Puritans.[5] The study of New England Puritanism has gone from documenting the intellectual history of elites to examining the ordinary and the marginalized.[6] With the current scholarship exploring masculinity, femininity, and the construction of language, the Puritans still have more to teach. Examining how they coded language and developed ideas around gender reveals much about how they understood and altered their world. Exploring the Puritans through this lens will also help twenty-first-century students "read" gender in deeper ways, to acknowledge the real ways in which gender constructs and language impact our society, business, politics, and daily lived realities.

[3] David D. Hall, *The Faithful Shepherd: A History of New England Ministry in the Seventeenth Century* (Williamsburg: Institute of Early American History, University of North Carolina Press, 1972), 1, 122; Bruce C. Daniels, *The Connecticut Town: Growth and Development, 1635–1790* (Middletown: Wesleyan University Press, 1979), 65; Theodore Dwight Bozeman, *The Precisianist Strain: Disciplinary Religion and Antinomian Backlash in Puritanism to 1638* (Chapel Hill: University of North Carolina, 2004), 239–40; Kai Erikson, *Wayward Puritans: A Study in the Sociology of Deviance* (New York: Wiley, 1966), 55–58. Erikson describes the relationship between church and state that "magistrates would act as a secular arm in the service of the church ... while the ministers would provide the final authority for most questions related to long-range policy."

[4] See R. S. Dunn, James Savage, and Laetitia Yeandle, eds., *The Journal of John Winthrop, 1630–1649* (Cambridge: Belknap Press of Harvard University Press, 1996). John Winthrop recorded his speech on the *Arabella*, describing the mission of the colony to be an example for all. "City on a hill" was his explanation of how Massachusetts Bay was supposed to be an example of a godly society for England. The leaders believed that they needed to show a corrupt England how a Christian society should operate. See also Edmund S. Morgan, *The Puritan Dilemma: The Story of John Winthrop* (Boston: Little Brown, 1958).

[5] See George Selement, *Keepers of the Vineyard: The Puritan Ministry and Collective Culture in Colonial New England* (Lanham: University Press of America, 1984), 3. In his introduction, Selement details that over 1,000 pieces have been written about the Puritans since Perry Miller.

[6] For example, Perry Miller, *The New England Mind: The Seventeenth Century* (Cambridge: Harvard University Press, 1939); David D. Hall, *Worlds of Wonder, Days of Judgment: A Popular Religious Belief in Early New England* (New York: Alfred A. Knopf, 1989); and Ruth Wallis Herndon, *Unwelcome Americans: Living in the Margins in Early New England* (Philadelphia: University of Pennsylvania Press, 2001).

The Puritan movement was the result of English challenges to the Catholic Church. The English Reformation began in 1534, when King Henry VIII issued the Act of Supremacy, which severed ties with the Catholic Church and proclaimed the king as the head of the Church of England. However, the Church of England retained many of the Catholic rituals and ceremonies. Once Henry VIII had the Bible translated into English, laypeople had access to its teachings, and some began calling for further reform. When Queen Mary ascended to the throne in 1553, she briefly returned Catholicism to England, executing Protestants and forcing the reformers to flee. When "Bloody Mary" died in 1558, the Protestant Queen Elizabeth succeeded her. The reformers returned to England, but to keep peace, Elizabeth limited changes to the Church of England.

It was during this time that critics coined the moniker "Puritan" to describe those reformers who wanted to rid the church of any sign of popish practices. English Puritans fought the corruption they saw in ceremonies, inept clergy, and open church membership. They believed the primary function of a church was to instruct people in the word of God as revealed in the scriptures. They countered the hierarchy of the bishops by arguing that individual congregations should have their own authority and choose their own ministers and elders. They decided that congregations should be joined together in an association of brotherly communion.[7] Puritans believed in the congregational way of church membership, which required individuals to have a conversion experience before they became full members, or visible saints. They affirmed that discipline was central to enforcing their virtuous standards. However, they did not arrive with a clear vision of how to institutionalize their religious expression. Different forms of Puritanism competed for primacy as they worked through how to establish and run a godly society.

In 1630 Puritans began migrating to New England in order to put their ideas into practice. Each congregation formed their own covenant, or social contract, that bound individuals together. A town's covenant firmly established its commitment to follow God's law in all civic, religious, and private matters. All members who signed the covenant pledged themselves to the community. The godly community subsumed all individual piety and service for the greater good.

A recent scholarly debate has revolved around the name "Puritan." At the time, critics belittling the movement developed the label "Puritans"

---

[7] Edmund S. Morgan, *Visible Saints: The History of a Puritan Idea* (Ithaca: Cornell University Press, 1963), 12.

because of its call for a pure church. In the early seventeenth century, elite ministers who helped define the movement called themselves the "United Brethren," which formed a union between the Presbyterians and the "Congregational way."[8] Yet the average brother or sister of the movement would not have referred to themselves as part of the "United Brethren." That term more aptly describes clerical ideology and development. Puritans referred to themselves simply as Christians, or the "godly." Historian Theodore Dwight Bozeman argues that the term Puritan should be used to describe this religious movement. He explains that the term "illustrates an obsessive trait of the quest for further reformation: a hunger for purity."[9] Bozeman emphasizes that Boston's famed Puritan minister, John Cotton, celebrated "the name of Puritans as the name of purity" in his writing.[10] Historian Charles Cohen is also in favor of the term, as Puritan describes "the people who looked with distress on the condition of their church and who covenanted together in groups of self-professed godly souls to reform what they considered an intolerable string of abuses."[11] Cohen asserts that the term Puritan is useful because it describes a "hotter sort" of Protestant: they were more zealous and determined than some of their counterparts. Part of the Reformed orthodoxy, this particular movement would get lost among the other religious groups if historians simply referred to them as Protestants or Reformed Protestants. Cohen argues that we "cannot lump together all English Protestantism." Protestant religious movements may have shared a certain set of beliefs, but they differed on how to interpret and implement these beliefs.[12]

In seventeenth-century Puritan writing, men and women expressed the centrality of their spiritual beliefs. The first female poet published in the colonies, Anne Bradstreet, illuminated many of the Puritan concepts familiar in American history:

> My soul, rejoice thou in thy God,
> Boast of Him all the day,
> Walk in His law, and kiss His rod
> Cleave close to Him always...

---

[8] Cotton Mather, *Magnalia Christi Americana, or the Ecclesiastical History of New England*, vol. I. 2 vols. (Hartford: Silas Andrus & Son, 1855), 272.

[9] Bozeman, *The Precisianist Strain*, 3.

[10] Bozeman, *The Precisianist Strain*, 214.

[11] Charles Lloyd Cohen, *God's Caress: The Psychology of Puritan Religious Experience* (New York: Oxford University Press, 1986), 4.

[12] Cohen, *God's Caress*, 7.

Thy tears shall all be dried up,
Thy sorrows all shall fly,
Thy sins shall ne'er be summoned up
Nor come in memory.

Then shall I know what Thou hast done
For me, unworthy me,
And praise Thee shall ev'n as I ought
For wonders that I see.

Base world, I trample on thy face,
Thy glory I despise,
No gain I find in ought below,
For God hath made me wise.

Come Jesus quickly, Blessed Lord.
Thy face when shall I see?
O let me count each hour a day
'Till I dissolved be.

Anne Bradstreet ("Meditation," no date)

Bradstreet rejected worldly interests for the promise of heavenly rewards and expressed her unworthiness of the favors God bestowed on her. She pined for the day her soul would reunite with God. Like her Puritan sisters and brothers, Bradstreet expressed a spiritual energy and commitment that would come to define the first three generations in New England.

Despite a common set of beliefs and principles expressed in Puritan theology and covenants, Puritans themselves were not of one religious mind that emanated from the clergy. In practice, Puritans understood religion in diverse ways that combined clerical and popular thinking.[13] Disagreements surfaced over membership, voting, and baptism, among other things. Towns and congregations developed some patterns and practices that differed from others, yet the versions of this movement that maintained religious authority over most of New England for three generations shared more in common than not. Because of their similarities, comparing their disciplinary actions makes it possible to see gendered patterns.

As Puritans founded New England, they also brought with them an unsettled gender system created by a changing European religious and cultural landscape. New ideas of spiritual equality, a spiritualized

---

[13] See David D. Hall, "Narrating Puritanism," in *New Directions in American Religious History*, ed. D. G. Hart and Harry S. Stout (New York: Oxford University Press, 1997), 70.

household, and marriage and family had the potential to undermine traditional authority.[14] Thus, they began their holy experiment with an untried religious prescript for running a commonwealth and a gender system challenged by the same religious and cultural energies that led to the Reformation. The lack of entrenched social institutions, combined with New World surroundings, led to family structures that loosened restrictions on women and tempered masculinity. This new world demanded more from both men and women. It required partners to handle business affairs, wives to run households and barter wares, and mothers to tend to neighbors and educate their children in moral virtue. Men had to head their families, run their farms and businesses, and safeguard their communities and churches. Puritanism mandated a tempered, sober, family-centered man, which conflicted with a more traditional masculinity of power and virility. It was a complex, changing gender system with the opportunity to significantly alter gender roles.[15]

---

[14] Historians debate whether the new ideas of marriage and a spiritualized household gave women more power in the home or increased patriarchal authority. For a discussion of the concept of a spiritualized household and new ideas about marriage, see Margo Todd, "Humanists, Puritans, and the Spiritualized Household," *Church History* 49 (March 1980): 18–34; Ian MacLean, *The Renaissance Notion of Woman: A Study in the Fortunes of Scholasticism and Medical Science in European Intellectual Life* (New York: Cambridge University Press, 1980); Keith Moxey, *Peasants, Warriors, and Wives: Popular Imagery in the Reformation* (Chicago: University of Chicago Press, 1989); and Edward Muir and Guido Ruggiero, *Sex and Gender in Historical Perspective* (Baltimore: Johns Hopkins University Press, 1990). For a discussion of the notion of spiritual equality in Protestant thought, see E. Jane Dempsey Douglass, *Women, Freedom, Calvin* (Philadelphia: Westminster Press, 1985); Mary Potter, "Gender Equality and Gender Hierarchy in Calvin's Theory," *Signs* 11, no. 4 (1986): 735–39; and Kathleen M. Davies, "The Sacred Condition of Equality: How Original Were Puritan Doctrines of Marriage?" *Social History* 2, no. 5 (1977): 563–79.

[15] Radical Protestant groups, such as Quakers, embraced the notion of spiritual equality and gave women access to leadership roles and power in the church. Puritan women did not gain such formal powers. See Mary Maples Dunn, "Saints and Sisters: Congregational and Quaker Women in the Early Colonial Period," *American Quarterly* 3, no. 5, Special Issue: Women and Religion (1978): 233–59; Phyllis Mack, *Visionary Women: Ecstatic Prophecy in Seventeenth-Century England* (Berkeley: University of California Press, 1992); Barry Levy, *Quakers and the American Family: British Settlement in the Delaware Valley* (New York: Oxford University Press, 1988); and Marilyn Westerkamp, *Women and Religion in Early America, 1600–1850* (New York: Oxford University Press, 1999). Not all radical Protestant groups enabled women to take equal roles in the church or social life. For a discussion of an Anabaptist group, the Hutterites, see Wes Harrison, "The Role of Women in Anabaptist Thought and Practice: The Hutterite Experience of the Sixteenth and Seventeenth Centuries," *Sixteenth Century Journal* XXIII, no. 1 (1992): 49–69.

Puritan theology added fuel to the contested gender fires with the radical Protestant ideas of a feminized spirituality and all souls being equal.[16] In striving to create a godly social order, New England ministers preached a doctrine of piety and communal devotion for all its members to follow equally. The concept of spiritual equality led Puritans to have the same requirements for men and women regarding church membership, baptism, admittance to the Lord's Supper, conversion, and church attendance. Yet laymen's ideas about gender influenced the "lived" religion experienced by men and women. Disciplinary cases reinforced a gendered piety, as laymen controlled censures and did not necessarily conform to the mandates of a feminized religion.

This study responds to several currents in the recent scholarship on Puritans. First, as scholars argue, there was not a single "Puritan mind"; rather, Puritanism varied, in that the daily "lived religion" of men and women differed from theological edicts, but it was also a gendered lived religion.[17] Second, this study explores the implications of the choices Puritans made in transforming doctrinal ideas into practices of community. Feminized spirituality had the potential to undermine patriarchal authority and gender roles, but church disciplinary practices reinforced a more traditional masculinity and femininity that compromised such potential. Third, this study identifies early contributions to the construction of the ideology of separate spheres. Historians first cited its emergence in the nineteenth century; however, recent studies find evidence in the eighteenth century. This study finds roots of separate spheres in the seventeenth-century meetinghouse, as laymen created a church disciplinary process that reinforced male religiosity through public service rather than internal piety and reinforced women's ties to the church and its private realm.

My interest in how gender influenced this Puritan experience focused my research on church records. I was already persuaded by historian David Hall, who argued that the daily "lived" religion of the common

---

[16] Joan Scott, "Gender: A Useful Category of Historical Analysis," *American Historical Review* 91 (1986): 1053–75.

[17] David Hall's concept of a "daily lived religion" was a response to the foundational history of Puritan theology by Perry Miller, who argued that Puritans were of one religious mind based on the theology of ministers. See Miller, *The New England Mind*; Hall, "Narrating Puritanism"; and David D. Hall, ed., *Lived Religion in America: Toward a History of Practice* (Princeton: Princeton University Press, 1997). See also Selement, *Keepers of the Vineyard*. Selement argues that while there were differences between intellectuals and the common Puritan, they shared collective mentalities; he argues that the clergy interacted daily with their congregations and were more influential in their thinking than Hall suggests.

Puritan subtly differed from the Puritanism preached by ministers.[18] It stood to reason, then, that men and women would fashion different ideas of religion based on ideas of gender. I started exploring church disciplinary records after reading this brief suggestion in the citation notes to *Good Wives: Image and Reality in the Lives of Women in Northern New England, 1650–1750*, by Laurel Thatcher Ulrich: "There is much more to be learned about the activities of women in churches from a close examination of membership patterns and disciplinary action."[19] These records offered vignettes of ordinary people's lives that inspired me to learn about their behaviors, struggles, transgressions, and choices. Disciplinary cases offer a unique opportunity to learn how congregations treated sinful men and women and, in turn, how they defined behavior for godly men and women.

Building on the work of historians examining Puritanism as a feminized religion, I wanted to further explore how the disciplinary process impacted not only women, but men as well. If we view women as the normative Puritan, what does that mean for laymen? What did it mean to be a man in this new world? Did men conform to and/or challenge ministerial expectations?[20] This study also draws upon Elizabeth Reis's *Damned Women: Sinners and Witches in Puritan New England*, which analyzes Puritan feminized spirituality. It also supports Reis's argument that women focused more on their sinful natures, whereas men tended to ignore their souls and focus on their actions. Reis found this in literature and witchcraft trials; I corroborate this further in disciplinary records. Reis argues that men were able to accept the feminized spirituality because of the distinctions Puritans made between the body and the soul. In their writing, Puritans split body and soul into distinct identities, describing the inferiority of the body, which houses the superior soul. A body decays, but a soul can live forever in the kingdom of heaven. Such literature described the souls of both men and women as feminine.[21] Reis asserts that the distinctions between the body and the soul permitted a greater gender fluidity. Men could safely adopt a feminized spirituality in private, while maintaining the outward masculinity of their bodies.

---

[18] Hall, *Worlds of Wonder*, 15.
[19] Laurel Thatcher Ulrich, *Good Wives: Image and Reality in the Lives of Women in Northern New England, 1650–1750* (New York: Vintage Books, 1980), 281.
[20] For explanation of gender history, see Scott, "Gender," 1053–75.
[21] Elizabeth Reis, *Damned Women: Sinners and Witches in Puritan New England* (Ithaca: Cornell University Press, 1997), 93–120.

In turn, women found status within the church because, Reis argues, Puritans constructed a gendered ideology and society that made women closer to God and Satan. Women could be both more virtuous and more sinful: their feminine nature could make them humble before God, but their weakness could also make them succumb to the Devil. Church disciplinary records show that laymen were not "comfortable" with their feminized inner piety, at least publicly. In censure cases, men rejected the feminized language of confession and adopted a masculine language that distanced themselves from their feminine souls; yet women and ministers continued to identify with and describe the attributes of the feminized soul. In the public space of church censures, men rejected the tenets of feminized spirituality, which distanced them from the church and ultimately compromised the potential Puritanism had to allow more gender fluidity.

Over the past several decades, historians have agreed that there was greater gender fluidity than previously thought in the seventeenth century, but debates continue about when and how gender lines became more rigid. Historians began to see colonial women's history not as some kind of "dark age" but as a set of gains and losses. In *Good Wives*, Ulrich explained women's history as a "convoluted and sometimes tangled embroidery of loss and gain, accommodation and resistance."[22] Cornelia Hughes Dayton illustrates the "loss" in compelling terms, describing how women enjoyed relative authority and power in the seventeenth century, only to lose such status in the early eighteenth century. Mary Beth Norton finds a similar trajectory for women, although she argues that they retained power later into the century than Dayton asserts.[23] Norton

[22] Ulrich, *Good Wives*, 240; Cornelia Hughes Dayton, *Women before the Bar: Gender, Law and Society in Connecticut, 1639–1789* (Chapel Hill: University of North Carolina Press, 1995), 10.

[23] Mary Beth Norton, *Founding Mothers and Fathers: Gendered Power and the Founding of Early American Society* (New York: Alfred A. Knopf, 1996), 3–4, 11–24. Norton describes New England as a Filmerian system, based on the philosophy of Robert Filmer: the family and state were analogous institutions. The hierarchy in the family – father, mother, children – resembled the hierarchy of the state. Thus, a woman had power as a mother, as a wife, and as a widow. The Filmerian system opened up power for women, but it also limited it. Wives submitted to the authority of their husbands. Yet, in their roles in informal public space, women had power and authority. Norton distinguishes between informal and formal public space and explains that the public/private dichotomy did not have the same meaning it would in the nineteenth century. It was only when the public/private split began to occur by the end of the eighteenth century that women became marginalized and lost ground. Norton and Dayton disagree over the timeline, but both assert that women lost public authority.

argues that women experienced a degree of gender fluidity in the seventeenth and early eighteenth century only to find themselves marginalized by the end of the eighteenth century.

My research on Puritan religious experience illustrates a public/private trajectory and timeline similar to what Dayton describes. This book spans the first three generations of Puritans in New England, beginning with the founding of the Massachusetts Bay Colony in 1630 and ending in the 1720s, as the generation born after the Half-Way Covenant of 1662 reached maturity.[24] For the first generation, the church was the center of town, with public authority over ecclesiastical and civic affairs. By the end of the seventeenth century, the third generation witnessed a decline in the public power and authority of the church as it became a private institution. This study contends that church disciplinary practices helped create that split, leading to a gendered Puritanism. Church discipline enforced different types of religious expression for men and women that distanced men from formal church membership while reinforcing women's ties to the church. Puritan lay practices, and not just the allure of the outside world, contributed to men not joining the church. However, men did not lose their religious intensity; instead, they redirected their religious duties to the world of commerce and civic life – the public world. There was no "decline" in religiosity even though men were not joining the church in the same numbers. Church disciplinary practices led to distinctly gendered religious experiences, which in turn led to more rigid gender roles and contributed to the creation of the modern gender ideology of separate spheres. The concept of separate spheres proffers that men had power in the public world of work and politics whereas women were relegated to the private world of domesticity. It divided gender into two realms with a clear delineation of power and import. It is used by historians to describe the more rigid gender roles that came to fruition in the nineteenth century. However, we can see the underpinnings of this gender system in censure practices in the seventeenth century.

By focusing on the first three generations of New Englanders, this study assesses how Puritans created and contested religion and identity as they moved from the ideals and expectations of the settlers to the behaviors,

---

[24] See Emil Oberholzer, Jr., *Delinquent Saints: Disciplinary Action in the Early Congregational Churches of Massachusetts* (New York: Columbia University Press, 1956). Oberholzer took his study of church discipline up through the 1830s, when he says church discipline dramatically declined. His time frame does not take into consideration the influence that such developments as revivalism, denominationalism, the American Revolution, the market revolution, and the expansion of the electorate in the 1820s had on church discipline and religious sensibilities.

beliefs, and structures of their children and grandchildren. What began in 1630 as a utopian religious experiment based on potentially radical Puritan ideals transformed by the 1720s into a more secular civil society. Religion lost public power and became part of the private sphere.[25]

Chapter 1 begins with the founding of the town of Dorchester in order to explain the roles, responsibilities, and expectations set by towns in both civil and ecclesiastical affairs. The first-generation church began with the utopian ideal of an association of saints, with men and woman as spiritual equals in the eyes of God. The town of Dorchester's founding minister, Richard Mather, the patriarch of the Mather family ministerial dynasty in New England, provides a window into the challenges of first-generation congregants and ministers. Son Increase and grandson Cotton have garnered most of the attention from historians. However, Richard Mather played a key role in making recommendations for congregational procedures, rules, and practices during the first generation and the transition in membership for the second generation. He helped write the Cambridge Platform in 1648 and supported the Half-Way Covenant long before it was adopted in 1662.[26] Because of his influence and adherence to strict church membership, he offers a compelling comparison between the ideas of ministers and those of laymen. This chapter then expands to explore towns and congregations throughout New England in order to illustrate the connections between civil and religious authorities and church discipline in implementing and enforcing a godly social order. While church discipline was central to maintaining Puritan standards, the practice also created fissures between ministers and the laymen who controlled the process.

Chapter 2 explores church censure practices by analyzing how congregations charged men and women with different sins, described sins in gendered terms, and created distinctive expectations for male and female confessions. By gendering sinful behavior, laymen created a different

---

[25] For a discussion of the role of narrative in community studies, see David Hall and Alan Taylor, "Reassessing the Local History of New England," *New England: A Bibliography of Its History*, ed. Roger Parks (Hanover: University Press of New England, 1989), xix–xlvii.

[26] See B. R. Burg, *Richard Mather of Dorchester* (Lexington: University of Kentucky Press, 1976), 135–44; Robert Middlekauff, *The Mathers: Three Generations of Puritan Intellectuals, 1596–1728* (New York: Oxford University Press, 1999 [1971]), 54–62; Hall, *The Faithful Shepherd*, 112–15; and Cotton Mather, *Magnalia Christi Americana; or, The Ecclesiastical History of New England* (Hartford: Silas Andrus & Sons, 1853), 211. The Cambridge Platform was a statement of doctrine agreed upon by congregations in Massachusetts and Connecticut. The Half-Way Covenant opened up partial membership to children of covenanted parents, allowing them to be baptized and fall under church discipline.

Puritanism for men than for women. Church discipline changed over the generations, as did the focus of the clergy. First-generation ministers preached communal obligation and individual piety. As discipline increased through the second and third generations, the focus of sermons changed. In the second and third generations, the emphasis on individual piety for women and communal responsibility for men led to the formation of different religious identities. By the third generation, women outnumbered men three to two in the feminized setting of the church, which more frequently focused on an individual's relationship to God. The Great Awakening would strengthen that focus on the individual.[27] The Puritan focus on female piety put more of an emphasis on individual spirituality for women, while contributing to the development of a male religiosity that focused on public and civic affairs. This is significant to recognize, because historians have previously related the concept of "the individual" to the rise of men in the public world.[28] While women stayed in the pews, men went out into the secular arena and expressed their religiosity through their sense of duty to their communities, their families, their businesses, and their country.

Chapter 3 explores the language of confessions, to explain how language affected religious practices. Ministers expected all confessions to use a feminized language of submission and humility. However, laymen diverged from the language prescribed by the clergy to accept a more masculine language for male confessants. In the public space of the meetinghouse, where laymen confessed their sins, they could not risk their masculine reputations by adopting a feminized verbal order espoused by the clergy. Women were the normative Puritan who fully adopted the

---

[27] For a discussion of the Great Awakening, which was an intense period of revival and religious fervor, see Patricia A. Bonomi, *Under the Cope of Heaven: Religion, Society and Politics in Colonial America* (New York: Oxford University Press, 1986); and Alan Heimert, *Religion and the American Mind: From the Great Awakening to the Revolution* (Cambridge: Harvard University Press, 1966).

[28] Gordon S. Wood celebrates the American Revolution and its political philosophy for making America the "most individualistic" society. Wood credits revolutionary republicanism with "offering new concepts of the individual, the family and the state, and the individual's relationship to the family, the state and other individuals." Yet, in his narrative of the revolution ushering people in from the darkness of monarchy to the light of democracy, Wood fails to address the more complex gains and losses and varied religious concepts of the individual. See Gordon S. Wood, *The Radicalism of the American Revolution* (New York: Vintage Books, 1991), 230, 96. Sacvan Bercovitch writes about the religious influence in the creation of the self; however, Bercovitch does not explore how gender affected the process. See Sacvan Bercovitch, *The Puritan Origins of the American Self* (New Haven: Yale University Press, 1975), 1–34.

language and demeanor of a feminized faith. Men created a more masculine verbal order that focused on their behavior instead of their souls.
Through this practice, the disciplinary process reinforced male duty and
female piety, which ultimately gendered Puritanism.

Chapter 4 focuses on the challenges Puritanism posed to masculinity
by examining the case of war hero Captain John Underhill. Famous for
his triumphant massacre of the Pequot Indians, Underhill was the definition of military manhood, or hypermasculinity. Trained by his father to
be a soldier, Underhill embraced a masculinity of power, sexual prowess,
pride, and heroism that did not fit in Puritan New England. The new
Puritan man needed to moderate some of the excesses of traditional
masculine norms. Shortly after his wartime heroism, Underhill found
himself excommunicated and banished from Massachusetts Bay, and
he clumsily navigated this gender terrain, ultimately gaining readmis-
sion to the church and colony by offering a thoroughly over-the-top
feminized, weeping confession. While Underhill fought for the status
and power he thought he deserved, other men faced similar problems
of competing masculinities. Some conformed, and others realized they
could not survive the New England way. Laymen in charge of church
discipline created a middle ground of masculinity that blended versions,
providing men a language and a sense of public duty that preserved
their manhood.

Chapter 5 examines what happened to women who did not conform
and the troublemakers and heretics who refused to adhere to the expectations of their faith and their societies. This chapter offers a case study of
Ann Hibbens, who exemplifies the dangers to women who transgressed
gendered boundaries. The wife of a wealthy and well-regarded man, Hibbens faced censure charges when she disputed the work and fees of a carpenter she hired. While negotiating such work fell within the boundaries
of wifely duties, challenging a man in business did not. In her censure
process, Ann did not adhere to the expectations for a female sinner and
was resolute that she was right, refusing to submit to the authority of
men. Any deviance or defiance of the social norms branded women as
suspect, and Ann's determination to spar with men made her very dangerous. When her husband died, leaving her unprotected, she went from
a troublesome woman to a witch. The costs were high for such women
in early New England.

Church records can be problematic sources for historians. They can
be incomplete due to either fire, damage, or poor record keeping, or
they may remain undiscovered in a forgotten corner of someone's attic.

There is also the issue of who documented church events; different men could have been charged with recording these events over time. What they recorded, left out, or embellished is hard to discern. Certainly the recorders were not infallible. Not every congregation recorded church censures, but others kept extensive notes. Some church records merely chronicle births, baptisms, admissions, and deaths, whereas others document sermons, fast days, disciplinary cases, and even the weather and notable controversies. Likely, congregations disciplined more men and women than appear in the records. Even with these flaws and occasional silences, church records across Massachusetts Bay reveal interesting gender patterns around disciplinary practices. This study includes records from Dorchester First Church, Boston's First and Second churches, Marblehead First Church, Plymouth, Salem, Cambridge, Reading, Northampton, Barnstable, Quincy, and Wethersfield. There are many stories these records cannot tell, but what they can tell us about the first three generations in New England reveals some of the complex ways in which gender and religion interacted, challenged, and influenced one another. The stories allow us to view the daily religious experience and read the language used to express the religious ideas and identities of community members.[29] Some individuals navigated the process with more ease than did others. Some men and women unabashedly challenged the system. And at least one young Puritan widow found herself stealing away in the middle of the night to escape the judgment of her congregation.

Twenty years after fleeing her father's house, Content Mason returned to Dorchester and confessed her sins. On May 25, 1712, the congregation forgave the 53-year-old woman and restored her from her excommunication. That summer, Content watched Reverend John Danforth perform the marriage ceremony for her daughter, the now-grown Eleanor Wood, and Comfort Foster, a man from a good-standing family. Over the next two decades, Mason continued to work on her salvation, and on June 1, 1728, the Dorchester congregation welcomed her into full communion. She was now a visible saint. When Content Mason died in 1749, aged almost ninety years, the once-wicked widow was among God's chosen.

---

[29] See Oberholzer, *Delinquent Saints*. This is the only study that examines Puritan church disciplinary records. See Susan Juster, *Disorderly Women: Sexual Politics and Evangelism in Revolutionary New England* (London: Cornell University of Press, 1994). Juster utilized censure records of a Baptist parish in the Revolutionary period, examining a single parish over a short time period in which some Baptist women attained formal power.

Through their censure practices, Puritans created a gendered religious experience by emphasizing different aspects of Puritan doctrine for men and women, and by censuring men and women for different types of sins. The gendering of Puritanism occurred as laymen reinterpreted Puritanism for male sinners, focusing more on civic duty than piety, while reinforcing women's sense of self and individual spirituality. For their public confessions, laymen created a masculine version of Puritanism; at the same time, women upheld the ministerial mandates of a feminized religion. This book explains how the censure process created a gendered lived religion that contributed to the creation of a modern separate-spheres ideology.

I

The Great Hen Squabble and
Regulating the Godly Path

The Dewy family's servant had not yet completed her morning chore of emptying the chamber pot when she dumped its contents on Goody Ingerson, their next-door neighbor. The unexpected assault was retaliation because Ingerson had killed some of the Dewys's hens. In 1714 the Dewys owned more than 120 chickens, and as their closest neighbor, Ingerson grew tired of the fowl scampering through her property. The Ingersons chased those chickens out of their garden, barn, and barley field, and even had to scurry the unwanted guests out of their house. To show her frustration and send a message about the wandering brood, Goodwife Ingerson wrung a few necks. Goodwife Abigail Dewy prepared her servant for the next attack by weaponizing their chamber pot. However, despite a stench-covered head, Ingerson managed to kill two more hens. She quickly passed them off to her daughter, with directions to run straight home. Tensions further escalated, and a small brawl almost erupted when Goody Dewy entered the fray carrying a whipping cord. Yelling from her front porch, Dewy ordered her chamber-pot-wielding servant to apprehend the young girl fleeing the scene. Luckily, the Ingerson daughter escaped the servant's clutches before Dewy could mete out a flogging, and both mother and daughter made it home safely (perhaps to a chicken dinner).

The case of the great hen squabble went to court, where the Connecticut magistrates ordered the Ingersons to pay for the dead chickens. However, when the court asked Abigail Dewy if she did indeed order her servant to drag Ingerson's daughter back to the Dewy house by the hair, she lied and said no. The Dewys may have won the court case over property loss, but Abigail's lie would not be forgotten. Soon thereafter, her Westfield congregation censured her for the sin of lying.[1]

Abigail's father-in-law, Thomas Dewy, had faced censure charges decades earlier, in 1683. Slow to repair his mill after a storm destroyed it, Dewy was upset when neighbors started building their own mill upstream, diverting his water supply. Late one night, he tore down their dam and hid their tools. His congregation censured him for the destruction of property. The minister even delivered a sermon on the irregularity of such behavior and the problems Dewy had caused the community.[2]

Like other New England families, the Dewys were subject to the scrutiny of civil and ecclesiastical forces to police their behavior. In order to regulate this godly path, Puritans formed church covenants, monitored families, patrolled communities, and created civil laws that enforced ecclesiastical rules. Officials utilized both the courts and the churches to reprove transgressions. Church discipline was an integral tool in recovering wayward men and women in a society that believed one sinner could be the ruin of all.

ESTABLISHING A COVENANT

The men and women of New England had a communal responsibility to watch over one another, lead their town down the Christian path, and direct public affairs in a Christian manner. When Governor John Winthrop gave his famous sermon, "A Model of Christian Charity," aboard the *Arabella* in 1630, he explicated the Puritans' community obligations: "In such cases as this the care of the public must over sway all private respects, but which not only conscience, but mere Civil polity doth bind us...having before our eyes our Commission and Community in the work, our Community as members of the same body."[3] Part of being a good Christian demanded taking responsibility for the public good.

When Puritans migrated to New England, their first task was to establish a covenanted church. As in the case of Dorchester, sometimes

---

[1] Edward Taylor, *Edward Taylor's "Church Records" and Related Sermons*, vol. I of the *Unpublished Writings of Edward Taylor*, ed. Thomas M. Davis and Virginia L. Davis (Boston: Twayne Publishers, 1981), 237–41.

[2] Taylor, *Church Records*, 183–85.

[3] John Winthrop, *Winthrop's Journal*, *"History of New England,"* 1630–1649, ed. James Kendall Hosmer (New York: Scribner's Sons, 1908).

founders formed a church before they even arrived in Massachusetts Bay. In Dorsetshire, England, minister John White organized the migration. On March 20, 1630, his group met at Plymouth, England, where White preached, held a day of fasting and prayer, and 140 passengers covenanted together and chose John Warham and John Maverick as their ministers.[4] Roger Clap, who boarded the *Mary & John*, wrote, "The Lord Jesus Christ was so plainly held out in the preaching of the gospel unto poor lost sinners, and the absolute necessity of the new birth,...that our hearts were taken off from Old England and set upon heaven."[5] They arrived in Mattapan, as Indians called it, on June 30, 1630, and began building their town.

Before they commenced building ships, roads, and fences, the people of Dorchester built a meetinghouse,[6] a crude building with a thatched roof (entry stairs added only years later). The residents also used this building as a depot for military stores and nightly guarded it from attack. Erected on Allen's Plain, near the corner of Pleasant and Cottage Streets, the meetinghouse was the center for town activities, and they scheduled weekly town meetings on Monday mornings, requiring every man to attend.[7] Believed to be the original town government in the colonies, Dorchester also pioneered the system of choosing male residents as selectmen to oversee civil matters and patrol the town to keep order.[8] The church stood as the center of the town's religious, social, and civic life.

[4] Records Commissioner, *A Report of the Record Commissioners of the City of Boston, Containing Boston Births from A.D. 1700 to A.D. 1800* (Boston: Rockwell & Churchill, City Printers, 1894), 7; Committee of the Dorchester Antiquarian and Historical Society, *History of the Town of Dorchester* (Boston: Ebenezer Clapp, Jr., 1859), 18.

[5] Captain Roger Clap, *Memoirs of Captain Roger Clap* (Boston: Greenleaf's Printing Office for Samuel Whiting, 1731), 6.

[6] James Blake, *Annals of the Town of Dorchester, 1750* (Boston: David Clapp, Jr., 1864), 12. Blake dates the meetinghouse to 1633, but other sources date it 1631. Carol Zurawski Whitney, "Seventeenth-Century Survey of Dorchester" (PhD diss., Boston University, 1979), 17; Committee of the Dorchester Antiquarian and Historical Society, *History of the Town of Dorchester*, 33; Dorchester Massachusetts Tercentenary Committee, ed., *Dorchester in the Old Bay Colony: 1630 Old and New 1930* (Dorchester: Chapple Publishing Company Ltd., 1930), 12.

[7] The meetinghouse did not actually move to Meetinghouse Hill until 1673. See Whitney, "Seventeenth-Century Survey of Dorchester," 107; *History of the Town of Dorchester*, 32; Record Commissioners of the City of Boston, *Dorchester Town Records* (Boston: Rockwell and Churchill City Printers, 1883), 3.

[8] *Dorchester Town Records*, 7.

Establishing a church and adopting a covenant were central to organizing a town. When founding a new congregation, colonists signed a "Profession of Faith and Covenant" pledging themselves as a Christian community to be responsible for one another. In the Dorchester covenant, founders outlined Christian conduct and duties:

Dorchester, the 23rd day of the 6th month, Annon 1636

Wee … joyne o'selves together in Church Comunion, from o' hearts ackowledging o' owne unworthines of such a priviledge of the least of Gods mercyes, & likewise acknowledging o' disability to keepe coven' wth God or to p'fourme any spirituall duty … bind ourselves solemnely … to walke together… [p]romising first & above all to cleave unto him as … o' onely spiritual husband and Lord … bewayling fro o' hearts o' owne neglect thereof in former tyme, and our polluting o'selves therein wth any sinfull inventions of men.

And lastly wee do hereby Coven' & p'mise to further to o' utmost power, the best spirituall good of each other, and of all and every one that may become members of this Congregacon, by mutuall Instruction reprehension, exhortacon, consolacon, and spirituall watchfulness over one another for good.[9]

Similar to those throughout New England, the Dorchester covenant affirmed the most important Puritan tenets: that members were bound together to fulfill the agreement with God, to watch over one another, and to be pious. Richard Mather explained that "our church covenants are with the Lord himselfe … For watch[under] & duties of edification one towards another are but branches of the Lords Covenant, being duties commanded by the Law … with that people of Israel … The neglect whereof … brought judgement upon them all."[10] Covenants were social contracts, and in congregations throughout Massachusetts Bay, people expected to fulfill their contract through communal service.[11] Each community member had the responsibility of maintaining the godly path by assuring that everyone in town was "walking orderly" and that the civil government would carry out its duties in a Christian way. Dorchester's covenant stressed the necessity of "binding together" as a "right ordered" community, and it was the members' duty to "further the spiritual good

---

[9] Charles H. Hope, ed., *Records of the First Church of Dorchester, Massachusetts, 1636–1734* (Boston: George H. Ellis, 1981), 6.

[10] Richard Mather, *An Apology of the Churches in New-England for Church Covenant* (London: T. P. & M. S. for Benjamin Allen, 1643), 7.

[11] Although John Cotton first created a covenant while still in England, covenant was distinct to New England Puritanism. New England clerics expended great energy defending the covenant to English nonconformists.

of each other." As a religion with communal and individual responsibilities, Puritanism required dual roles for its congregants.

The other side of Puritan responsibility dealt with personal religiosity and the state of one's soul, or piety. Puritanism required everyone to examine their souls and sinfulness on a daily basis, ever striving for signs that they were saved and ever plunging themselves into a state of despair over their sinful natures. Because of this, creating a covenant was not a rote exercise and could be fraught with challenges to prove that members were sincere and pious. Puritans even passed a law that allowed new congregations to form only with the approval of a council composed of magistrates and church elders from nearby towns. When one of Dorchester's original ministers, John Warham, left with half the congregation to establish the town of Windsor, the remaining residents were concerned that they were no longer covenanted. When the other Dorchester minister, John Maverick, died soon thereafter, residents immediately sought a new minister who could rectify the situation and save their godly mission. They turned to Richard Mather, who had just arrived from England. On the advice of respected Massachusetts Bay ministers John Cotton and Thomas Shepard, Mather accepted the offer from Dorchester. He felt pressured to accept the ministry and believed that if he did not relent, "a tribe...should perish out of Israel" because they were essentially without a formal church. On April 1, 1636, the people of Dorchester assembled before the ministers and magistrates of nearby communities who would examine their worthiness. To some of the examiners, including Thomas Shepard, most of the individuals questioned had not experienced a true spiritual awakening and instead based their knowledge of salvation on unsound religious tenets.[12] Shepard and others believed that the Dorchester applicants failed to define salvation in terms of God's grace and instead based it "upon dreams and ravishes of spirit by fits; others upon the reformation of their lives; others upon duties and performances."[13] They ruled that the Dorchester congregation verged on heresy by confusing sanctification as a path to justification, rather than a sign of it.[14]

[12] Middlekauff, *The Mathers*, 50; B. R. Burg, *Richard Mather* (Boston: Twayne Publishers, 1982), 33.

[13] John Winthrop, quoted in Burg, *Richard Mather*, 33.

[14] Bozeman, *The Precisianist Strain*, 3; Edmund S. Morgan, *The Puritan Family: Religion and Domestic Relations in Seventeenth-Century New England* (New York: Harper & Row, 1944 [1966]), 1; Cohen, *God's Caress*, 10.

The decision to deny the request humiliated Mather.[15] He immediately began to hold religious meetings, teaching the correct doctrine on grace. Later that year, the council approved the gathered church at Dorchester. This experience left Mather all the more determined to keep his congregation pure.

The covenant of grace is central to understanding Puritan theology. Puritans believed God made several agreements with people. The first agreement was the covenant of works that God made with Adam. In exchange for eternal life, Adam had to obey God's laws. Humans broke that covenant with Eve's original sin, losing their immortality. Puritans believed that although mankind broke the covenant of works with their wicked sins, through his grace, God formed a new covenant, which he did not base on human behavior. The second agreement was the covenant of grace that Abraham originally formed in the Old Testament when he promised his faith alone. In the covenant of grace, God predestined some people, called "the elect," to be saved. Sanctification, or good works, was not a path to salvation, but a sign of election. Thus, Puritans continually searched for signs that they were among the elect – or what they would call "visible saints."

The uncertainty of whether one would be saved to rest in heavenly peace with God or be doomed to eternal hellfire caused a great deal of anxiety for Puritans. Predestination had its costs. One could never be sure. Historian Charles Cohen describes an anxious cycle: "Sorrow over sin, intensifying into hatred of it, despair of perceiving one's incapacity to achieve salvation, awareness of faith, despondency passes into joy, peace of conscience, and love of God."[16] Such assurance of salvation led to the sin of pride, and thus the course resumed, in search for signs of justification.[17] Dorchester's Roger Clap exemplified this cycle of hope and doubt. When he believed he was saved, he said that God "transport[ed] me as to make me cry out upon my bed with loud voice

---

[15] It was Mather's second humiliation in Massachusetts Bay. He applied for membership in the Boston First Church and was originally denied the request based on his defense of his ordination in England by a bishop. It took him months to accept the Boston standard belief of a "laying on the hands." He did finally gain membership to the church.

[16] Cohen, *God's Caress*, 76.

[17] For a discussion of this cycle, see Morgan, *Visible Saints*, 69–70; and Cohen, *God's Caress*, 110. For an example, see Thomas Shepard, *Confessions of Thomas Shepard*, ed. George Selement and Bruce C. Wooley (Boston: Colonial Society of Massachusetts, 1981).

He is come, He is come. And God did melt my heart at that time so that I could, and did mourn and shed more tears for sin."[18] This anxiety was reflected in many Puritan diaries. With much consternation over his fourteen-year-old daughter, Betty, Samuel Sewall recorded in his diary the grief and angst she experienced. Throughout 1696, Sewall expressed grave concerns over his daughter, who showed "signs of depression and sorrow" as she prayed to work through her salvation. She would burst into tears after reading a sermon, convinced she would burn in hell. If her father tried to offer solace with a biblical reading, her fears increased with newfound sins. Her parents eventually called in a pastor to counsel her. Betty's mother encouraged her to pray more, but Betty believed she was too much of a sinner for God to hear her. She would wake with nightmares, inconsolable. Spring brought Betty some comfort, as if through her constant prayer she finally believed she was among the elect. However, on a Sabbath day in May, tears prevented Betty from reading her Bible. She cried hard, because she feared she had once again fallen into sin. Her father tried several methods to relieve her anxiety. He prayed with her and eventually decided to send her to Salem for a summer sojourn. But through the fall, Betty's anxiety continued. Sewall recorded, "she weeps so hard that she can hardly read: I talk with her and she tells me of the various temptations she had, and that she was a reprobate."[19] It was a painful process that was never ending for the true "moral athletes" concerned about their salvation (Figure 1.1).[20]

The second generation of Puritans renewed their covenants during times when they were especially anxious about the spiritual health of their communities. On March 4, 1677, the Dorchester congregation gathered to renew their covenant and reinforce its call to duty and piety. They "rebuked" themselves for all the violations of the covenant and vowed to "reform our owne hearts, by endeavoring to recover ye spirit life & power of godliness." In addition to increasing piety, the congregation promised to reform their families and the "general

---

[18] Clap, *Memoirs*, 13.

[19] Samuel Sewall, *The Diary of Samuel Sewall, 1674–1729* (New York: Farrar, Straus and Giroux, 1973), 356–59.

[20] Charles Cohen describes Puritans as moral athletes because of the continuous cycle of fear and doubt that Puritans put themselves through in contemplating their salvation. See Cohen, *God's Caress*.

FIGURE 1.1. Public worship in Plymouth. *Source:* Print Collector/Hulton
Archive/Getty Images.

growing evil of this time," confronting sins such as profanity, vanity,
drunkenness, idleness, uncleanness, lasciviousness, and slander.[21] The
renewal was a vow to correct the transgressions that occurred over
the past two generations and to refocus the congregation on its godly
endeavor.

To ensure that the next generation's children were bound to the
same responsibilities, pastor Josiah Flint held a special meeting the day
after they renewed the covenant. On March 5, 1677, Flint met with
the "seed of the church," the young people of Dorchester over the age
of sixteen, and gave a short speech urging them to accept church discipline even though they were not yet full church members. He asked
them to consider that they had already benefited from living under a
covenant and that God now called them to submit. Sixty-one young
men and thirty-five women personally gave their assent to government
by the church.

[21] Hope, *Records of the First Church of Dorchester*, 18–20.

CHURCH MEMBERSHIP

Defining church membership was an early debate. John Warham agreed with ministers such as Thomas Hooker who favored open church membership, while John Maverick supported other Boston clerics, led by John Cotton and John Davenport, who restricted membership to visible saints. By 1633, due to pressure from Cotton and other Boston ministers, it was increasingly difficult for those congregations favoring open membership.[22] This debate was the main reason Warham left Dorchester and, along with Hooker, moved to Connecticut, where leaders could institute their own membership practices.[23] Richard Mather adopted the Boston clerics' idea of limiting church membership to visible saints, the elect. He was so concerned about the purity of his church that while some colleagues asserted it was better to admit ten hypocrites than to keep out a single Christian, Mather argued just the opposite. He quoted Ecclesiastes, "One sinner destroyeth much good," and lectured from the pulpit about the grave misfortunes of those who did not gain membership:[24]

As dolefull & dreadfull as it is, yet till a man attain this benefit of justification, all his sins do remain in Gods sight as fresh & clear as the very day when they were first committed...the guilt of those sinnes did cleave unto them, fresh in the sight of God...all unbelieving sinners, unjustified persons, whether alive or dead, the guilt of all their sinnes doth remain upon them to this day.[25]

To become a visible saint, a person had to have an experience (or knowledge) that they were saved. Such conversion experiences frequently involved visions or dreams during prayer.[26] The pastor and church elders would interview the potential member about the experience and his or her ideas of faith. The laymen then voted on the person's acceptance into

[22] Burg, *Richard Mather*, 28–29; Hall, *The Faithful Shepherd*, 98; Morgan, *Visible Saints*, 86–90; E. Brooks Holifield, *The Covenant Sealed: The Development of Puritan Sacramental Theology in Old and New England, 1570–1720* (New Haven: Yale University Press, 1974).

[23] For John Winthrop's account of the move, see Winthrop, *Winthrop's Journal*, 173. See also Maude Pinney Kuhns, *The "Mary and John": A Story of the Founding of Dorchester, Massachusetts, 1630* (Rutland: Charles E. Tuttle, 1943), 3.

[24] Middlekauff, *The Mathers*, 53.

[25] Richard Mather, *The Summe of Certain Sermons upon Genes:15.6* (Cambridge: Samuel Green, 1652), 32.

[26] See Patricia Caldwell, *The Puritan Conversion Narrative: The Beginnings of American Expression* (New York: Cambridge University Press, 1983). For a discussion on the psychology of conversion, see Cohen, *God's Caress*.

the congregation. As Dorchester's John Spur and Nathaniel Wiet realized in 1678, acceptance through that process was not guaranteed. When the men met with the pastor and church elders, their answers were so vague and insincere that the congregation issued a censure for contemptuous carriage. Neither Spur nor Wiet ever addressed the censure and eventually were excommunicated.[27]

FAMILY GOVERNMENT

A godly society required not just a covenanted church, but also pious and well-regulated families. Historian John Demos described the Puritan family as "a little commonwealth": they were the first line of defense for an orderly society.[28] Ministers believed that a good father ensured the religious, social, and economic welfare of his family. In 1659, Increase Mather explained to a council of ministers that it was "the duty of the elders and the church to call upon parents to bring up their children in the nurture and admonition of the Lord."[29] In 1669, the Boston First Church empowered its elders to inspect families for adequate religious edification.[30] Indeed, Cotton Mather referred to the family as the "first society," and, as patriarchs, men were to lead the family in its religious education and prayer. Ministers emphasized that families needed to be pious and orderly, fulfilling both aspects of the covenant.

Throughout Massachusetts Bay, both civil and ecclesiastical authorities were charged with policing family. With the focus on male lapses in family order, the courts enforced the duties and responsibilities men held as the heads of family government.[31] Courts considered family government so crucial to a community's holy commonwealth that they routinely intervened in family affairs. In 1639, the court ordered a young man to marry a woman he sullied. After first being whipped, branded

---

[27] Hope, *Records of the First Church of Dorchester*, 79–80. By 1678 many young people who were baptized signed documents attesting that they were under church government even though they were not full members. John Spur would be released from his excommunication in 1696 and dismissed to the church in Taunton.

[28] John Demos, *A Little Commonwealth: Family Life in Plymouth Colony* (New York: Oxford University Press, 1970).

[29] Increase Mather, "A Disputation Concerning Church-Members and Their Children," cited in Morgan, *The Puritan Family*, 140.

[30] Morgan, *The Puritan Family*, 133–40.

[31] For a discussion of family government, see Demos, *A Little Commonwealth*; and Norton, *Founding Mothers and Fathers*.

with an R on his cheek, and made to pay a fine to her parents, Aaron Starke then married Mary Holt.[32] The court issued several fines to protect Goodwife Egleston when her husband bequeathed her to another man, who then disparaged her with unkind words.[33] Courts routinely ordered men to pay child support. In 1645, the Hartford court had Leonard Dyks whipped, sent to jail and hard labor, and his wages held until he agreed to pay child support to a young woman, Ruth Fishe. That same year, the court ordered that Matthew Williams should have his wages held until he paid child support to Susan Cole.[34] The courts thus sought to protect the communal good through well-ordered families.

Congregations also upheld the tenets of family government. For example, when the Plymouth church censured Abigail Billington for fornication, a church elder used that opportunity to warn fathers "to keep up family government."[35] If fathers lived up to their Puritan duty of running an orderly and godly family, then pious daughters would not stray.[36] Historian M. Michelle Jarret Morris tells the story of Daniel Gookin, a respected Massachusetts Bay leader, who was infamous for his wayward dependents. His children and servants were charged with a host of lascivious and raucous sins – from dancing and drinking to fornicating.[37] Gookin was accused of having a disordered household.

Family order extended to servants as well. William Chapman challenged the social and moral order when he married Elizabeth Bateman, a fellow servant of Captain John Cullick, after failing to get permission from their master. Causing further disruption, Chapman became angry over Cullick's response and "said diverse unsufferable scandals and reproaches" about the captain and his family. The courts fined Chapman, sent him to jail for two weeks, ordered family discipline, and bound him to good behavior.[38]

---

[32] Connecticut Historical Society, *Records of the Particular Court of Connecticut, 1639–1663* (Hartford: Connecticut Historical Society, 1928), 54, 56.

[33] Connecticut Historical Society, *Records of the Particular Court,* 34.

[34] Connecticut Historical Society, *Records of the Particular Court,* 35.

[35] *Plymouth Church Records, 1620–1859* (New York: John Wilson & Son, 1920), 197.

[36] For a discussion of family, see Demos, *A Little Commonwealth*; Philip Greven, *The Protestant Temperament: Patterns of Child-Rearing, Religious Experience, and the Self in Early America* (New York: Alfred A. Knopf, 1977); Norton, *Founding Mothers and Fathers*; and Lawrence Stone, *The Family, Sex, and Marriage in England, 1500–1800* (New York: Harper & Row, 1977).

[37] M. Michelle Jarret Morris, *Under Household Government: Sex and Family in Puritan Massachusetts, 1660–1700* (Cambridge: Harvard University Press, 2013), 13–14.

[38] Connecticut Historical Society, *Records of the Particular Court,* 124–25.

With the "little commonwealth" as the cornerstone of social order, Puritans created laws forbidding single men from living alone. In 1669, the Massachusetts General Court passed a law that placed single men in family homes so they could "walk orderly and submit to family government." Dorchester selectmen followed the court's direction and found homes for the sixteen single men on their list. The selectmen were fulfilling their duties to the community described in the covenant. What began as "Christian watchfulness" became civic service. Town officials also placed single men in families so they had models for proper manly behavior and industry. These men may have been very pious, but the town wanted assurances they would also work hard and conduct themselves properly in public. Of course, it was unthinkable for single women to live alone. Under the laws of femme covert, women were the property of their fathers, and afterward their husbands. Widows were the interesting, and sometimes complicated, exception.[39]

Towns also policed how parents instructed their children. The Dorchester selectmen and church elders conducted a joint survey of their residents in 1669 to "inquire of persons as to their manner of living, and whether they profited by public or private instruction."[40] Certainly the civil and church leaders were interested in the same issue: how to keep people walking on the orderly path of godliness. If men failed in their Christian duty as fathers, it was up to the community to help. Courts, selectmen, town officials, and churches all sought to discipline wayward Puritans.

CREATING LAWS FOR A GODLY SOCIAL ORDER

Churches had no formal power over civil government, but they did have significant informal power to influence legislation, town meetings, and judicial decisions. Puritan men and women expected their civil authorities to follow the word and law of God. New England ministers developed such expectations from John Calvin's teachings, which explained

---

[39] For a discussion on the challenges and issues concerning widows, see Carol F. Karlsen, *The Devil in the Shape of a Woman: Witchcraft in Colonial New England* (New York: Norton Press, 1987). Karlsen links widowhood to witchcraft, arguing that property-owning widows without male heirs were especially prone to witchcraft accusations. Without sons, a widow controlled her own wealth.

[40] Committee of the Dorchester Antiquarian and Historical Society, *History of the Town of Dorchester*, 211.

that the church and state must be separate, but both must work in the service of God.[41]

In a sermon delivered in 1638, Thomas Hooker preached that choosing public magistrates was a right that belonged to the people, through God, but that they must follow God's law and will in choosing their officials. Hooker connected the duty to God with the duty to community. Early colonial laws were influenced by Puritans' ideas of God's laws. Ideas such as Hooker's became the groundwork for the Fundamental Orders of 1638, written by one of Connecticut's founders, Roger Ludlow. The Orders were a series of laws agreed upon by the three river towns, Windsor, Hartford, and Wethersfield. The Orders established the process for holding elections and calling meetings for general assemblies or courts. Ludlow clearly rooted the government in a godly endeavor:

> The word of god requires that to mayntayne the peace and union of such a people there should be an Orderly and decent Government established according to God ... Doe therefore ... conjoyne our selves to be as one ... Commonwealth ... enter into Combination and Confederation together to mayntayne and presearve the liberty and purity of the gospel of our lord Jesus wch we now professe, as also the discipline of the Churches whch according to the truth of the said gospell is now practiced amonst us.[42]

Under Ludlow, the Connecticut courts expanded the Orders of 1638 into the Code of 1650. Similar to the Orders, the Code established civil law based on the law of God. The Code of 1650 mandated due process, protecting the liberties and privileges granted by God. The Code protected individuals from arbitrary power by creating a series of laws and General Court orders. It also made clear that the word of God was superior to any civil law. It outlined death sentences for anyone who worshipped another God, anyone deemed to be a witch or consort of the Devil, and anyone who blasphemed the name of God.

Moreover, the Code of 1650 created a series of laws that regulated religious practices and behaviors. It allowed civil government to mandate church attendance and ensure that "the peace, ordinances and rules of

---

[41] Hall, *The Faithful Shepherd*, 1, 122; Bruce C. Daniels, *The Connecticut Town: Growth and Development, 1635–1790* (Middletown: Wesleyan University Press, 1979), 65; Bozeman, *The Precisianist Strain*, 239–40; Erikson, *Wayward Puritans*, 55–58. Erikson describes the relationship between church and state that "magistrates would act as a secular arm in the service of the church ... while the ministers would provide the final authority for most questions related to long-range policy."

[42] Daniels, *The Connecticut Town*, 65–66, 177.

Christ be observed in every church, according to His Word." The Code explained that if a resident had contempt for the word of God, it was an attack not only on the church, but on civil government as well. Anyone in contempt of God's holy ordinances could face charges before the court *and* his congregation. As a warning to others, officials would stand an offender upon a pillory during lecture day, with a sign that read, in capital letters, "AN OPEN AND OBSTINANTE CONTEMNER OF GOD'S HOLY ORDINANCES." The Code also described the duty of Christian watchfulness to keep a "vigilant eye over their brethren and neighbors" to assure godly behavior. The Code was deeply invested in creating a godly social order; however, there were also lines that separated civil from ecclesiastical powers. The Code explained that civil authority could not strip someone from an ecclesiastical position, and nor could the church relinquish anyone from a civil position.

The Fundamental Orders and the Code of 1650 resembled the Massachusetts Bay Colony's 1641 Body of Liberties.[43] Each document detailed individual liberties and protections, along with laws regarding religious practice and observance. Each strived for a godly community, with tight social controls and a clear ecclesiastical interest in civil affairs. Leaders in Massachusetts and Connecticut disagreed about voting status and membership, but they shared ideals about Christian watchfulness, a civil government based on the word of God, and a system of censures and punishments for those who transgressed.

Throughout New England, town governments and courts also enforced godly standards set forth in church covenants and Puritan doctrine. In Dorchester, each elected selectman policed a group of families and was responsible to maintain order. Selectmen summoned residents for a host of offenses, including idleness, drinking, entertaining sin, corruption, and even playing kettle pins. In 1679, the First Church of Dorchester censured Abigail Merrifield for fornication. The civil court also found her guilty and sentenced her to a fine of "three pounds or whipt with twelve stripes."[44] Merrifield was a repeat offender, eventually excommunicated.

---

[43] It was either written or cowritten by Rev. Nathaniel Ward. Edward J. McManus argues that most of the form and content came from proposals by John Cotton. See Edward J. McManus, *Law and Liberty in Early New England* (Amherst: University of Massachusetts Press, 1993), 9. However, according to Winthrop's journal, they chose Ward's draft. See Winthrop, *Winthrop's Journal*, 279–80.

[44] See Hope, *Records of the First Church of Dorchester*, 81–82, 106; Allyn Bailey Forbes, ed., *Records of the Suffolk County Court, 1671–1680*, vol. I, 2 vols. (Boston: Colonial Society of Massachusetts, 1933), 1018.

Between 1674 and 1679, Samuell Rigby sometimes served as a constable, but more often he appeared in court and church to answer to various censure charges. In 1674, he first appeared in town records for neglecting his "calling, living a dissolute life, [and being a] trouble to the selectmen."[45] Similarly, Robert Styles appeared twice before the Suffolk County Court on charges of not attending church and neglecting his calling. This was after the selectmen cited him for his idle ways. Styles must have ignored their orders, for on his second appearance, the court added a charge of "not submitting to authority."[46]

The selectmen scoured the town for idle men, as Puritans believed that "idleness was the Devil's work." In a godly society, everyone should be busy working to serve God. The selectman tried to force an entire family out of Dorchester in 1673. Thomas, Jonathan, and Joseph Birch plagued the town with their lack of employment, industry, and godliness. Selectmen questioned Thomas about his public behavior, had the court order Jonathan out of town, and had frequent meetings with Joseph over finding a trade. The selectmen finally had to refer them to the county courts. At one point the selectmen ordered Constable Samuell Rigby to place Joseph Birch with a good master. In another instance Birch complained that he "had no iron nor coals" but promised that "he would endeavor to reform." In 1677 the court finally ordered Joseph to pay a fine or sit in the stocks for his drunken conduct.[47]

The selectmen focused on outward conduct – public displays of behavior that could be witnessed by the community. Dorchester selectmen had several interactions with the widow Elizabeth George, who kept an ordinary. The widow faced court and church censures for "entertaining sin," for often allowing sundry visitors to get drunk, and occasionally for "selling drinke without a license." However, the selectmen contended

---

45 Committee of the Dorchester Antiquarian and Historical Society, *History of the Town of Dorchester*, 226; Record Commissioners of the City of Boston, *Dorchester Town Records*, 195.

46 Committee of the Dorchester Antiquarian and Historical Society, *History of the Town of Dorchester*, 223; Forbes, ed., *Records of the Suffolk County Court*, 915. The court ordered that he "put forth" his children, presumably because his idleness resulted in poverty and he could not take care of them. When the Selectmen met with Styles again in 1679 about his idleness and placing his children, he refused because his wife did not want to give up her children. Record Commissioners of the City of Boston, *Dorchester Town Records*, 181.

47 See Committee of the Dorchester Antiquarian and Historical Society, *History of the Town of Dorchester*, 223–30; Forbes, *Records of the Suffolk County Court*, 258, 266; Record Commissioners of the City of Boston, *Dorchester Town Records*, 182, 214.

that she kept the ordinary better than her husband had, and in fact, they held their meetings at her tavern. In 1679 selectman William Sumner even offered to help oversee the ordinary because she was getting so old.[48] The Dorchester selectmen policed residents' behavior as part of their covenant to watch over one another, to ensure that each person "walk[ed] orderly."[49]

Idleness represented a failure not just of Puritan duty, but also of manly expectations. Dorchester men who could not provide for their families threatened ideas about what it meant to be a man. The town provided relief to those suffering financially because of a family death, old age, disability, or other problems that might prevent a man from working, but men did not receive it without a cost to their reputations. In 1679 the selectmen called on Francis Ball to discuss his "outward estate" after he requested town assistance. They told him to place his children in another home, something Ball explained that his wife was unwilling to do. He received free shoes that year from a widow's donation to the poor, and the church collected money and two half bushels of corn for him. Frances Ball appeared on relief records as early as 1655 and received rent and money for the next three decades. Ball lived in the town for at least seventeen years and was a member of the church, but his small "outward estate" and his failure to live up to male expectations as the head of a family worried the selectmen.[50]

Civil and ecclesiastical authorities were also concerned with residents running their household economies properly, as evidenced not only in the great hen squabble, but in records of the earliest generation of settlers as well. In Dorchester, the settlers named the original commons "Cow Pastures" and another common area "Calf Pastures," for cows

---

[48] See Committee of the Dorchester Antiquarian and Historical Society, *History of the Town of Dorchester*, 206, 240; Hope, *Records of the First Church of Dorchester*, 92; Forbes, *Records of the Suffolk County Court*, 814, 957, 1015, 1160. See also Sharon Salinger, *Taverns and Drinking in Early America* (Baltimore: Johns Hopkins University Press, 2002), 115, 164–65, 168. Salinger explains that many widows ran ordinaries to escape "poor relief" when their husbands died.

[49] For an analysis of deviant Puritans, see Erikson, *Wayward Puritans*. Erikson does not distinguish between deviant men and women but argues that Puritans used discipline/policing to permanently exclude a deviant class. While certainly there were some "misfits," most censured individuals were not permanently excluded from church and did include some people of status.

[50] Frances Ball appeared on relief records as early as 1655 and received rent and money for the next three decades. See Record Commissioners of the City of Boston, *Dorchester Town Records*, 119, 177, 220, 236, 247, 261, 319.

were plentiful, as were hogs.[51] By 1633 they enacted "many orders...and penalties" regarding cattle and fences.[52] Problems with fences became a recurrent theme throughout New England's history. In 1647 the selectmen organized a committee to view the fences in the great lots and "apportion each man his share" to control the damage.[53] Hog control first appeared in a 1633 order. As late as 1673 an order by the selectmen required Robert Spur and Obediah Hawe to watch for hogs unringed or unhooked and to demand payment from the owners for wayward swine.[54] Additionally, selectmen paid hunters to kill wolves that preyed on livestock. However, it was not just wild animals that impeded the colonists' livelihood. In 1657 the selectmen enacted a penalty of twenty shillings to "offending parties" who polluted roads by "lumbering them up with manure, wood, timber, stones, building of hovels, styes for swine, saw-pits, and clay-pits."[55] Cows on the roads sometimes caused trouble, such as on the night of September 17, 1661, when Major General Humphrey Atherton traveled home from Boston and was fatally thrown from his startled horse when it ran into a cow in the middle of the road.[56] Many of the people admonished by the courts and selectmen found themselves also being disciplined by their congregations.

CHURCH DISCIPLINE

Most Massachusetts Bay churches followed similar standards when censuring their members. In 1644 John Cotton wrote that church discipline represented the "key of order." Such a key "is the power whereby every member of the Church walketh orderly himself...and helpeth his brethren to walk orderly also."[57] In 1648 Puritan minister Thomas Hooker explained the necessity of church discipline: "[God] hath appointed Church-censures as good Physick, to purge out what

---

[51] Whitney, "Seventeenth-Century Survey," 17.
[52] Record Commissioners of the City of Boston, *Dorchester Town Records*, 3.
[53] Committee of the Dorchester Antiquarian and Historical Society, *History of the Town of Dorchester*, 179.
[54] Record Commissioners of the City of Boston, *Dorchester Town Records*, 3.
[55] Committee of the Dorchester Antiquarian and Historical Society, *History of the Town of Dorchester*, 186–88.
[56] Committee of the Dorchester Antiquarian and Historical Society, *History of the Town of Dorchester*, 191; Winthrop, *Winthrop's Journal*; Blake, *Annals*, 22.
[57] John Cotton, *The Keyes to the Kingdom of Heaven and Power Thereof* (London: M. Simmons, 1644), B7.

is evill, as well as Word and Sacraments, which, like good diet, are sufficient to nourish the soul to eternal life." Hooker believed that church members must watch over one another, "each particular brother (appointed) as a skillful Apothecary, to help forward the spiritual health of all in confederacy with him."[58] John Cotton explained that the church put this power in the hands of the laity to prevent abuse of power by the clergy.[59] Voting on censure cases meant that the laity had some authority over their fellow church members. They had to determine the merits of an accusation, judge the sincerity of a confession, and mete out a judgment.

Censure cases included a consultation with the minister, intervention by the elders, and a final vote from the male laity. Often, prior to a censure case appearing before the congregation, the church elders would meet with the sinner to give counsel and urge confession. Ministers consulted the elders on the nature of the sin and discussed those who refused to repent. Ministers and elders were supposed to handle private sins, while only public sins were tried before the congregation. Generally, public sins were those transgressions committed in front of one or two witnesses. In reality, the distinction was blurred, and "public sin" became any sin that people found out about. Congregations dropped censure cases when witnesses could not substantiate the sin. In 1727, when the Plymouth congregation tried censuring Lydia Cushman for drunkenness, she swore that an illness caused her strange behavior. Without witnesses to corroborate her inebriated state, the congregation dismissed the charges. Four years later Cushman faced another censure for drunkenness, and this time witnesses were able to describe her antics and the congregation suspended her.[60]

Sinners did not face their congregations for most private sins, which often dealt with impiety and struggles with faith. Congregations never charged a sinner with impiety. When Samuel Sewall wrote in his diary about his struggles over his "spiritual weakness and temptations," he met with his pastors, who encouraged him to pray. However, when Thomas Sargeant uttered "blasphemous" words about the Holy Ghost in a public

---

[58] Thomas Hooker, *A Survey of the Summe of Church-Discipline* (London: Printed by A. M. for John Bellamy, 1648), 33.

[59] See Cotton, *Keyes to the Kingdom of Heaven.* This practice of lay voting power was unique to the congregational churches of the Puritans. Presbyterians had elders and lay leaders meet privately to discuss and decide censure action.

[60] *Plymouth Church Records*, 235.

meeting, he was censured.[61] One man kept his struggles to himself, while the other expressed his outwardly.

A sinner had to confess in front of the entire congregation. While women frequently had the option of having their confession read for them, the brethren and the sisters in the meeting hall still focused their attention on her. As the minister or deacon read her confession, all eyes were on the sinner. Censure cases were supposed to be lessons for everyone, to encourage the entire community to walk orderly by using the sinner as an example. Each censure became part theater and part religious edification. The congregation listened for key words and phrases that displayed humility, sincerity, and penitence. The sinner had to convey true remorse in front of neighbors, family, friends, and foes. There was a fine line between displaying the humility necessary for forgiveness and humiliating yourself in front of your community. More than one sinner cracked under such social pressure. Men lost their voices, women cried, and some simply refused to appear for years on end.[62]

Over three generations, Puritans consistently emphasized the need for church discipline. In 1680, the second-generation Puritan churches adopted the Cambridge "Platform of Church Discipline," which further explained the purpose of censures:

The censures of the church are appointed by Christ for the preventing, removing, and healing of offenses in the church; for the reclaiming and gaining of offending brethren; for the deterring others from the like offences; for purging out the leaven which may infect the whole lump; for vindicating the honor of Christ, and of his Church, and the whole profession of the gospel; and for preventing the wrath of God.[63]

---

[61] Sewall, *Diary of Samuel Sewall, 1674–1729*, 4, 32–33.

[62] For a discussion of Puritan psychology, see Cohen, *God's Caress*; and Erikson, *Wayward Puritans*. For a discussion on social controls, see E. Brooks Holifield, "Peace, Conflict, and Ritual in Puritan Congregations," *Journal of Interdisciplinary History* XXIII (Winter 1993): 551–70; Raymond A. Mentzer, *Sins and the Calvinists: Morals, Control, and the Consistory in the Reformed Tradition* (Kirksville: Sixteenth-Century Journal Publishers, Inc., 1994); Gerald F. Moran and Maris A. Vinovskis, *Religion, Family and the Life Course: Explorations in the Social History of Early America* (New York: Harper & Row, 1992); William E. Nelson, *Dispute and Conflict Resolution in Plymouth County, Massachusetts, 1725–1825* (Chapel Hill: University of North Carolina Press, 1981).

[63] *The Cambridge and Saybrook Platforms of Church Discipline, with the Confession of Faith of the New England Churches, Adopted in 1680* (Boston: T. R. Marvin, 1829), 54–55.

In 1701 Westfield's minister, Edward Taylor, wrote that censures "recover the Poore Soule from his wound [of Satan], and take the Captive out of the hand of the adversary; As also to keep the Holy Place clean from being defiled."[64] Hooker, Cotton, and Taylor all emphasized the importance of church discipline for maintaining a holy community.[65]

Even though ministers could not formally direct the course of accusations, censures, or confessions, some ministers tried to use their influence more than did others.[66] Edward Taylor frequently offered to instigate a censure case or help write a confession. He had varied results. While several congregants used his help with their written confessions, many in the congregation did not readily accept his intrusions into disciplinary matters. In 1712 Benjamin Smith petitioned to have his aging father-in-law legally put under his care. Taylor sided against Smith, going so far as to write a letter to the court at North Hampton. Smith, frustrated, called for Taylor's letters to be read at a conference held to handle the matter, whereupon an irate Taylor argued that he did not intend the letters to be read publicly. In his diary he fumed that Smith had belittled him to the committee. Taylor tried to have Smith censured for "disobedience, provoking a minister, impenitency, false speaking, and threats." When his congregation refused to call a vote on Smith's alleged sins, Taylor threatened to suspend church services. He did not administer the Lord's Supper during the entire seventeen-week ordeal. Five months after the case ended Taylor issued two disciplinary sermons to his congregation. Although Taylor wanted Smith to repent, the laymen held the ultimate power of censure and did not honor their minister's strong demands.[67]

At times the male laity explicitly admonished the clergy for trying to sway the disciplinary process. In 1709 colonial leader and magistrate

[64] Taylor, *Church Records*, 174.

[65] For a discussion of church discipline, see Charles Francis Adams, *Some Phases of Sexual Morality and Church Discipline in Colonial New England* (Boston: Massachusetts Historical Society, 1891); Gerald Harris, "The Beginnings of Church Discipline: 1 Corinthians 5," *New Testament Studies* 37 (1991): 1–21; Oberholzer, *Delinquent Saints*; Wilberforce, *Church Courts*.

[66] For a discussion of lay and ministerial power, see Nehemiah Adams, *The Autobiography of Thomas Shepard* (Boston: Pierce and Parker, 1832); Hall, *The Faithful Shepherd*; Hall, *Worlds of Wonder*; Hall, *Lived Religion*; Selement, *Keepers of the Vineyard*; and Selement, "The Meeting of Elite and Popular Minds at Cambridge, New England, 1638–1645," *William and Mary Quarterly* 41, no. I (1984): 32–48.

[67] See Taylor, *Church Records*, 215–25.

Samuel Sewall was particularly upset when Pastor Pemberton had a young woman, Hannah Butler, renew her baptismal covenant by offering a confession of faith, which the congregation accepted with a silent vote. During the process, Pemberton revealed that she had sinned against the seventh commandment, "thou shalt not commit adultery." Sewall was outraged that Pemberton did not give the congregation previous notice so they could have the opportunity to fully investigate whether or not Butler had sufficiently repented. "Ignorant Consent is no Consent," Sewall wrote in his journal. Pemberton must have had a history of bypassing the process, as Sewall was clearly not the only member angered over Pemberton's maneuver. Sewall also noted that he heard that Pemberton promised the congregation he would never do it again.[68]

Exchanges could get tense when the male laity disagreed with ministers, elders, or each other. In 1640 when Boston's notorious scoundrel Richard Wayte was accused of stealing, overcharging for goods, lechery, keeping evil company, and drunkenness (more on him later), the male laity refused to take the minister's advice to remove his admonishment. Historian Helle Alpert explains that "many members independently formed their own opinions and voiced them, even though they differed from the recommendation of the elders: they simply did not share the elders conviction of Wayte's sincerity."[69] While some were unmoved, other men argued that they needed to learn more about Wayte's late-night antics with "wicked" people. The pastor, John Wilson, and church elders were angry when two brethren, Goodman Button and James Johnson refused to vote. Even Governor Winthrop intervened to convince the laymen to accept Wayte's confession, attempting to reason with them that "searching other men's souls could be uncertain." Winthrop's suggestion is interesting, because searching other men's souls was exactly what the congregation was mandated to do as a covenanted church. But, clearly, Winthrop's comment illustrated the discord within the congregation on how exactly to discern sincerity. In Winthrop's estimation, Wayte met the standard: "For my owne part...I cannot but acknowledge my self satisfied and my heart, it ready to imbrace him...The church may doe what they will."[70] The disgruntled laymen prevailed

---

[68] Sewall, *Diary of Samuel Sewall, 1674–1729*, 627.

[69] Helle M. Alpert, "Robert Keayne: Notes of sermons by John Cotton and Proceedings of the First Church of Boston from 23 November 1639 to 1 June 1640" (PhD diss., Tufts University, 1974), 89.

[70] Alpert, "Robert Keayne," 313.

and excommunicated Wayte, but not without some hard feelings in the
congregation.

High status or wealth could not shield a sinner from censure. Famed
minister John Cotton's son was excommunicated from the Boston First
Church in 1644 for "uncleane practices" with three women.[71] Thomas
Dudley served as governor of Massachusetts Bay and was one of the
founders of the town of Cambridge and Harvard College. His eldest
daughter, Anne Bradstreet, was a poet and the first New England woman
to be published. His son Joseph would also serve as governor. However,
Boston First Church excommunicated Governor Dudley's daughter
Sarah in 1647, after a series of scandalous events. Sarah was married
to Benjamin Keayne, son of merchant Robert Keayne. Benjamin went
on a business trip to England, and when he was reunited with Sarah, he
accused her of giving him syphilis. Her well-connected father was seemingly able to get her a divorce, but she was eventually excommunicated
for "evil carriage" with another man.[72] And, as Chapter 5 illustrates,
money and social position did not protect Ann Hibbens from excommunication or hanging.

At times families discreetly dealt with wayward children to protect
them from censure. Governor Joseph Dudley and Judge Samuel Sewall
found themselves at odds as they each tried to protect their own children
from the rebuke of censure and public ridicule. Sewall's son Samuel was
married to Dudley's daughter Rebekkah, and their marriage grew rocky
from multiple miscarriages and infant deaths. While Samuel turned to
drink, Rebekkah found comfort with another man and gave birth to an
illegitimate son. The families fought and hurled accusations at both parties, and Samuel lived off and on with his parents as the family patriarchs
negotiated. After one trip to visit the unhappy couple and an encounter

---

[71] Richard D. Pierce, ed., *The Records of the First Church of Salem, Massachusetts, 1629–1736*
(Salem: Essex Institute, 1974), 60–61; Richard Godbeer, *Sexual Revolution in Early
America* (Baltimore: Johns Hopkins University Press, 2002), 98. He was readmitted a
month later after a sincere confession.

[72] Pierce, *Records of the First Church of Salem*, 25; Bernard Bailyn, ed., *The Apologia
of Robert Keayne: The Self-Portrait of a Puritan Merchant* (Boston: Colonial Society
of Massachusetts, 1964), 576; T. H. Breen, *The Character of the Good Ruler: A Study of
Puritan Political Ideas in New England, 1630–1730* (New Haven: Yale University Press,
1970), 37. There are no records of what could be the first divorce in the colony; however,
Sarah did eventually remarry, indicating she did divorce Benjamin.

with Rebekkah's alleged lover, Judge Sewall lamented of his son, "Lord save him and us."[73] Eventually the families reached an agreement that kept the couple together – and out of the church or courts.[74]

MINISTERIAL EXPECTATIONS AND PURITAN DOCTRINE

Puritan ministers called on all their congregants to be both pious and dutiful, to watch over the community, and to be humble, passive, and meek before God. The clergy defined a single Puritanism for both the men and women in their congregations, following Calvin's edict of a "priesthood of all believers."[75] Puritan doctrine asserted that souls were spiritually equal and had equal access to church membership, redemption, and God.

Puritan doctrine described souls as feminine. When minister Thomas Shepard lamented the sinful nature of human souls, he compared the soul to a woman. "When the soul sees that all its righteousness is a menstrous cloth, polluted with sin ... it begins to cry out, How can I stand or appear before him with such continual pollutions."[76] In their call for a feminized piety, ministers used feminine metaphors to explain a Puritan's relationship to Christ.[77] When William Brattle delivered sermons in Cambridge in the late seventeenth century, he described conversion as the process of turning a lion into a lamb, explaining that "for tho men before conversion may be compared to wolves, lions and after conversion he is lambs & kids." And he compared the "marriage of ye lamb" to Christ, the bridegroom. He lectured that "ye bride makes herself ready ... fit for ye entertainment of a great king; it is ye solemn marriage of ye lamb." Brattle lectured, "When Christ comes as a Bridegroome he comes personally ... There is great preparation of ye wedding ... Is ye solemn marriage of ye Lamb to ye whole church ... he comes as husband to dwell with his wife." Brattle described a feminine supplicant congregant who waited for Christ as an eager bride.[78] Historian Amanda Porterfield argues that

[73] Sewall, *Diary of Samuel Sewall, 1674–1729*, 728, 732, 815, 835–36.
[74] Part of the negotiations ensured that the illegitimate son would have no claim to the Sewall inheritance.
[75] Leslie J. Lindenauer, *Piety and Power: Gender and Religious Culture in the American Colonies, 1630–1700* (New York: Routledge, 2002), xvi.
[76] Thomas Shepard, *The Sound Believer*, quoted in Mack, *Visionary Women*, 19.
[77] See Reis, *Damned Women*, 39, 101.
[78] William Brattle, Sermons Delivered in Cambridge, ms., William Brattle II, Misc. Volume, Massachusetts Historical Society.

ministers demanded female piety from their congregations as a vehicle for social cohesion.[79] All Puritans needed to be supplicant to Christ, and thus the church, to ensure order in this new society.

Many Puritan clerics utilized the metaphor of the laity as bride and Christ as bridegroom, including John Cotton, who wrote about waiting for Christ. In a 1651 sermon, Cotton asked his congregation, "Have you the strong desire to meet him in the bed of loves … and desire to have the seeds of his grace shed abroad in your hearts and bring forth the fruit of his grace?"[80] John Oxenbridge of Boston described a "royal reception" that Christ the bridegroom would offer his bride.[81] Shepard also expressed his submissiveness to Christ as a bridegroom, writing that he received Christ as a "husband" who he "lusted" for. When Shepard's wife lay sick in childbed, he felt guilty because he lusted more for his wife than for Christ. "I began to grow secretly proud and full of sensuality delighting my soul in my dear wife more than in my god."[82]

Edward Taylor, who was also a poet, frequently used feminized imagery to describe one's relationship with Christ. In his poem "Let Him Kiss Me with the Kisse of His Mouth," he prayed for a kiss and Christ's "sweet love." He wrote erotically that "the prayers of love ascend in gracious tune to him as musick, and as heart perfume." Taylor described a feminized spiritual eroticism. He wrote that he would "prepare his soul as a 'feather bed … with gospel pillows, sheets and sweet perfumes' to welcome Christ the lover." Historian Richard Godbeer asserts that Taylor described the soul as a womb waiting to be implanted by Christ's seed. Joseph Rowlandson preached a jeremiad, "The Possibility of God's Forsaking a People," in which he compared Christ to a father and Puritans to a wife: "He is a Father, and a tender-hearted Father … Can children be willing their Father should leave them? He is a Husband … a loving, careful, tender husband too; can the Wife be willing to part with

[79] Amanda Porterfield, *Female Piety in Puritan New England: The Emergence of Religious Humanism* (New York: Oxford University Press, 1992), 7.

[80] Donald E. Stanford, ed., *The Poems of Edward Taylor* (New Haven: Yale University Press, 1960), 142, 164, 212, 230, 248, 259, 295, 362–63, 448; John Cotton, *Christ the Fountain of Life*, 36–37, quoted in Godbeer, *Sexual Revolution in Early America*, 54; and Cotton, *Practical Commentary*, 131, quoted in Godbeer, *Sexual Revolution in Early America*, 54.

[81] John Oxenbridge, "Conversion of the Gentiles," ms., Ms. SBd-56, Massachusetts Historical Society, 1690.

[82] Adams, *Autobiography of Thomas Shepard*, 27, 39.

her husband?" He warned his listeners that they could be left orphans and widows if they abandoned Christ.[83]

Ministers also expected their followers to be self-critical and debasing, a demeanor considered feminine. Even in his own autobiography, Shepard used such feminine language, consistently describing himself as unworthy, torturing himself with doubt and loathing. He wrote, "He is the God that convinced me of my guilt, filth of sin, self-seeking, and love of honor…and humbled me…and to loath myself the more."[84] As he considered joining the ministry, he wrote that he was "like a vile wretch in the use of God's gifts" and that he was "so unholy" that his "spirits began to sink."[85] When lecturing on prayer, Brattle reminded his listeners of the need for a feminized demeanor: "They ought to pray unto God with an abasing and humbling sense of [guilt] upon their hearts…they ought to pray with a deep sense of their unworthiness…and even thus with ye deepest of self-abasement and inward humility." In one of John Cotton's sermons, he urged his listeners to "break open the stony doores of your heart…and to give you an heart to give up your soule and body and spirit" to Christ.[86] In another sermon he preached how patience, humility, and zeal could lead to righteousness, and he pointed to faith, love, knowledge, and meekness as the path to purity of heart.[87]

Sermons consistently extolled the virtues of humility, submissiveness, and a childlike dependence on Christ. In 1631 William Perkins described his parishioners as children breastfed with the milk of the scriptures.[88] Ministers used metaphors of pregnancy and motherhood to describe the relationship with Christ. John Rogers taught that "every child is pregnant…with the seeds of all sin." The metaphor of pregnant sin called on a Puritan to imagine his body nourishing sin, like a pregnant woman nourishes her child. Such imagery blurred the distinction of body and

---

[83] Neal Salisbury, ed., *The Sovereignty and Goodness of God, Together with the Faithfulness of His Promises Displayed: Being a Narrative of the Captivity and Restoration of Mrs. Mary Rowlandson* (Boston: Bedford Books, 1996), 149–52.

[84] Adams, *Autobiography of Thomas Shepard*, 73.

[85] Adams, *The Autobiography of Thomas Shepard*, 24–25.

[86] Everett H. Emerson, ed., *Gods Mercie Mixed with His Justice; or His Peoples Deliverance in Times o Danger by John Cotton, 1641* (Gainesville: Scholars Facsimile Reprints, 1977), 25.

[87] Emerson, *Gods Mercie*, 40–42.

[88] William Perkins, *Works*, quoted in Stephen Baskerville, "The Family in Puritan Political Theology," *Journal of Family History* 18 (1993), 161.

soul and asked the godly to feminize themselves. Ministers expected such feminized piety from both male and female congregants.[89]

Ministers may have called for a feminized piety, but New England men were not going to adopt such a demeanor publicly and would seek to regulate social behavior in a more gendered fashion.[90] Doctrine did not define censure in any gendered way; the same rules regarding sins and confession should have applied to men and women alike. However, as a public performance, the laity developed different standards for both. It was easier for them to expect women to be obedient, humble, and self-critical. Laymen did not necessarily want to humiliate their fellow man in the same way. As Puritans created new social norms, ideas of masculinity varied between laymen and ministers. More traditional gender concepts won out over the theological ideas of the feminized soul.

TRADITIONAL GENDER ROLES

Although gender ideologies were in flux in the seventeenth and early eighteenth centuries, the strong pull of patriarchy continued to maintain that women were weak and men were strong. Several historians – including Phyllis Mack, Elizabeth Reis, Amanda Porterfield, Susan Juster, and Carolyn Merchant – have examined the understanding of masculinity and femininity during that time. Protestant reformers, philosophers, and scientists explained how women's bodies and souls were unstable, causing them to be irrational, weak, emotional, and dependent. Mack explains how society believed that female bodies were more "wet and spongy," which made her "lustful, irrational, emotional…moody, and impulsive, which is why men needed to control them."[91] Protestant John Knox, in a 1558 tract to discredit women as political rulers, asserted that

---

[89] John Rogers, *Death the Certain Wages of Sin,* 95, quoted in Godbeer, *Sexual Revolution in Early America,* 68. For a discussion of the body/soul and feminized soul, see Reis, *Damned Women,* 93–120; and Marilyn J. Westerkamp, "Engendering Puritan Religious Culture in Old and New England," *Pennsylvania History* 64 (1977): 105–77.

[90] Recent historians of early American religion have called attention to the disjuncture between lay-cleric belief systems in the scholarship, such as Hall, *Worlds of Wonder;* Cohen, *God's Caress;* and Jon Butler, *Awash in a Sea of Faith: Christianizing the American People* (Cambridge: Harvard University Press, 1990). Countering this recent historiography, and asserting that the laity agreed with their ministers, is Selement, *Keepers of the Vineyard.*

[91] Mack, *Visionary Women,* 25–26. See also Juster, *Disorderly Women,* 5.

because women were physically and mentally weaker, they were meant to be obedient servants to their husbands.[92] John Calvin argued that it was because of Eve's original sin that women were forced into the role of the subservient wife.[93] Seventeenth-century society viewed men as strong and rational. Men were not judged by their inherent nature, but rather by their social status and public reputations. Men were public beings, associated with the material world, while women were understood to be private, internal, and spiritual.[94]

The male laity charged with church discipline did not conform to the clerical prescriptions, instead developing a different pattern of ideas and practices that can be traced through the church records. Censure cases illustrate how laymen did not accept the requirements of feminization and created censure patterns that allowed men to retain their public masculinity by focusing not on their personal piety but on their public actions and duties. The laity used church discipline to define and fix rules, which consequently gendered souls, sins, and censure practices.

Through courts, town governments, and churches, Puritans policed behavior to ensure that congregants honored their contract with God. Whether it was Goodwife Dewy, censured for lying about the great hen squabble, or members with other sinful offenses, church discipline was central to regulating the godly path. As the following chapters will explore, how laymen enforced church discipline had important consequences for men, women, and Puritanism itself.

[92] John Knox, "The First Blast of the Trumpet against the Monstrous Regime of Women," quoted in Carolyn Merchant, *The Death of Nature: Women, Ecology and the Scientific Revolution* (San Francisco: Harper Row, 1980), 145.

[93] Merchant, *The Death of Nature*, 146.

[94] For a further discussion of "weak" women, see also Karlsen, *Devil in the Shape of a Woman*; and Merchant, *The Death of Nature*.

2

Drunkards and Fornicators on Meeting House Hill

Gendered Sin and Discipline

Wandering home after a night at the taverns in the summer of 1688, a young man swayed and fell from his horse, passed out drunk. About an hour later, a church elder traveling along the road with a group of women came upon him lying face down, unconscious. The group easily recognized the man as Consider Atherton, the son of one of Dorchester's founding fathers. Consider's hat lay crumpled at his side, and his horse fed on some nearby grass, nonplussed by the ordeal. When Elder Blake tried to wake Atherton, he hardly budged. Once roused, "he was soe drunk & reeled & staggered" off.[1] As the group watched his retreat, they must have thought of Consider's late father, the decorated Major General Humphrey Atherton. The senior Atherton was a war hero who took a fatal fall from a horse while returning from negotiations with a nearby Indian tribe – a huge loss to the community. On his tombstone the town inscribed a poem:

> Here lied our Captain Major of Suffolk was withal,
> A godly Magistrate was he, and Major General.
> Two troops of horse with him here came his worth such love did crave,
> Ten companies of foot also, mourning marched to his grave.
> Let all that read be sure to keep the faith as he had done:
> With Christ he lives now crowned, his name was Humphrey Atherton

The back of the tombstone read, "The memory of the first Captains and officers of the Ancient and Honourable Artillery Company; may their

---

[1] Dorchester First Parish Church Records (1636–1981; I.A. Loose Church Records, 1680–1981), Massachusetts Historical Society, Boston.

succesors, to the latest era, be remembered as first on the list of valour, patriotism, and virtue." The Atherton family legacy must have been on everyone's mind as they watched Consider stagger down the road, an unheroic and notorious drunkard.

This was not the first time Consider's congregation had had to deal with his drunken behavior. They first censured Atherton for drunkenness in 1683, but he had already established a pattern, the church records indicating he "had fallen into ye sine of drunknes both formerly & now againe of late." Even before his first church disciplinary action, the Suffolk County Court had convicted Atherton in 1678 for breaking into Nicholas Bolton's house to steal cider.[2]

By the summer of 1688, he had a lengthy record. On a humid July Sunday, he stood before his congregation and explained that his untimely nap on the road was caused by his trip to taverns, or ordinaries, in Roxbury and Boston. Unsatisfied with his brief answer, the church brethren reminded Consider of his previous censure earlier that spring and sent him home to contemplate a more penitent confession suitable for a man with his pattern of sinfulness. When he made yet another failed attempt at a confession, the laity decided he needed an intervention and scheduled a meeting with the pastor. Unfortunately, when Consider met with Pastor John Danforth, he was in no shape to reflect on his sins and quickly excused himself, immediately passing out drunk on the highway by Hawkins Brook. People who found him could not budge him awake, and the story circulated that he had been up all night with friends at the local Chaplin's ordinary.[3]

By his fifth attempt at a sincere confession, the brethren had lost patience with Consider. On July 15, 1688, they admonished him and contemplated excommunication. The church judged him to be "an obstinate ofendor & an incoridgable drunkard" and proclaimed that his sin resided in his "idlness, his breach of former promises, his rebellion against ye church."[4] The congregation was especially offended by Atherton's failure to live up to his duty to his community, keep his promises, and behave as a godly Dorchester man. It must have been a disappointment that an Atherton had been so publicly shamed. Consider's father helped found the church and town, became an important Indian negotiator, and was a celebrated war hero. Consider's brother, Hope, attended Harvard, taught

---

[2] Forbes, *Records of the Suffolk County Court*, 957.
[3] Hope, *Records of the First Church of Dorchester*, 91, 96.
[4] Hope, *Records of the First Church of Dorchester*, 91, 92, 97, 957.

school in Dorchester, and then took over the pulpit in Hadley. Regrettably, Consider started his own family tradition: his son Humphrey faced five censure charges for drunkenness in later years.[5]

During his life, Consider Atherton had watched the congregation censure other sisters and brothers who did not "walk orderly." The ministers of the Dorchester meetinghouse, like those throughout Massachusetts Bay, stressed a path of duty and piety for all their members, but through the course of the seventeenth century, this became a gendered road.

GENDERED PATTERNS OF CHURCH CENSURES

Throughout the church disciplinary process, men and women were treated differently with regard to the types of sins they were censured for, the expectations for their confessions, and the judgments they received. Several patterns emerge in the records, illustrating that the male laity focused on dereliction of duty and behavior for men, while reprimanding women for their sinful souls. Church records show how congregations viewed sinners, as they documented what elders or brethren said about the accused during the disciplinary process.

Male laity censured men and women for a wide variety of sins. The most common sins are listed in Table 2.1, and, as indicated, the top three male sins were drinking, Sabbath breaking, and business fraud, while the top female sins were fornication, drinking, and lying.

MISCREANTS

Failure in their dedication to the community was a main focus for male censure cases. When men misbehaved during church services, they would be subject to censure. In 1659 the male laity censured Jeremi Haaws for misbehaving in the meetinghouse during a Day of Humiliation. Similarly, the church records described Daniel Ellen and Joshua George, censured for contemptuous carriage, as "negligent" in their duties and noted their "miscarriage." Attending Sabbath services was mandatory, and if someone moved to a different area, they were required to register with their new congregation or face censure charges. In 1682, when Patience Blake experienced a problem switching congregations, the Dorchester congregation discussed it as "her great sin."[6] Because she was a woman, the

---

[5] Hope, *Records of the First Church of Dorchester*, 29, 131, 223, 227, 237.
[6] Hope, *Records of the First Church of Dorchester*, 89–90.

TABLE 2.1. *Most frequent sins*

Sin	Men	Women	Couples
Business Fraud/Ethics	11	1	0
Defamation	4	1	0
Drunkenness	62	13	0
Entertaining Sin	5	4	0
Fighting	5	0	0
Fornication	4	75	13
Lascivious Carriage	6	4	0
Lying	8	12	0
Neglect of Family	7	3	0
Offense against a Person	8	1	0
Quarreling	4	1	0
Sabbath Breaking	28	7	1
Slander	4	5	0
Swearing/Cursing/Profanity	7	0	0
Multiple Sins Charged	27	16	0

congregation treated her transgression differently than those of her male counterparts. Just two years later, in 1684, Ebenezer Lyon tried to join the church, but a few parishioners were offended by remarks he had made. He offered a written confession but denied some of the accusations, and the congregation rejected his admittance, instructing Lyon to "watch his life and conversation." Malachi Halloway stood before his former Dorchester congregation in 1691 because he refused to be under the watch of the church in his new home in Taunton. The brethren did not question his Christian piety, but listened to him exclaim about the Taunton church being "covenant breakers" and talked to him a great deal about his "conflict" with the church, but not a conflict within his soul. They pursued discussions with him for a year,[7] yet they did not comment on his lack of piety, instead urging him to consider his actions more carefully.[8]

One of the most important religious duties a male church member had was to vote in congregation matters. In 1681 the laity met to decide between two candidates for pastor – John Danforth of Roxbury and

---

[7] Hope, *Records of the First Church of Dorchester*, 15, 32, 80, 82; Forbes, *Records of the Suffolk County Court*, 915.
[8] Hope, *Records of the First Church of Dorchester*, 69, 91.

Reverend Jeremiah Cushing of Hingham. John Breck, although not a full member, felt strongly that he deserved a voice in the matter and therefore cast a vote for minister. This caused quite a scene in the meetinghouse, and every member except Henry Leadbetter voted to expel Breck from the meeting. The next week, the elders announced that they had spoken with Breck and that he "was sorry yt he had acted soe as he did in yt manner & yt if any elce weer unsatisfied" they could talk to him directly.[9] Again, Breck offers an example of a man who "acted" in poor judgment and offered to heal relationships rather than discuss his sinful soul.

Congregations censured men for dereliction of public duty, whether it was filing false lawsuits, arguing over property lines, charging inflated prices, tearing down a neighbor's mill, whaling on the Sabbath, committing land fraud, or behaving poorly during military exercises. In 1681 church elders went to Thomas Davenport's house to counsel him over fraud in a land deal.[10] In 1696 Boston's Second Church censured James Fowl for neglecting his militia watch.[11] In the winter of 1682, when the Westfield congregation censured John Maudsley for "dishonoring God," they were speaking of a lawsuit he filed against the town because he was upset about a recent land distribution deal and the subsequent speculation about a new highway going through his property. In censuring him, his congregation believed he broke the fifth, eighth, ninth, and tenth commandments. Regarding the fifth commandment to "honor thy father and thy mother," they cited his unrighteous lawsuit against the town. Under the eighth commandment, "thou shalt not steal," the congregation argued Maudsley was "stirring up authority" to protect his land and did not follow "lawful proceedings." As for the ninth commandment of "not bearing false witness," they decided Maudsley lied when he argued that he did not get proper satisfaction in the land deal. Finally, they cited the tenth commandment about coveting thy neighbor's house, to argue that he would not have proceeded with the lawsuit if he had adhered to such guidance. The congregation accepted his promise "to meddle no more in this matter," and they warned him to "be more watchful."[12] His congregation chose to address the legal and business ventures of Maudsley, emphasizing how his actions had disrupted the public order. In this

---

[9] Hope, *Records of the First Church of Dorchester*, 85.
[10] Hope, *Records of the First Church of Dorchester*, 86.
[11] Boston Second Church, Book of Second Church Records (1689–1717), Massachusetts Historical Society, Boston.
[12] Taylor, *Church Records*, 178–79.

new "experiment in the wilderness," Puritan men were the foundation of a well-ordered society. In regulating their behavior through the disciplinary process, laymen continually emphasized the primacy of their public responsibilities.

One of the more noteworthy censures involved an influential but infamous merchant, Robert Keayne. In 1639 the Boston First Church censured the merchant for inflating prices to the dishonor of God. He was charged "for selling his wares at excessive Rates, to the Dishonor of Gods name, the Offence of the Generall Cort, and the Publique scandall of the Cuntry."[13] By the time of this action, Keayne had already developed a bad reputation as a heartless businessman and had been sued for allegedly stealing a neighbor's pig. Although the General Court ruled in Keayne's favor, rumors persisted that he did indeed steal the sow (he was the son of a butcher, after all).[14] Although he held prominent offices upon his arrival in Boston – including as surveyor, selectman, and representative of the General Court – he was nonetheless highly unpopular. Keayne took the censure very seriously – not as a warning that he endangered his soul but rather believing that his reputation, and thus his business, would suffer.[15] It took him almost a year, but Keayne finally offered up a penitent confession, even though he never forgave his community for disparaging him. Keayne was further humiliated when his daughter-in-law, Sarah Dudley, was excommunicated for an adulterous relationship with one Nicholas Tauton.[16] His son Benjamin, Sarah's husband, left for England shortly thereafter. Perhaps it was the family drama that led him to drinking, for in 1652 Keayne was charged in court and in church with the sin of drunkenness and was forced to resign his public posts. In his last will and testament, he defends his faith and his actions:

It was the greife of my soule (and I desire it may ever be so in a greater measure) that any act of mine (though not justly but by misconstruction) should be on occasion of scandall to the Gospell and pfession of the Lord Jesus or that my selfe should be looked at as one that had brought any just dishonor to God (which

---

[13] Boston First Church Records, 12; Bailyn, *Apologia of Robert Keayne,* 573.

[14] Bailyn, ed., *Apologia of Robert Keayne,* 572.

[15] Boston First Church Records, 1639. For a discussion about how this censure humiliated and disgraced him, see Bailyn, *Apologia of Robert Keayne,* vii–viii. Also see Richard Archer, *Fissures in the Rock: New England in the Seventeenth Century* (Hanover: University Press of New England, 2001), 111–33; and Mark Valeri, *Heavenly Merchandize: How Religion Shaped Commerce in Puritan America* (Princeton: Princeton University Press, 2010), 14–38.

[16] Boston First Church Records, 25, October 1647; Bailyn, *Apologia of Robert Keayne,* 576.

I have endeavored long and according to my weake abilitie desired to prvent) though god hath beene pleased for causes best knowne to himselfe to deny me such a blessing, as if it had been in my owne power I should rather have chocen to have prished in my cradle than to have lived to such a time.[17]

Keayne was angry about how the charges had damaged his reputation and continued to suggest that people misunderstood him. His will was an extended self-defense stating that his soul was grieved that people misunderstood him, not that it was sinful.

Women rarely faced charges regarding business practices and deals, since they lacked formal power in the secular world. Even when commercial disputes did arise, a congregation treated a woman differently than they would a man. They did not charge women with breaking contracts or fraud but instead made women's business transgressions personal failures of character. For example, Dorchester's Sister Chaplain borrowed money from John Green to buy a shipment of wine. When Green died and his estate tried to collect the debt from Chaplain, she refused. In 1696 the congregation did not cite her with breaking a contract, but rather with lying. Like Abigail Dewy and the great hen squabble (Chapter 1), Chaplain's censure was not about property or debt; it was about a personal lie. Lying was considered a weakness of the soul. The belief in the innate weakness of women was powerful, and it meant that women constantly posed a threat of becoming corrupt. Puritan ideology offered women greater gender fluidity than traditional gender rules, but if they challenged those boundaries and transgressed, they presented even a greater social threat to social norms. If they failed in their tasks as "deputy husbands," their sin was even more dangerous to the social order.[18] As we will see in Chapter 5 with the story of Ann Hibbens, women who meddled in business affairs could find themselves under deep suspicion.

DRUNKARDS

If the character of a colonial town depended on its village drunkards, then Dorchester could be counted among the most colorful.[19] Whether from a prominent family, the servant class, the military, or whether

---

[17] Bailyn, *Apologia of Robert Keayne*, 573–74.

[18] For a description of "deputy husband," see Ulrich, *Good Wives*, 9, 36–40.

[19] For a discussion of colonial taverns, see David W. Conroy, *In Public Houses: Drink and the Revolution of Authority in Colonial Massachusetts* (Chapel Hill: University of North Carolina Press, 1995); and Salinger, *Taverns and Drinking in Early America*.

young or old, a man sometimes found himself too drunk to "walk orderly" – or even to walk home. The church, the selectmen, and the courts were not interested in the quiet men who drank themselves to sleep at night in their own homes. They censured the drunks who made public spectacles of themselves, those found face down in the mud, those intoxicated during Sunday services, or those too drunk to speak when approached on the street.

Public drunkenness was viewed as a miscarriage of duty and responsibility. Consider Atherton caused his community great concern. They discussed his idleness, his "breach of former promises ... ye horrible refactoryness to & contempt of & rebellion against ye Church." Men faced over 86 percent of the censure charges for drunkenness. Congregations could have discussed the sin in terms of a "wicked heart" or an "evil or weak nature." Yet over and over again when censuring drunkards, congregations emphasized their failure of religious conduct, focusing on their outward behavior and not on the weakness of their souls that led them to the temptations of overindulgence.

Puritans did not condemn drinking. On the contrary, they believed moderate drinking promoted good health and considered liquor a dietary supplement. For breakfast, lunch, and dinner, or whenever thirst needed quenching, a person would likely drink beer, mead, or hard cider. During celebrations, recreation, funerals, or births, Puritans served alcohol. Drinking large amounts of alcohol became a mark of a man's worth: masculinity was linked with the ability to drink. A gentleman could be insulted if a man refused his offer of a drink. While Puritan men and women drank at home or at celebrations, the tavern or ordinary was a male institution. They became a social meeting ground, serving as the first post offices and news outlets. They were a focal point for travelers, as well as a place for locals to get the latest news or gossip, listen to music, play sporting games, or even gamble. Elite men formed clubs that met in taverns. Communities did not legally ban women but socially prohibited them. Frequenting a local ordinary could destroy a woman's reputation. This held especially true for elite women. Women could own and operate taverns, and usually widows ran such establishments to support themselves, but taverns were primarily places where "men could be men."[20] As such, drinking was a predominately male sin (Figure 2.1).

---

[20] Salinger, *Taverns and Drinking in Early America*, 3–4, 67–70, 126, 161.

FIGURE 2.1. Public drunkenness, seventeenth-century tavern. *Source:* Print
Collector/Hulton Archive/Getty Images.

Church records frequently listed a sinner as "overtaken" with drink
or noted the "miscarriage" of drinking and the "neglect of duty."[21] To be
overtaken with drink suggested that blame did not rest on one's internal
strength but on the force of outside evil. When the Plymouth congregation
censured John Grey in 1703, the brethren had tried repeatedly to res-
cue him from his sin: "Sundry times Solemnly admonished by ye church
and all due paines taken with him to Endeavour to reclaim him from the
Ill course of life as swearing drunkenness." Unable to save him, they excommunicated Grey as an "unprofitable branch and declare yt ye church
would have no more to do with him." By labeling Grey as "unprofitable,"
the congregation focused on his inability to contribute to the community.
An investment in him would not yield benefits to the whole. However, they
prayed that he might still be saved: "Ye pastor concluded ye work with a
word to ye Assembly ... with prayer both for ye man yt it might be for ye
destruction of ye flesh that ye spirit might be saved in ye day of ye Lord
Jesus ... and for others yt ye might hear and fear." He may have served as

[21] For examples, see Hope, *Records of the First Church of Dorchester*; and, Boston Second
Church, Records of the Second Church (vol. III, 1675–1685), Massachusetts Historical
Society.

an example to other wayward drinkers, as a communal lesson, but the congregation did not urge him to reflect on his own soul and piety.[22]

Men censured for drunkenness "acknowledged" their sin or their "neglect of duty," or they "manifested repentance," but they did not pray for more piety. Westfield's Stephen Kellog acknowledged he was a "sinful creature," but he did not ask for internal strength or a closer relationship with God; nor did he promise to search his soul. Instead, he asked for outside help, by "hoping God would enable him to walk with greater watchfulness."[23] Men continually emphasized the external, whether it be outside temptations, responsibilities, or assistance. Even a repeat offender such as Boston Second Church's Henry Dawson did not offer any reflection on the state of his soul. Dawson not only frequently imbibed, but he failed to attend church, kept questionable company, lied, broke promises, and "evilly spoke." When he appeared before his brethren, he "expressed sorrow, both for his Drunkenness and for ye obstinancy & Rebellion against ye Church." In this way male sinners sought to repair their standing in the community.[24]

Samuell Rigby stood before his congregation and the court at various times for cursing, excessive drinking, idleness, neglect of the law, "disorders" in his family, and beating his wife. In 1677, 1678, and 1679, the congregation called Rigby to answer for his sins. The court sentenced him in 1677 to be whipped or to pay a fine for his drunkenness, sundry behavior, and absenting himself from church. When the court called him in 1678 for excessive drinking and family problems, including hitting his wife, he asked for a jury trial. Because no witnesses would testify against Rigby, the jury found him not guilty. His congregation and the court labeled Rigby's sins as a breach of duty and a failure of public behavior.[25]

Often a drunkard earned a well-known reputation before the congregation or the courts officially censured him.[26] William Danforth's problem with drinking must have been so evident that town officials simply warned him to stop frequenting ordinaries altogether and to "set himself in a way of constant employment in some lawful calling."[27] Selectmen admonished Danforth for a failure of duty in being idle and drunk.

[22] *Plymouth Church Records*, 97.
[23] Taylor, *Church Records*, 211.
[24] Records of the Second Church, 1700.
[25] Hope, *Records of the First Church of Dorchester*, 75, 80, 81; Forbes, *Records of the Suffolk County Court*, 846, 940.
[26] Salinger, *Taverns and Drinking in Early America*, 111.
[27] Committee of the Dorchester Antiquarian and Historical Society, *History of the Town of Dorchester*, 246.

While most drunkards battled the bottle their entire lives, at least one young man learned an early lesson. Famed minister and founder of the First Church of Cambridge, Thomas Shepard, recalled in his autobiography his dissolute college years. Attending Cambridge University in England at age fifteen, Shepard admitted he drank and partied with "loose company" and recalled a particularly hard night when he woke up in a stranger's bedroom, not knowing where he was. "I awakened late on Sabbath and sick with my beastly carnage." He was so embarrassed that he left the bedchamber and wandered into the cornfields, where he hid the rest of the day. But it was while lying in the field that he considered his sorry state: "The Lord who might justly have cut me off in the midst of my sin, did meet me with much sadness of heart and troubled my soule for this and other my sins ... and made me resolve to set upon a course of dayly meditation about the evill of sin and my own ways."[28] Shepard mended his ways and turned to the ministry, but most men did not have such epiphanies in cornfields, and congregations and courts had to repeatedly castigate them.

Families of high and low status had to contend with drunkards in the family. The sad tale of the fall of Samuel Stone exemplifies how families struggled to rein in their wayward sons. Samuel was the son of the Revered Minister Samuel Stone, who helped settle the towns of Cambridge and Hartford. The younger Samuel started out in the ministry but did not last long. The Hartford community had implored Samuel to change his ways. Ministers, town leaders, and magistrates tried to help him. Samuel feigned some ambiguous illness to argue that he needed strong drink. Over the course of time, his reputation as an egregious drunkard grew. His famous father died in 1663, and his widowed mother was left to entreat him alone. She was terrified her son would die before the congregation could forgive him for his sins. In 1681, because of their reverence for her and the family name, the congregation held a special meeting to deal with Samuel. He refused to attend, believing he was blameless. Despite his mother's protestations, Samuel was excommunicated. He would not live to repent. In the summer of 1683, Samuel spent the day drinking with friends at various homes and taverns, his antics almost landing him in a fight. It was a very dark night as he stumbled home. Crossing the bridge that divided Hartford was apparently too perilous for the drunken young man, as Samuel's body was found the next morning floating down

---

[28] Thomas Shepard, Diary of Thomas Shepard, Ms S-62, Massachusetts Historical Society, 21–22.

the river. Although he had inherited his famous father's house, land, and library, on the day his body was fished out of the water, Samuel was penniless and in debt.[29]

Concerned over such excess drinking, Puritans struggled to regulate their taverns. In 1664, at a Dorchester town meeting, residents turned down a request to open an ordinary. But in 1666 they relented to pressure and allowed Nicholas George and his wife Elizabeth to open an establishment. Dorchester officials also prosecuted men who tried to sell alcohol without a license. In 1681 the court sentenced Arthur Cartwright to ten stripes of the whip for selling cider without a license.[30] And as late at 1696, the Dorchester church elders petitioned the General Court to refuse any more taverns in the town. In his memoirs, Roger Clap warned the younger generation about the dangers of ordinaries: "Flee the lusts of uncleanness, and the occasions of it. Abhor drunkenness and excessive drinking. Come not into a tavern but on just and weighty occasions."[31] Before resorting to censure, the town would try to dissuade drunkenness through private counsel, by neighborly advice, or by posting the names of the drunkards on the tavern door.[32] In 1711, as residents of East Haven began to form a church, they put a ban on alcohol sales in their founding documents in order to combat the problem of drunkenness:

Whereas the baneful effects of the use of intoxicating liquors as a beverage are abundantly proven by experience; and whereas the traffic in the same for such purposes, is a prolific cause of misery and woe, we therefore regard it a sin for any member of this Church to engage in such use or traffic. And any person seeking admission to our number who is thus engaged, shall be regarded as unworthy of our fellowship and communion.[33]

In his lengthy journal, Judge Samuel Sewall expressed a great deal of scorn for drunkards. In 1680 he wrote about an investigation of a woman found dead in her bed, covered in blood. She had been known to drink, and when the autopsy found no evidence of violence, Sewall wrote, "Her death

---

[29] John Whiting to Increase Mather, letter, published in vol. VIII, Massachusetts Historical Society Collections, 469–72; First Church of Hartford Records, Connecticut State Library.

[30] *Abstract and Index of the Records of the Inferior Court of Pleas (Suffolk County Court) Held at Boston, 1680–1698* (Boston: The Historical Records Survey, 1940), 113. The court respited his sentence for good behavior.

[31] Clap, *Memoirs*, 37.

[32] Salinger, *Taverns and Drinking in Early America*, 87.

[33] Records Old Stone Church, East Haven.

puts in mind of the proverb wherein we say such as one hath drunk more than he hath bled today." In 1713 Sewall even refused to attend the funeral of an acquaintance, noting that "he had been such a Drunkard and Idler that I went not to the Funeral, having no heart to it." And several times he wrote about trying to warn away his son Samuel from visiting taverns.[34]

Female drunkards faced less sympathetic congregations than did men. The Boston Second Church noted that Mary Cox "abandoned herself in a course of drunkenness and other scandals"[35] – that is, she abandoned herself in her sinfulness. Her struggle was not to be "profitable" to the community, but to regain herself. When six members of the Boston Church testified that they saw Ruth Fuller drunk on various occasions, four of them said she "disguised herself" with drink. Again, for a woman, the congregation put an emphasis on how this sin prevented her from being true to herself. Drinking caused Fuller to become unrecognizable; the sin changed her. In the dozens of male cases between 1630 and 1725, not one censure record used such internal, individual language about a man's body, heart, or soul. Yet continually for women the congregation emphasized the internal nature of her sin. The feisty and defiant Fuller had other ideas about her own body and argued that she "would be hanged on ye gallows" before she said anything. Sister Hix must have been one of the few well-known female drunkards. When she confessed her sin in January 1687, the records simply noted she was "often taken in yt sin," while accepting her confession.[36]

The majority of women censured for drinking also committed other "scandalous" sins. When Boston's First Church cited Anne Walker for drunkenness in 1638, they listed her "sundry scandallls, as of drunkenish, intemperate, and uncleane or wantonish behaviors, and likewise of Cruelty towards her children & also manifold lyes."[37] For women, drunken behavior was an indicator of a deeper sinful nature rather than an aberration caused by a night of partying.

FORNICATORS

Puritans defined illicit sex as a sin against the body. Ministers believed that the body "was set up to be a house for the soul to dwell and act in."

---

[34] Sewall, *Diary of Samuel Sewall*, 48, 707, 815.

[35] Boston Second Church Records, 1706.

[36] Hope, *Records of the First Church of Dorchester*, 96.

[37] Boston First Church Records, ms., Boston First Church, Massachusetts Historical Society, 1638.

Boston minister Samuel Willard explained that the "temptation of sex threatened to taint 'bodily members. Lust endeavors to keep them in its service and slavery to do its drudgery, but grace obliges them to be the servants of righteousness and employed in the glorifying of God.'" To defile the body was to contaminate the soul. Cotton Mather prayed over his concerns about his body. He wrote in his diary to "consider every part of my body, and, with as explicit an ingenuity as may be, consider the several actions and uses thereof, and then go on to consider on what methods I may serve the glorious God with them." He wanted God to save him "from ever perverting my body unto any employments forbidden by him."[38] The weakness of the body endangered the soul. Censures emphasized that a sinful soul was one that succumbed to temptation. When Experience Holiar offered her penitent confession for fornication, she quoted the first book of Corinthians: "Every other sin a person commits is outside the body, but the immoral person sins against his own body."[39] 1 Corinthians 6:18 also explains, "The body is not for immorality, but for the Lord, and the Lord is for the body ... glorify God in your body."

Ideas of the body followed the gendered lines of weak women and strong men. Puritans viewed men's bodies as strong and women's bodies as delicate, vulnerable to illness, and prone to sin.[40] Since Eve's fall in Genesis – which condemned humans to mortality – Christians viewed women's bodies as "weaker vessels" unable to withstand the temptations of sin.[41] As punishment for Eve's original sin in the Garden of Eden, all women were condemned to the pain of childbirth. In the seventeenth and early eighteenth centuries, a woman between the ages of twenty and forty years was pregnant or nursing for nineteen of every twenty-four months. Her body's cycle of pregnancy, birth, and lactation determined much of her adult experience. The poet Anne Bradstreet (1612–1672) made 522 references to the human body and 238 to illness and death in her poetry.[42]

---

[38] Mitchel, Continuation of Sermons upon the Body of Divinity; Willard, *Complete Body of Divinity*, 502; Cotton Mather, *The Pure Nazarite: Advice to a Young Man*, quoted in Godbeer, *Sexual Revolution in Early America*, 62–63.

[39] Hope, *Records of the First Church of Dorchester*, x–xi.

[40] Reis, *Damned Women*, 93, 106–107.

[41] For a discussion of gendered notions of the body, especially in relation to witchcraft, see Reis, *Damned Women*, 96–108.

[42] Joseph R. McElrath and Allen P. Robb, eds., *The Complete Works of Anne Bradstreet* (Boston: Twayne Publishers, 1981), 24.

Midwives and older women in the community were the ones who served as arbiters of sexual mores and issues about the body.[43] Midwives offered testimony in church and court on pregnancy and paternity. For example, in 1722, when the Dorchester congregation charged William Hersey, Jr., and his wife with fornication before marriage, Hersey denied the charge, arguing that he had no "carnal knowledge of her body before that day they were married." However, the church took sworn testimony from midwives, who provided evidence that their full-term baby arrived after only five months of marriage.[44] The midwives explained that they "believed no child ever attained such ripeness & perfection at 5 months & nine days from ye conception."[45] Courts consistently honored these women as experts, and such examinations of the body rested firmly within the feminine domain.[46] Thus, it was in the realm of normative female behavior to talk about the body, admit sin about the body, and fill church confessions with self-abasing language regarding women's sinful bodies.

As a sin against the body, fornication was primarily a female censure. Women were involved in 90 percent of all censure cases, and 77 percent of the time they were censured without a man being charged. By contrast, most men involved in fornication cases were charged alongside their wives. The censuring of Patience Lawrence was typical of fornication cases. On July 17, 1692, the Dorchester congregation gathered for Sacrament Day. Three days earlier they had met together for a public day of thanksgiving for the settling of government in England, the victory over Indian enemies, and their hopes for a fruitful harvest. However, on that summer day they were not counting their blessings, but confronting their transgressors. Besides excommunicating the runaway Content Mason, they also censured the pregnant and unwed Patience Lawrence twice for fornication. Unfortunately for her, the baby died shortly after childbirth. Patience offered a penitent confession and was forgiven.[47]

---

[43] See Norton, *Founding Mothers and Fathers*, 191–92; Laurel Thatcher Ulrich, *A Midwife's Tale: The Life of Martha Ballard, Based on Her Diary, 1785–1812* (New York: Vintage, 1991), 150; Monica D. Fitzgerald, "'Safely Delivered': Social Childbirth and Female Authority in Colonial New England" (master's thesis, California State University, Hayward, 1996).

[44] Hope, *Records of the First Church of Dorchester*, 137.

[45] Hope, *Records of the First Church of Dorchester*, 137.

[46] Women could also examine men's bodies for signs of familiarity with the Devil or in other cases that involved a dispute about paternity or the body. See Norton, *Founding Mothers and Fathers*, 183–97.

[47] Hope, *Records of the First Church of Dorchester*, 123, 130; Sanford Charles Gladden, *An Index to the Vital Records of Dorchester, Massachusetts through 1825* (Boulder: Empire Reproduction and Print Company, 1970), 125.

Married couples may have confessed to censure as a vehicle to enter the church and baptize their children, yet husbands often went unwillingly to such confessions. When the Dorchester congregation called Samuell Blake to confess in 1679, "he made some kind of acknowledgment but his voice was soe low yt scarce any hert yt little wch he spake."[48] Confessing in front of his uncle, Deacon James Blake, may have embarrassed the newly-wed, but he also likely never saw a man stand alone to confess to such a sin. Since Puritans viewed fornication as a female sin, such censures feminized men in ways that a censure for drunkenness or idleness did not. Men would go to great lengths not to have to confess to this intimate charge. In August 1716 Hannah Abrams addressed the Salem congregation after Sabbath services with hopes of regaining her membership. The congregation had suspended her for fornication, evident by her early pregnancy. She explained that she avoided confession because of "the perverseness of her husband, who would not suffer her to make a confession" out of fear that he would face censure as well. During a particularly difficult illness, she swore that if God spared her, she would find a way to confess. The empathetic Salem congregation reinstated the weary goodwife.[49] In 1654, when John Smith and his wife tried to conceal the fact that their child was born five months after their marriage, the Dorchester church excommunicated them. When they sought readmittance, some members of the congregation expressed concern about Goody Smith's scruples and deferred the decision. The subsequent vote split on the wife's behavior, not the husband's.[50]

Congregations pursued censures against women even in cases where they did not voluntarily confess. The Dorchester congregation called Mary Modesly to address her sin in 1681, and she appeared but would not offer up a confession. "She did appear but being put to it to speak by way of acknowledgment of ye sin, she gave noe answer but weept whether for ye shame or ye sin yt was not known."[51] It took six months to get her written confession. If women simply denied the charge, they could still be censured. In 1698 someone in the Charlestown church complained against Mary Eades. When the minister visited her, she denied the charge. The minister told the church about his efforts and "how obstinate and impenitent ye offender was" and decided to admonish her.[52]

---

[48] Hope, *Records of the First Church of Dorchester*, 83.
[49] Pierce, *Records of the First Church of Salem*, 247.
[50] Hope, *Records of the First Church of Dorchester*, 166.
[51] Hope, *Records of the First Church of Dorchester*, 87.
[52] Hunnewell, ed., *Records of the First Church in Charlestown, 1632–1789*, xii–xiii.

Congregations even called separate meetings to discuss women's fornication charges. When the Dorchester congregation gathered to discuss the sins of Abigail Merrifield after evening exercises on May 3, 1679, many wanted to excommunicate her, but others thought they should wait until after she delivered her baby. The courts, however, had no such quandary; one month prior, they had convicted her of fornication and sentenced her to a whipping or a fine. She eventually admitted that Joseph Belcher had fathered her child.[53] But even after she recovered from childbirth, Merrifield refused to appear before her congregation, so they cast her out of the church. They excommunicated Merrifield not because she had a child out of wedlock, but because she was not repentant. Fourteen years later, when Merrifield was on her deathbed, she finally wrote a confession and expressed "great conviction of her sin." The congregation released her from excommunication, and she died in peace.[54] Elizabeth Weeks, another Dorchester fornicator, was simply admonished by the congregation, but some members thought that she should be excommunicated for her sins of sex before marriage. They decided that if someone in the Weeks family could get her to come forward and show repentance, they would withhold the excommunication. She refused.

At times women were admonished without even being asked to appear before the congregation. In 1713 the Dorchester congregation voted to admonish Sarah Weeks, Elizabeth's second cousin, for fornication. She was never asked to appear but received a letter from her church elders informing her of the censure. There were no cases of the congregation censuring a couple without offering them the opportunity to stand before the church to repent. In fact, there was only one case of a couple who did not confess voluntarily. The study of fornication censures exemplifies the progression of gendering sin, as these censures focused almost exclusively on women.

[53] Joseph Belcher got himself in trouble not only with Merrifield but with Robert Spur's daughter as well. Belcher's wife left him in 1674 and moved to Braintree. In 1677 her father, John Gill, sued Joseph Belcher's father's estate for not performing the "promise made upon the marriage of [the Belcher's] son with the plaintiff's daughter." The jury found in favor of the Belchers. See Hope, *Records of the First Church of Dorchester*, 12; Forbes, *Records of the Suffolk County Court*, 874.

[54] Hope, *Records of the First Church of Dorchester*, 81, 106; Forbes, *Records of the Suffolk County Court*, 1018. Another Weeks cousin, William, and his wife, Sarah, were charged with fornication before marriage in 1727 and afterward were both accepted as members of the Dorchester church; Hope, *Records of the First Church of Dorchester*, 239.

TABLE 2.2. *Censure rulings*

Censure Ruling	Men	Women	Couples
Forgiven	57	71	23
Admonished and Then Forgiven	19	17	0
Admonished with No Further Action Recorded	19	10	1
Admonished and Suspended	1	3	0
Excommunicated	33	20	2
Excommunication Removed	8	6	1
Excommunicated because of Failure to Appear	10	4	1
Reappeared One Time	1	3	0
Reappeared More Than Once	12	4	0
Refused to Confess	1	1	0
Note of Illegitimate Birth	2	20	3

CENSURE RULINGS

Women navigated the church disciplinary process easier than men. As Table 2.2 shows, women were more easily forgiven, had to reappear fewer times, and were excommunicated less often. Women were also more likely to work to remove their excommunication. Men were more likely to fail to appear at their censure hearing, to reappear multiple times, and to be excommunicated. Some sinners waited years before getting their admonishment, suspension, or excommunication lifted – such as Content Mason, who took decades to regain her church membership. It could take men, too, years to repent. William Coleman, of Boston's Second Church, found himself suspended because of his drunk and disorderly life in 1696 but did not offer a penitent confession until 1711, when the congregation restored him to membership.[55]

Twice as many men than women had to reappear before their congregations because their confessions were insufficient. Men were also excommunicated at a much higher rate than women, likely because men's identities were not tied to church membership the same way as

[55] Book of Second Church Records 1689–1717.

women's were. Church membership was not the only vehicle men had to express their religiosity. Men could demonstrate their sense of Puritan duty through public service. Women did not have the same opportunities, however, and their membership in the church became an important space for validation. This feminized religion provided women a sense of self as the normative Puritan, and thus they would work harder than men to maintain their connections to their churches.

Puritanism offered women a greater degree of fluidity in their gender roles. Acting as good Christians, women could mediate different spheres in the seventeenth century to help maintain a godly society and individual piety.[56] They spoke, testified, and conducted business – all under the auspices of religious obligations. However, Puritanism also enacted modes of controlling the godly. Congregations expected everyone to submit to God, but that submission also served as a metaphor for social hierarchy: servants to masters, poor to wealthy, children to parents, wives to husbands. While this hierarchy certainly applied to men of varying status, laymen refused to further devalue their masculinity by publicly embracing a feminized piety.

Censures sought to control women's bodies, but at the same time, Puritan discipline appealed to women by celebrating piety and offering access to God, status, and self-awareness. Unlike men – who were linked to the community through godly duty, civil service, and town affairs – congregations viewed women, their piety, and their bodies in a more in-dividual way.[57] Puritan congregations reinforced the male obligation to public duty and communal watchfulness and thus linked male religious identity to a corporate Puritan identity as the "keepers of the religious social order." However, by feminizing piety and the Puritan soul, con-gregations reified the religious self for women, developing patterns that

---

[56] For a discussion of female piety, see Westerkamp, *Women and Religion*, 26; Reis, *Damned Women*, 3–5; Ann Braude, "Women's History Is American Religious History," in *Retelling U.S. Religious History*, edited by Thomas A. Tweed (Berkeley: University of California Press, 1997), 87–107; and Porterfield, *Female Piety in Puritan New England*. All agree that piety elevated women. Porterfield maintains that men found spiritual sat-isfaction in female piety. Braude contends that the ideals of masculinity were in conflict with the Christian values of piety.

[57] For a discussion of Puritanism and women's bodies, see Reis, *Damned Women*, 93–120; and Westerkamp, "Engendering Puritan Religious Culture in Old and New England," 105–27.

reinforced personal reflection, self-examination, and an internal struggle with their faith. Puritans judged women on their individual spirituality, while they judged men on their performance of their communal obligations. Through the disciplinary process, laymen contributed to the creation of the public/private or separate-spheres modern gender ideology.

THREE GENERATIONS OF DISCIPLINE

Censures increased during the second and third generations of Puritanism as an expression of Puritans' anxiety about their godly path and as a result of the Half-Way Covenant in 1662, which put more people under church discipline. The Half-Way Covenant was a compromise ministers devised to confront declining church membership. Although nonmembers could not vote or partake in the Lord's Supper, they could now be disciplined by the church and have their children baptized. The church considered them "half-way" members.[58] Table 2.3 shows that censure numbers were relatively few in the first generation but increased over the second and third generations.

As the church membership changed to reflect a dominant female audience drawn to the messages of individual piety, women had already been a part of the ethos of self-examination for three generations.[59] This helped create the concept of a religious self. The notion of an individual relationship with God and self-examination of one's soul found an audience with women. The congregation reemphasized internal self-abasement through their censures of women. By the eighteenth century, men had not become less religious because their numbers had dropped in church membership, but rather because they had refocused their religious energy toward civic duty.

Dorchester church founder Richard Mather died in 1669, and as more first-generation settlers approached death, they urged their children to continue to walk "orderly." In 1690 Roger Clap wrote,

---

[58] Morgan, *Visible Saints*, 131–32.
[59] Early records indicate equal numbers of men and women as church members, but by the eighteenth century women outnumbered men by as much as two to one. See Westerkamp, *Women and Religion*, 17, 79; and Anne Speerschneider Brown, "'Bound Up in a Bundle of Life': The Social Meaning of Religious Practice in Northeastern Massachusetts, 1700–1776" (PhD diss., Boston University, 1995).

TABLE 2.3. *Total censures over time*

Generation	Total Censures	Men	Women	Couples	Unknown
1630–1662	27	18	7	2	0
1663–1690	153	90	52	3	8
1691–1725	184	72	82	23	7
TOTAL	364	180	141	28	15

what I have fired in my heart...I here charge you solemnly...sons, daughters, and grand children...I charge you that every one of you fear the Lord...and obey his commandments which is the duty of every man...whom he hath graciously taken into covenant...and hath promised to be a God to you in your generations.[60]

The second generation needed to heed the message of the covenant and the Puritan dual responsibility of duty and piety.[61]

By the third generation, ministers began to alter their emphasis from Puritan duty and covenant to a discussion of individual piety. Cotton Mather propounded his notion of "Maxims of Piety" from early in the eighteenth century until his death in 1727. The "new piety" embraced three concepts (although never concretely defined): fear of God, acceptance of Christ's justification, and honoring God through love of man.[62] During the last two decades of his life, Mather rarely mentioned the covenant but stressed "working on the souls of people."[63]

This shift to Maxims of Piety by the clergy was the result of a conflation of changing social and political realities. In 1684 England revoked the Massachusetts Bay Charter. King James II restructured the government in the entire region to form the Dominion of New England, which included Massachusetts, Connecticut, Rhode Island, Plymouth, New York,

[60] Clap, *Memoirs*, 30.
[61] For a discussion on second-generation jeremiads and ministerial concerns, see Virginia DeJohn Anderson, *New England's Generation: The Great Migration and the Formation of Society and Culture in the Seventeenth Century* (New York: Cambridge University Press, 1991), 177–221.
[62] See Middlekauff, *The Mathers*, 227. For a discussion of this shift of emphasis, see Middlekauff, *The Mathers*, 253–61. For a discussion about the loss of ministerial authority in government, see Hall, *Faithful Shepard*, 227–48. Colonists did not become less religious, but ministers lost authority in civil government in the 1690s.
[63] See Mather, *Magnalia Christi Americana*, 656.

New Jersey, and New Hampshire.[64] James II appointed Sir Edmund Andros as Royal Governor, who quickly alienated the colonists by suspending town meetings, appointing judges, enforcing the Navigation Acts, and issuing taxes. Puritan magistrates lost their authority and influence over government affairs. With England's Glorious Revolution in 1689, in which James II was deposed and his daughter Mary and her husband William were crowned, the colonists overthrew Andros. In 1691 King William disbanded the Dominion of New England and offered a new royal charter to Massachusetts. However, that charter gave more power to the king and changed the basis of franchise from church membership to personal property. Additionally, the 1691 Act of Toleration ordered that Massachusetts Bay allow other religious denominations. With the alteration of franchise and the Act of Toleration, English law removed Puritanism from the center of public life and relegated it to personal practice.[65]

Puritan ministers shifted their focus from the covenant dual prescriptions of duty and piety to a congregant's individual faith. Such an emphasis appealed to women, who had piety reinforced as a path to grace.[66] But the message of piety was not as poignant for laymen, who for most of the colonial life of New England had been indoctrinated by the church with a religious ethos of communal duty.

In 1712 Dorchester's minister John Danforth published *Holy Striving against Sinful Strife* in London. He stressed to his audience the individual sinfulness in such things as not paying taxes, avoiding court claims or discipline, hating a neighbor, too much self-love, envy, anger, vanity, hatred, spitefulness, and vengefulness. While he alluded to his listeners as God's chosen by calling them the "children of Abram," this was Danforth's only vague illusion to the covenant. He argued that to overcome sinful

---

[64] See Selement, *Keepers of the Vineyard*, 80–81, for a discussion of the "dissolution of collective culture." Selement's chapter, "From a Puritan to a Yankee Culture," examines arguments from Miller, Dunn, and others about "secularizing" forces. Selement argues that the Puritans were outnumbered by other religious factions, dissenters grew, and worldly interests increased. See Middlekauff, *The Mathers*, for a discussion of the shift to a theological emphasis of piety and not covenant with Cotton Mather. For a discussion of third-generation ministers, see Hall, *Faithful Shepard*, 270–78. Hall argued that what we think of as the eighteenth century actually began in the 1690s, when ministers had to accept toleration, Massachusetts became a royal province under the new charter of 1691, and third-generation ministers refashioned Puritanism for their generation.

[65] For a discussion of the transition from 1686 to 1691, see Breen, *Character of the Good Ruler*, xii, 37. Breen describes how Puritan rulers viewed themselves as Moses, as keepers of the covenant, during their time in public power.

[66] See Middlekauff, *The Mathers*, 243, 256–60.

strife, visible saints needed "the exercise of mutual holy love, meekness, humility ... and ... their constant ... expression of ... submission and affectionate love one to another in the bowels of Christ."[67] Danforth focused on individual church members, and not on the congregation as a community. He emphasized piety, not duty – a departure from the practice of first- and second-generation clergy.

From first arriving on the shores of Massachusetts Bay through three generations of Puritan practices, men's civil duties had been infused with religious meaning. As keepers of Puritan duty, men upheld the "we" aspects of Puritanism (those of the community), while women embraced the "I" notions in Puritanism (those of the individual). Disciplinary practices reinforced these identities, which created a gendered religious practice.

---

[67] John Danforth, *Holy Striving against Sinful Strife* (London: Eleazer Philips, 1712).

3

"Wicked Tongues and Wayward Behavior"

The Language of Confession

Rachel Ashley's lying-in following the birth of her daughter in 1707 did not follow the normal course of social calls, neighborly assistance, and celebration.[1] Instead, within a month of delivery, the new mother appeared before the General Court and was fined for the crime of fornication. Upon hearing of her transgressions, the Westfield congregation allowed her a little more time to rest before they censured her for the same sin. The young mother appeared before the congregation to confess:

Where as to my greate sorrow, publick shame & greate Sin I have been Carryed away by overbearing temptation to the transgressing God's law ... & hereby have indeed given Gods people just ground to ... turn me out of the hearts & respect of Gods people whose Charity I have wounded by my Sin, as well as my own Soule. Wherefore in Sorrow of heart, & sense of so great a sin & Evill against God & my own Soule, as Whoredom ... the great dishonour to God herein & other Considerations that come upon me of an Heart burdening Nature ... pitty me & my poor Soul.[2]

Ashley filled her confession with the feminized language expected of her, using words such as *shame, wounded, great sin, nature, pity, evil, poor,* and *grief.* The word *sorrow* also appeared three times. With debasing

---

[1] For information about New England childbirth practices, see Richard W. Wertz and Dorothy C. Wertz, *Lying-In: A History of Childbirth in America* (New York: The Free Press, 1977); Catherine M. Scholten, *Childbearing in American Society: 1650–1850* (New York: New York University, 1985); Ulrich, *A Midwife's Tale.*

[2] See Taylor, *Church Records,* 219.

and demoralizing language, she focused on her nature and the state of her heart and soul. The confession conveyed a sense of self-examination, penitence, and a personal inner struggle with sin. While concerned with the specific charge laid before her, Ashley's confession revealed a deeper acknowledgment of her sinful nature.[3]

The male laity had no expectations that men would offer a confession similar to Ashley's. No church recorder transcribed a fornication confession from a man. Yet, through analyzing the language men and women used when they confessed, distinct patterns emerge. Over the course of a three-year period, the Salisbury congregation confronted several men involved in a land dispute who offered up confessions. In 1699 Major Robert Pike complained that his brethren Nathaniel Brown and John Eastman had claimed some land that was rightfully his. After much insistence from Pike, Brown and Eastman offered a joint confession:

Tho we were not conscious to our own souls that have we wittingly transgressed the rules...and yet if in any of these we have been guilty of a breach in ye church rules in words or actions we do profess [we are] sorry for them and beg forgiveness of your self and of all the church desiring to live in love and unity with you.

Brown and Eastman did not debase themselves. They expressed concern about community and neighborly relations. They do not even use the word sin, but apologized if their actions broke rules. Not agreeing with the congregation's resolution, Major Pike refused to go to communion. The congregation grew tired of his continued obstinacy after a few years and finally demanded he repent in 1702. Pike offered a confession:

With denying and absenting from communion from church, I have so offended as to incur a censure...I hereby desire of all my brethren charity and pass by my offense...I desire to embrace in charity and in covenant unity with the church.[4]

---

[3] For a description of the experiences of Puritan religious cycles of conversion, confession, grace, sin, redemption, etc., see Cohen, *God's Caress*, 5, 76, 119. For more on how women internalized sin, see Reis and Westerkamp; see also Margaret W. Masson, "The Typology of the Female as a Model for the Regenerate: Puritan Preaching, 1690–1730," *Signs* 2, no. 2 (1976).

[4] Records of the First Church of Salisbury, ms., Massachusetts Historical Society, 1687–1750.

He was more concerned with his relationships in the community and that his actions had transgressed acceptable boundaries. Male confessions used words such as *rules, breach, offense, desire forgiveness, actions*, and *brethren*. Men expressed fear of jeopardizing their ties to their community or marring their honor and reputations.

This chapter analyzes the words and performances of confession to illustrate how laymen veered from ministerial prescripts. While spelling was haphazard at best, the meaning behind words carried weight. Words mattered in Puritan New England. In the public performance of censure confessions, congregations listened for key words that could manifest forgiveness or lead to an admonishment. In the same way that sins were gendered through the disciplinary process, Puritans gendered confession. Scholar Sandra Gustafson explains that in seventeenth-century New England there existed socially accepted linguistic practices. "Verbal forms" were critical in shaping social identity. In the public act of socially acceptable speech, women and men employed different voices. Laymen expected women to show humility and express their sinful natures.[5] However, in the daily lived practice of confession, men were required to demonstrate a verbal order that focused on the covenant demand of duty and communal responsibility, avoiding any unpleasantness and emasculating inward reflection.[6]

According to ministers, there was a single set of expectations for all visible saints. As the normative Puritan, women actually modeled the clerical mandates of a feminized language.

---

[5] Sandra M. Gustafson, *Eloquence Is Power: Oratory and Performance in Early America* (Chapel Hill: University of North Carolina Press, 2000), 31, 25.

[6] While historians have not comprehensively examined the language of church disciplinary records, several historians have studied the language of conversion narratives and Puritan language in general. See Caldwell, *Puritan Conversion Narrative*; Shepard, *Confessions*; and Harry S. Stout, *The New England Soul: Preaching and Religious Culture in Colonial New England* (New York: Oxford University Press, 1986). For a discussion of gender and language, see Jane Kamensky, *Governing the Tongue: The Politics of Speech in Early New England* (New York: Oxford University Press, 1999); Robert St. George, "'Heated' Speech and Literacy in Seventeenth-Century New England," in *Seventeenth-Century New England*, ed. David D. Hall (Boston: Colonial Society of Massachusetts, distributed by the University Press of Virginia, 1984), 275–317; Lad Tobin, "A Radically Different Voice: Gender and Language in the Trials of Anne Hutchinson," *Early American Literature* 25 (Fall 1990): 353–70; Kathleen Brown, *Goodwives, Nasty Wenches, and Anxious Patriarchs* (Chapel Hill: University of North Carolina Press, 1996); Jill Lepore, *The Name of War: King Philip's War and the Origins of American Identity* (New York: Alfred A. Knopf, 1998); and Juster, *Disorderly Women*.

THE IMPORTANCE OF WORDS AND
THE GENDERING OF LANGUAGE

The work of historians Jane Kamensky and Robert St. George is critical to understanding language in early New England. Both historians assert that speech was much more important to seventeenth-century Puritans than it is to twenty-first-century Americans. Kamensky views the import of speech as part of the narrative of New England "exceptionalism."[7] She finds that New Englanders spent a great deal of time "speaking of speaking." Whether meeting in taverns, churches, fields, town halls, courthouses, parlors, or streets, the "power of talk" was a favorite subject of conversation.[8] St. George agrees, explaining that "speech in New England was the principle means of discourse" and that "words were how individuals constructed and maintained social reality and conveyed specific social meaning that were immediately understood."[9] The Puritan central emphasis on the word of God, and that everyone should have access to it, not only led to high literacy rates for men and women, but also meant that people spent an inordinate amount of time thinking and discussing such words. Discussions about a pastor's recent sermon, for instance, could last days. The New England archives are filled with diaries of transcribed sermons, as men recorded the sermons to later ponder their meaning and beauty.[10] But when words were used harshly or to utter false statements, they could put the speaker in danger. St. George contends that "illegal speech acts were as base as sermons and prayers were eloquent."[11] Words could elevate a person or put them in dire straits.

Speech was a marker of identity, status, godliness, and social order. St. George asserts that in seventeenth-century New England, "speech was an indicator of control, reason, mastery; but also a source of misrule and social conflict most difficult to control." Words spoke to a commitment to family, town, government, and God. Words conveyed one's understanding of scripture, devotion to God, and respect for authority. As St. George explains, "Speech was a principal sign of progress in the ongoing battle between God and Satan." Words "conveyed the Word of God and Belched

---

[7] Kamensky, *Governing the Tongue*, 6; St. George, "'Heated' Speech and Literacy in Seventeenth-Century New England," 285.

[8] Kamensky, *Governing the Tongue*, 5.

[9] St. George, "'Heated' Speech and Literacy in Seventeenth-Century New England," 278.

[10] Kamensky, *Governing the Tongue*, 31, 33.

[11] St. George, "'Heated' Speech and Literacy in Seventeenth-Century New England," 278.

forth the flames of hell."[12] Further, there was a fine line between speaking with authority and being too severe. For example, a husband was ruler of his "little commonwealth" family, but he could not speak too harshly to his wife or children.[13] Words also signaled an alarm that someone was threatening the peace, through gossiping, lying, slander, blasphemy, or contempt. Offensive words could put you in front of a magistrate or the congregation; a person could be fined, censured, or sued.[14] In the most severe cases, someone's words could result in banishment or hanging. In 1663 the Connecticut court sent Abigail Bets to the gallows for calling Christ a "bastard."[15] Kamensky argues that this contested space of public speech was fraught with paradoxes between liberty and control.[16] Context also mattered in speech. A person could speak out of turn, out of order, or too loudly or softly, not enough or too much. Women had a smaller circumference of acceptable speech. Anne Hutchinson, who was

[12] St. George, "'Heated' Speech and Literacy in Seventeenth-Century New England," 279, 285.

[13] For a discussion of family life and literacy rates, see Demos, *Little Commonwealth*; Greven, *The Protestant Temperament*; Morgan, *The Puritan Family*; and Kenneth A. Lockridge, *A New England Town: The First Hundred Years, Dedham, Massachusetts, 1636–1736* (New York: W. W. Norton Books, 1970).

[14] St. George, "'Heated' Speech and Literacy in Seventeenth-Century New England," 278. St. George examines the Essex County court records from 1640–1680 to explore the importance of speech. George explains that the General Laws of 1641 included punishments for lying, blasphemy, cursing, slander, and swearing, 280. See Kamensky, *Governing the Tongue*, 7.

[15] Connecticut Historical Society, *Some Early Records and Documents of and Relating to the Town of Windsor Connecticut, 1639–1703* (Hartford: Connecticut Historical Society, 1928), 268.

[16] Many historians have studied the impact of the dissenting religious language on the colonies and early republic. See William McLoughlin's key study on religious dissent, *New England Dissent, 1630–1833: The Baptists and the Separation of Church and State* (Cambridge: Harvard University Press, 1971); Bernard Bailyn's foundational study of the impact of religious thought on the American Revolution, *The Ideological Origins of the American Revolution* (New York: Belknap Press, 1968, 1992); and Ruth Bloch on the influence of the rhetoric of the Second Great Awakening on public discourse, *Visionary Republic: Millennial Themes in American Thought, 1750–1800* (Cambridge: University of Cambridge, 1986). See also Rhys Isaac, *The Transformation of Virginia, 1740–1790* (Chapel Hill: Omohundro Institute of Early American History and Culture; University of North Carolina Press, 1999); Juster, *Disorderly Women*; Butler, *Awash in a Sea of Faith*; Bonomi, *Under the Cope of Heaven*; and Christopher Grasso, *A Speaking Aristocracy: Transforming Discourse in Eighteenth-Century Connecticut* (Williamsburg: Omohundro Institute of Early American History and Culture, 1999), all of whom study the connections between public speech and religious influences. See Norton, *Founding Mothers and Fathers*, for a discussion of gendered discourse.

a midwife and popular spiritual adviser, hosted women in her home to discuss scripture. She raised the ire of Boston officials when her audience went beyond the common circle of women and started to include men.[17] Part of the larger Antinomian crisis that threatened to destabilize the colony, Hutchinson was banished and excommunicated in 1637–1638.

As Puritans began to settle in New England, they brought with them "verbal order" in flux. Prior to the Protestant movement, the English viewed speech in both legal and social contexts as dangerous, and speech dictated expectations by age, class, and gender. Most laws and prescriptive literature were about avoiding harmful speech. Men were to think before they spoke, showing restraint with measured words. Ideally, women would not speak at all.[18] However, as Kamensky explains, the loud and dissenting English Puritans upturned tradition by "investing the medium of speech with a new gravitas."[19] Kamensky argues that the "Puritan impulse was…a fundamental redefinition of both the spiritual and the social meaning of speaking" that called for "new freedoms for the tongue and new demands for its government."[20] There was to be more openness of speech to convey the word of God, yet the very religious emphasis that allowed for more discourse also meant that violating the codes of speech was more problematic. The Puritans who crossed the Atlantic were the "hotter" sort of English Puritan. After all, they left England and its church to become the model of Christianity, their more feverous brand of Protestantism creating severe expectations about behavior. "Speech was to be the central marker of what many dared to hope would be not just New England's distinctiveness, but its superiority."[21]

In addition to the new parameters for language, there were also distinctions between male and female speech. This "gendered verbal order"

[17] For a discussion of dissenters, Antinomians, and Anne Hutchinson, see Louise A. Breen, *Transgressing the Bounds: Subversive Enterprises among the Puritan Elite in Massachusetts, 1630–1692* (Oxford: Oxford University Press, 2001); Michael Winship, *Making Heretics: Militant Protestantism and Free Grace in Massachusetts, 1636–1641* (Princeton: Princeton University Press, 2002); Bozeman, *The Precisianist Strain*; Marilyn J. Westerkamp, "Anne Hutchinson, Sectarian Mysticism, and the Puritan Order," *Church History* 59 (December 1990): 482–96.

[18] Kamensky, *Governing the Tongue*, 25.

[19] Kamensky, *Governing the Tongue*, 29. Kamensky's chapter on English Puritans describes the distinction between English and English Puritan ideas of speech, 17–42.

[20] Kamensky, *Governing the Tongue*, 29.

[21] Kamensky, *Governing the Tongue*, 44. Kamensky uses the concept of American exceptionalism in arguing that the verbal order of New England Puritans was distinct from that of old England, 6.

that Kamensky describes called on men to speak "forthright," convey respect, and use words that were "forceful but governed." Women had to employ a language of humility and submission.[22] Kamensky explains, "New England goodwives were well versed in the language of submission. Self-shaming appears to have come easily to them – more readily than it did perhaps to their husbands, sons and brothers."[23] In analyzing damaging speech, St. George notes an important gender distinction. Men used defamation to attack a man's reputation, whereas women used "heated" speech as a "moral rebuke."[24] Both Kamensky and St. George agree that speech was used to defend and critique men and women differently.[25]

To understand how church discipline gendered Puritanism requires a reframing from the male experience as normative. First-generation Puritan ministers challenged the "gendered verbal order" with their expectations that all Puritans should be humble and submissive before God.[26] For ministers, women were the normative Puritan.[27] With emphasis on a feminized soul and a submissive demeanor, the clergy expected men, as well as women, to present a "feminized verbal order." However, laymen did not comply with such expectations, preferring a "gendered verbal order" that allowed them to retain masculine speech. In so doing, Puritanism became less radical, and more distinctly gendered.

SIGNIFICANCE OF THE CONFESSION

The censure confession was integral to continuing in fellowship, and congregations listened intently for important signals and words that would justify forgiveness. A worthy confession had to directly address the sin, show sincerity and repentance, and offer a promise to mend ways.

---

[22] Kamensky, *Governing the Tongue*, 158, 74, 77; Benjamin Wadsworth, *The Well-Ordered Family: Or, Relative Duties* (Boston: Printed by B. Green, for Nicholas Buttolph, at his shop in Corn-Hill, 1712), cited in Kamensky, *Governing the Tongue*, 77.

[23] Kamensky, *Governing the Tongue*, 134.

[24] St. George, "'Heated' Speech and Literacy in Seventeenth-Century New England," 308.

[25] St. George includes a list of defamatory words used for men and women, arguing that the types of heated speech targeted at men and women were gendered. He suggests that "women seem to have regulated the community of morality, men the community of commodity exchange," 314.

[26] Masson agrees that Puritan mandates challenged traditional gender expectations and that both men and women were expected to behave as brides of Christ, 305. See also Westerkamp and Reis.

[27] See Braude, "Women's History Is American Religious History." She argues that women were the normative Puritans.

Sincerity and repentance were not only about the words one chose, but also about one's demeanor. A confessant had to look the part. Dorchester's minister, Josiah Flint, explained that people's inward sincerity should be reflected in their outward actions. He observed that "the professing people of God make a very fair show of Repentance and yet fall very short of wh God expects & requires of them. An externall visible fair profession & the internall reall & true work of Repentance are not inseparable."[28] Cotton Mather exhorted that the confession must display "humility, modesty, patience, petition, tears, with reformation."[29]

Meetinghouse confessions were also supposed to serve as lessons for the entire congregation, so it was important that laymen reject subpar performances. The process of accepting or rejecting confessions reinforced the standards and expectations for everyone.[30] A young girl who sat beside her siblings and mother listening to Rachel Ashley's confession would learn that bad things happen when girls stray, but she would also absorb what her congregation expected from her if she found herself in a similarly unfortunate situation. How a congregation censured a sinner, and how that sinner confessed, revealed much more about the community than anything else. If a congregation became lax in the disciplinary process, they ran the risk of ridicule from other parishes, and all the while the more daunting threat of God's wrath loomed overhead (Figure 3.1).

It was not uncommon for sinners to appear more than once to meet the standards for penitence and sincerity. In 1678 when Samuell Rigby stood before his Dorchester congregation to confess his sin of drunkenness, the male laity rejected his confession, finding that it "did not come up to satisfaction."[31] The congregation did not see or hear genuine regret and remorse. Later that year, the same congregation listened

---

[28] Josiah Flint, Notes on Sermons, ms., Josiah Flint Papers (1669–1672), Massachusetts Historical Society.

[29] Cotton Mather, *Ratio Discipline Fratrum Nov-Anglicorum* (Boston: Printed for S. Gerrish in Cornhill, 1726), cited in Oberholzer, *Delinquent Saints*, 30. Oberholzer confirmed that "the sincerity of the penitent must be outwardly manifest."

[30] For a discussion of the relationship between lay and clerical beliefs, see Selement, *Keepers of the Vineyard*; Hall, ed. *Lived Religion in America*; and Hall, *Worlds of Wonder*. Hall argues that daily religious practices, or lived religion, varied from the religion espoused from the pulpit and that New Englanders created a religion to meet their needs, not one dictated to them. Selement counters that ministers and laity interacted on a daily basis, the laity accepting most ministerial ideas of theology. This study argues that laity veered from ministerial ideas of censure, which gendered Puritanism.

[31] Hope, *Records of the First Church of Dorchester*, 79.

FIGURE 3.1. Men at a Puritan prayer meeting. *Source:* whitemay/DigitalVision Vectors/Getty Images.

to Nathaniel Mather confess to dishonoring the church. Dissatisfied, the members ordered him to reappear. The congregation saw his confession as "falling short of what he should have attained unto and he 'missing to doe his best to attain more.'"[32] In the spring of 1714, Westfield's Stephen Kellog faced a censure for drunkenness. During his confession, he apologized but claimed it was an upset stomach that caused his behavior. His congregation did not accept the confession and waited until the fall of that year for a more appropriate display of remorse.[33]

At times, a sin could be exceptionally egregious or the confession so weak that the laity needed additional assurances or testimonies that the sinner was truly penitent. In 1665, the Salem congregation charged Remember Samon with fornication. The records noted that her confession expressed "shame before the Lord and his people, desiring her soul

[32] Hope, *Records of the First Church of Dorchester*, 80.
[33] Taylor, *Church Records*, 236–7.

might be washed from her sins by the blood of Christ and that the people of God would pray for her." However, the pastor and several deacons had to appease the congregation by confirming that they had received an even more "enlarged penitential confession" from Samon before the laymen accepted it. In 1669 the Salem congregation listened to Joseph Williams confess to theft, yet they noted that his confession was "more dry and more general than was desired." It took several laymen in good standing to testify on his behalf for the congregation to accept his confession.[34]

In every confession, a person's reputation was at stake. Neighbors, business associates, family members, friends, and those of varying social status were listening and judging. The congregation would likely forgive the sinner, but how would his or her confession be remembered outside the meetinghouse? Those confessing had more at stake than meeting pious clerical requirements. They had to face the men and women in the community and protect their reputations. Men could not jeopardize their public image and good standing by appearing weak or effeminate. The New England man needed to be sober, rational, and a respected member of his community. Weeping in public was not acceptable for a man. Besides the dramatic case of John Underhill, whose story appears in Chapter 4, there is not a single recorded case of a man weeping during his confession. A woman crying during her confession showed she was truly repentant; such displays of emotion validated women's sincerity.

THE PERFORMATIVE ASPECT OF CONFESSIONS

Confession was not a rote exercise. Each confessor needed to ask God and the community for forgiveness and include a promise not to stray again. If the sin impacted one's family, the confessor was expected to ask them for forgiveness as well. A bad business deal, theft, or slander required words of atonement to the victims and the larger community.

The performative aspect of the confession required several steps. In his work on cultural rituals, Victor Turner describes "social dramas" as involving a four-step process: the breach of social norms, the crisis, adjustments or redress, and reintegration or permanent breach. The ritual of church discipline fits within this Turnerian definition: the accusation of sin; calling the sinner to confess; the confession to the congregation; and

---

[34] Pierce, *Records of the First Church of Salem,* 122.

then acceptance, admonishment, or excommunication. The congregation participates in this social drama not only to witness and judge (officially and otherwise), but also to heed a lesson. In the stage of adjustment or redress, Turner asserts that an individual enters a stage of "liminality," where normal rules and roles are suspended and reversed. In such a model, at the moment of confession, the sinner would become liminal – a man would become feminine and a woman would become masculine. Caroline Bynum Walker argues that Turner's model of liminality only applies to men and that women do not reverse their roles, but instead reinforce their existing attributes. Walker's contention is applicable to female censures, as congregations expected female confessions to contain a feminized language and demeanor. However, Turner's model is also not applicable to male sinners. While doctrine, sermons, conversions, and covenants may have required a liminal state for men, the laity in charge of church discipline did not. The audience participating in the social drama influences the liminality of the redress. The male laity refused to enter such a stage. Within their public confessions, men affirmed their masculinity and women affirmed their femininity.[35] However, the concept of liminality is tricky for New England Puritans, whose clergy espoused a feminized faith. If the normative faith is feminine, what is liminal? We are so used to assuming the norm is male that when you turn it on its head, as

---

[35] Victor Turner, *The Ritual Process: Structure and Anti-Structure* (Chicago: Aldine Publishing Company, 1969), 166–203; Caroline Walker Bynum, "Women's Stories, Women's Symbols: A Critique of Victor Turner's Theory of Liminality," in *Essays on Gender and the Human Body in Medieval Religion* (New York: Zone Books, 1991, 1996), 29, 32, 35, 37–40. Where Turner's liminality does apply is in witchcraft accusations. As Kamensky explains, a female witch transgressed her femininity by using speech that was disruptive. Essentially, the female witch was masculinized. However, the male witch was often viewed as being "cowed" by his wife; the male witch was feminized, viewed as controlled by a woman; see Kamensky, *Governing the Tongue*, 158. See also Reis, *Damned Women*, 156–7, who equates male witches with failing in duties as husbands and fathers, while women often "displayed some sort of offensive carriage as wives, mothers or daughters." She also notes that men did not feel the same compunction to confess in elaborate ways, but offered more "tentative and tactical admissions" or denied accusations entirely. Reis contends that men did not defer to the court as women did. Even into the eighteenth-century revivalist period, historians note how accused witches or women possessed used such disruptive speech. Historian Kenneth Minkema examines the case of Martha Roberson. Accused of being possessed by the Devil, her speech, or "tongue," was angry and spiteful. However, when she was not possessed, she was humble and quiet. See Kenneth P. Minkema, 'The Devil Will Roar in Me Anon': The Possession of Martha Roberson, Boston, 1741," in *Spellbound: Women and Witchcraft in America*, ed. Elizabeth Reis (New York: SR Books, 1998), 99–119.

Puritans did, what happens? For ministers and laity the norm and liminal were in contention. Was a feminized man the norm as ministers suggested? If so, did men enter the liminal when they used masculine speech? All of this makes the performance in the meetinghouse complicated, with multiple audiences and tensions between contested gender systems, confusing expectations, and challenging norms.

The sinner as neighbor, the expectations and fears of the audience, and religious pressures all converged during a confession. Gustafson describes how in the "performance of semiotic speech and texts, claims to authenticity and relations of power were given meaning and form."[36] Both the listener and the confessor entered the meetinghouse with certain expectations and roles, and both needed to perform to meet such expectations. In 1664 Samuel Archer failed to meet the requirements of his Salem congregation. Called for his sin of drunkenness, Archer's confession was "far from manifesting any repentance in his expression." The congregation had him serve as a warning to others by excommunicating him.[37] Gustafson explains that "verbal forms manifested social tensions."[38] The confession was mediated by all of the pressures of the performance in facing the audience, meeting their expectations, and maintaining composure.[39]

Congregations weighed the attitudes and demeanor of the confessor. Robert Spur, his son John, and his son-in-law Nathaniel Wiet all faced censure charges in 1678 stemming from disagreements with the pastor Josiah Flint. The Dorchester congregation called Robert Spur to answer for his "withdrawing from church, not partaking in the Sacrament," and having some "p'judice" against Flint." Robert Spur was already a visible saint, but John and Nathaniel were still in the process of gaining full membership. The members censured John for "petulant carriage" toward Flint and a church elder when the three of them met privately about John becoming a church member. They also wanted to hear Wiet's confession before he gained membership. Flint and the church elder did not like the

---

[36] Gustafson, *Eloquence Is Power*, xvii.

[37] Pierce, *Records of the First Church of Salem*, 100.

[38] Gustafson, *Eloquence Is Power*, xvi.

[39] For a discussion of seventeenth-century gender roles, see Brown, *Good Wives, Nasty Wenches, and Anxious Patriarchs*; Juster, *Disorderly Women*; Norton, *Founding Mothers and Fathers*; Reis, *Damned Women*; Ulrich, *Good Wives*; Westerkamp, *Women and Religion in Early America*; Diane Willen, "Godly Women in Early Modern England: Puritanism and Gender," *Journal of Ecclesiastical History* 43 (October 1992): 561–81.

young men's answers or attitudes, which they both contended did not show sufficient penitence. The church excommunicated John Spur and Wiet in 1679, but Robert continued to work to regain his membership. The congregation summoned Robert three more times over the course of a year to answer his admonishment. He "did not come up to the satisfaction" of his brethren twice. It was only when he wrote a confession about the effect the censure had on him that the congregation removed his sentence. On March 21, 1680, the congregation welcomed Spur back into the fold.[40]

PUBLIC VERSUS PRIVATE SPEECH

Men may have adopted masculine speech in their confessions, but in their private spaces they were more apt to use a feminized verbal order. When no prying eyes were watching (or reading), men were more free to express their piety. New England men kept diaries and journals, recording events in their families, communities, businesses, and meetinghouses. They noted news from nearby towns, transatlantic affairs, and the weather. They transcribed sermons, jeremiads, and court hearings. They also ruminated on the state of their souls and their relationship to God.

The archives abound with private journals of ministers using highly feminized language, reflecting on their spiritual inadequacies and faulty relationship with God. We see this in the diary of Thomas Shepard.[41] He described his "warfare against" sin with a language of submission, obedience, and sexual desire for Christ: "I was also how my soule did seeke union to Christ & God by obedience to his will."[42] Over seventy years later we continue to find clerical diaries with the same language. In Boston minister Joseph Sewall's 1711 diary entry, he wrote, "Humble me...Show me my sinfulness of nature...vanity of heart."

---

[40] Hope, *Records of the First Church of Dorchester*, 79–81, 84.

[41] Thomas Shepard migrated to Massachusetts in 1635 and became one of the leading and most influential ministers of his time. He was minister for the First Church in Cambridge until his early death in 1649, at the age of 44. For analysis and biography of Thomas Shepard, see David Hall, *Puritanism in Seventeenth-Century Massachusetts* (New York: Hold, Rinehart, and Winston, 1968); Selement, *Keepers of the Vineyard*; Winship, *Making Heretics*; Michael McGiffert, ed., *God's Plot: Puritan Spirituality in Thomas Shepard's Cambridge* (Amherst: University of Massachusetts Press, 1994).

[42] Shepard, *Diary of Thomas Shepard*, January 23.

He continued to write about how he was a "frail, miserable and sinful creature." He spent much of his time in meditation and prayer, worried over his barren soul, his sin, and his negligence in duty. "I have reasons to bewail the prevalency of my sins. O wretched man yt I am." He prayed for humility and communion with God, and even asked for a "new heart," while lamenting his vanity, lazy sloth, wickedness, dullness, corrupt nature, carnal mind, and unclean lips. "How unworthy I am … a miserable sinful creature almost continually wandering from God."[43] Such feminized language was standard in public and private ministerial writing.

No minister agonized over his own vile heart and sinful soul more than Michael Wigglesworth, a notable leader, famed poet, medical doctor, constant worrier, and a fairly accomplished hypochondriac. Edmund Morgan, editor of Wigglesworth's published diary, explains, "If worrying would have saved New England, Wigglesworth would have saved it."[44] A typical entry is very self-critical: "Blind man! Carnal heart! I am afraid, ashamed, heavy laden under such cursed framed of heart … My soul groans, my body faints … Behold I am vile … Lord, what wouldst thou have me to doe?"[45] He would verbally upbraid himself for a mere thought or dream that was ungodly. He used the word "vile" consistently in describing both his body and soul. He criticized his weak and sinful body, and even ridiculed specific body parts – heart, tongue, and eyes. According to his diary, his heart was vile, wicked, loathed, weak, whorish, deceitful, discouraged, vane, profane, filled with enmity, impotent, unthankful, stupid, deadened, impenitent, cursed, carnal, brutish, and swinish.[46] He believed his various physical illnesses (both real and imagined) were manifestations of his vanity, pride, and corrupt soul. He was ashamed of a "filthy dream" or "carnal thoughts" that distracted him from communion with God, which he described with a great deal of sexual imagery: "Open though my mouth wide and fill it with thy son. I need him … I desire to take him … I desire him … that he may subdue … my heart."[47] Wigglesworth was a model of the self-debasing

[43] Joseph Sewall, Papers, 1703–1716, ms., Joseph Sewall Family Papers, Massachusetts Historical Society.
[44] Edmund Sears Morgan, ed., *The Diary of Michael Wigglesworth, 1653–1657* (New York: Harper & Row, 1946), vi.
[45] Morgan, *Diary of Michael Wigglesworth*, 53.
[46] Morgan, *The Diary of Michael Wigglesworth*, 3–121.
[47] Morgan, *The Diary of Michael Wigglesworth*, 25.

feminized Puritan.[48] "The fact that Michael Wigglesworth...does not look like the average New Englander of the seventeenth century, may simply mean that he accepted the demands of Puritanism more wholeheartedly than most of his countrymen." Morgan explains that Wigglesworth was "closer to the ideals of Puritanism" than his contemporaries.[49] Few ministers and no laymen compare in his use of debasing, feminized language. Wigglesworth mastered the feminine.

Puritan laymen were not able to maintain the feminine soul in public. However, they wrote with feminized language and emotion in their private reflections.[50] One of the most useful diaries of early New England because of its detailing of personal, social and political issues, is that of Judge Samuel Sewall.[51] The famed jurist in the Salem witchcraft trials, Judge Sewall was the chief justice of the Massachusetts Superior Court and a successful merchant and investor. He was married to Hannah Hull for over forty years and fathered fourteen children. His diary is remarkable in its detail about daily life in the colony – including pregnancy, birth and childrearing, injuries and illnesses, deaths and funeral rituals, food, weather, government and church affairs, business transactions, friendships and quarrels. Throughout his diary, Sewall was self-reflective and expressed his fears over his salvation and the love and heartache he felt for his family.

The month before Sewall became an official member of Boston's Second Church, he intently labored over his soul. He worried he was

---

[48] See Alan Bray, "To Be a Man in Early Modern Society: The Curious Case of Michael Wigglesworth," *History Workshop Journal* 41(Spring 1996): 155–65. Alan Bray writes about how Wigglesworth's sexual dreams troubled him; he actually thought he contracted a venereal disease from his sinful dreams. Bray argues that Wigglesworth demonstrates how gender was "threatened and contingent," 6.

[49] Morgan, *Diary of Michael Wigglesworth*, ix, xiii.

[50] See Reis, *Damned Women*, 93–120; Cohen also discusses the popularity of the topic of the separation of the body and soul in Puritan theology, *God's Caress*, 40.

[51] Sewall's diary is the basis for Judith Graham's examination of Puritan family life. See Judith Graham, *Puritan Family Life: The Diary of Samuel Sewall* (Boston: Northeastern University Press, 2000). Through Sewall's diary, Graham argues that Puritan parenting was not authoritarian, but based on love, affection, and care. In their studies on early American masculinity, both Anne Lombard and Lisa Wilson utilize Sewall's diary as evidence of the tempered Puritan man. See Ann S. Lombard, *Making Manhood: Growing Up Male in Colonial New England* (Cambridge: Harvard University Press, 2003); and Lisa Wilson, *Ye Heart of a Man* (New Haven: Yale University Press, 1999). For more on Sewall's participation in the witchcraft trials and his later apology, see Eve LaPlante, *Salem Witch Judge: The Life and Repentance of Samuel Sewall* (New York: HarperCollins, 2007).

not fit to be a church member because of his sinfulness and hypocrisy. "Since I had thoughts of joining to the Church, I have been exceedingly tormented in my mind...with my own unfitness and want of Grace... I resolved to confess what a great Sinner I had been."[52] He described meetings he had with his minister to talk about his "grieving spirit," and his minister advised him to pray.[53] He also described his anxiety and fear, and how overwhelmed he felt:

I was almost overwhelmed, as thinking that he deemed me unfit for it. And I could hardly sit down to the Lord's Table...I never experienced more unbelief. I feared at least that I did not believe there was such a one as Jesus Christ and yet was afraid that because I came to the ordinance without belief...I should be stricken dead." He pleaded to love Christ with all his "heart and soul.[54]

In his diary, Judge Sewall revealed an emotional vulnerability unseen in the public eye. When Solomon Stoddard wrote a condolence letter after Sewall's wife died, Sewall recorded, "I soaked it in tears."[55] Historian Eve LaPlante notes Sewall's self-criticism and self-reflection. She explains, "Unlike some early Congregationalists, who described a vivid flash of engagement with the divine that converted them to Christ, Samuel's piety was the less dramatic but daily effort to pray sincerely and to understand religious texts. Still, he was often assailed internally by a sense of his own sinfulness."[56]

Puritan men also used a "feminized verbal order" in their conversion narratives.[57] Unlike confessions, descriptions of someone's conversion experience were private.[58] Men and women wrote down conversion experiences in order for their ministers to consider them for membership. The ministers and the church elders privately evaluated the experiences and did not share

---

[52] He also expressed in this passage his concern about the split between the Second and Third churches.

[53] Sewall, *Diary of Samuel Sewall*, 38–42.

[54] Sewall, *Diary of Samuel Sewall*, 39.

[55] Sewall, *Diary of Samuel Sewall*, 872.

[56] LaPlante, *Salem Witch Judge*, 7, 13.

[57] See Reis, *Damned Women*, 39. She argues that male conversion narratives did not lament the men's depravity. However, this study shows how private conversion narratives used a feminized verbal order not found in public confessions.

[58] See Caldwell, *Puritan Conversion Narrative*. Caldwell explains that conversion narratives had patterns and were arranged in a particular order: they were concise, were specific to an experience of grace, and relied on scripture, 5–6. She also explains that "ministers encouraged a certain freedom and emotionalism," 24.

them with the entire congregation. When a Dorchester man presented his relation experience to his minister, he called himself "a vile and abominable sinner." He described how "God comforts and delights" his soul and how he was engaged in a fight with the Devil for control of his body. "There shall be weeping, wailing and knashing of teeth, amist these, satan has been endeavoring to entangle me by his strategies."[59] But men did not present these relations to their entire congregation; their peers did not read them.[60] While men may have privately expressed their piety and questioned their souls, publicly they had to contend with other social expectations of masculinity. Even with the New World realities and contested gender systems, laymen did not embrace public displays of feminized spirituality for other men.

EXPECTATIONS FOR CONFESSIONS

A sinner's confession was also judged in gendered ways. The church records show much more of an emphasis placed on women's penitence. Even without the self-debasement, men had a harder time constructing a confession that met the standards set by the other male laity. Men failed in their confession much more frequently than women. Tellingly, women demonstrated remorse or penitence more regularly than men. Men's confessions were more likely to be deemed unacceptable, and they were required to return with a new and improved confession. The feminized language women used, and were expected to use, made their confessions easier to accept. Men walked a fine line between protecting their masculine reputations and delivering an acceptable confession of their sins. The following chart illustrates the language in church records used to describe male and female confessions (Table 3.1).

GENDERED DESCRIPTIONS OF SIN

The language found in church records describing male and female sinners indicates a clear emphasis on women's bodies and souls – their evil hearts, tongues, and nature(see Table 3.2). When the Westfield congregation

---

[59] Unknown, "Relation Experience," ms., Collection of the Dorchester Antiquarian and Historical Society Collection, Massachusetts Historical Society.

[60] Evidence of these more emotive conversion narratives by men can be found into the eighteenth century as well. Minkema analyzes the conversion narrative from the 1730s by Samuel Belcher and highlights the "emotive" and "heartwrenching" narrative. See Kenneth P. Minkema, "A Great Awakening Conversion: The Relation of Samuel Belcher," *William and Mary Quarterly* 44, no. 1 (1987): 121–27.

TABLE 3.1. *Church notes on confessions*

Notes Recorded on the Confession	Men	Women	Couples
Lacked humility	1	0	0
Lacked sincerity	2	0	0
Lacked penitence	7	3	0
Lacked remorse	3	0	0
Showed remorse	1	0	0
Showed penitence	12	30	2
Showed sincerity	1	0	0
Dry and general	1	0	0
Words without words	0	1	0
Unacceptable	7	1	0

TABLE 3.2. *Gendered descriptions of sin/sinner*

Only Used for Male Sinners	Only Used for Female Sinners	Language Used for Both
Acknowledge	Evil (heart, tongue, language)	Scandalous
Excuse	Horrid	Incorrigible
Miscarriage	Vile	
Transgressed	Sorrow	
	Heinous	
	Humble	

censured Abigail Dewy for lying about the neighborly hen squabble in 1714, the issue was not just her lying words, but also her lying tongue. Both men and women faced censure charges for lying or slander, but their congregations gendered their censures. The Dorchester congregation called Sister Patten more than a sinner when they censured her for slander in 1696. Patten "cast contempt" on the whole process of private business deals by saying Brother Hix had lied and perjured himself. The congregation accused her of "often indulging in Corruptions & passions of her Evill heart and evill language of her hasty tongue." When the wife of the celebrated captain Thomas Clark aimed her spurious comments against the General Court and the governor, the Dorchester congregation censured her for "slanderous and lying expressions of her tongue."

Yet when William Sumner uttered offensive remarks about the Committee of the Militia in 1675, his congregation noted "offensive speech." Boston's Second Church censured Brother Blackman for slander and obscenity when he made a joke about another man's wife being his whore, yet his congregation noted that his *words* (not his tongue or his heart) were morally evil. Women examined their "evil hearts" and their "wretched souls"; men apologized for their "poor actions" or their "neglectful ways." Congregations focused on men's behavior, not their bodies.

Congregations adopted gendered language in their own descriptions of male and female sin. In a sampling of church records that offer descriptive language of 50 men and 32 women, congregations accuse 66 percent of men of neglecting duty, breaking rules, or disturbing the peace with their behavior, while such language was used for only 19 percent of the women. Church records employ words such as "sorrow," "wicked heart," "shame," "body," "tongue," or "soul" in 8 percent of the male censures, compared with 60 percent of female censures. Congregations warned men to stay on the godly path but exhorted women to search their souls. Although the Plymouth congregation dropped the censure charges against Lydia Cushman for lack of evidence, they sternly reprimanded her: "And in the Name of Christ do advise and exhort her to consider that the Lord is a Jealous God, whose Eyes are as a Flaming Fire, who searcheth the Rains and the Heart and will give to every man according to his work."[61] In 1699 the Westfield congregation warned Samuel Bush after his censure for lying: "Brief advice was given to him...watchfulness and chiefly to see that the beginning of matters be laid right, in not commonly temptation will rush over things."[62] Cushman's congregation urged her to keep her heart pure, while Bush's brethren issued recommendations to conduct his business properly to avoid any outside temptations.

A woman's speech could be more dangerous, because society viewed her as less rational, more prone to passions of the heart.[63] When Sarah Stevens faced censure for her "evil words," the Boston Second congregation described her as "vile and heard hearted." Magistrates found her "uncivil carriage" so disturbing they sentenced her to the House of

---

[61] *Plymouth Church Records*, 235.
[62] Taylor, *Church Records*, 201.
[63] For a discussion of gender ideas about reason and passion, see Merchant, *The Death of Nature*.

Corrections and two whippings. However, in 1677, when the church at Plymouth censured a brother for "evil words and carriage," they privately sent elders to reprove him. Not a single congregation called a man "hard hearted" or referred to his "evil heart." The Plymouth congregation recorded how a brother's "heart melted" and made him a "more profitable member of society." However, their emphasis rested not on his soul, but rather on his contributions to the community. Yet when that same Plymouth congregation censured a sister for a neighborly fight, they did not talk about her actions in the community, but instead how she "carried herself offensively."[64]

GENDERED ANALYSIS OF CONFESSIONS

In their symbolic public performance, men tried to protect their manhood by using "speech as a signifier" of their masculinity. Sandra Gustafson describes how "local language communities" created moral, social, and institutional transformation.[65] Laymen reinterpreted the religious edicts to construct their own masculine religious identity. Joseph Pomery of Westfield confessed his sins for failing to collect all the town taxes:

> I have not manifested a greater conscientious attendance upon the Duties I were bound, both unto the Town & Countrey respecting the same ... Help me with your prayers that the Remainder of my Life might be more to the glory of God, I am Your Brother and Unworthy Fellow Servant in the Fellowship of the Gospell.[66]

Absent from Pomery's confession were the feminized words of humiliation, suffering, sorrow, and grief. He did not even use the word *sin*. Table 3.3 gives the most common words used in confessions, by gender.

When Thomas Dewy stood before his congregation for destroying his neighbor's mill and dam in 1683, he confessed,

> I desire the people of God & especially the Church whereof I am an unworthy member, to lay by whatever Offence they may have taken hereat; & to help me with their prayers, that God may shew himselfe gracious to me herein: & for the time to come to defend me against all overbearing temptations.[67]

---

[64] *Plymouth Church Records*, 160, 164.
[65] Gustafson, *Eloquence Is Power*, xvii, 16.
[66] Taylor, *Church Records*, 183.
[67] Taylor, *Church Records*, 183–5.

TABLE 3.3. *Common words used in confessions*

Most Commonly Used Words in Women's Confessions	Most Commonly Used Words in Men's Confessions
Sin/sinful	Watchfulness
Soul	Dishonor
Shame	Duty
Hearts	Community
Sorry	Promise

While Dewy did refer to himself as an "unworthy member," he focused on asking for help from his community. For this man, sin was not a battle he fought with his inner soul, but one he needed to gather external forces to defend against. He asked the congregation to forgive his offense using language more familiar to a courtroom. Male dialogue in the legal, commercial, and political realm created a common "masculine verbal order" that laymen also adopted for their public religious voice.[68]

Male confessions sought to reestablish a good standing in the community. In February 1664 Stephen Fosdick appealed to his Charlestown congregation to release him from the excommunication he had been under since 1643 for neglecting services. Fosdick analyzed his "offense" in speaking against the church and acknowledged his willingness to reform and repent. It was his outward ties to his brethren that became the focus of his confession. He confessed to breaking a "solemn promise or engagement."[69] Men admitted to similar lapses of obligation in civil courts when associates sued them for bad faith, contractual disputes, or property issues. The cases centered on an external issue or problem, without comment about a man's nature.

Male confessions frequently admitted to bad conduct or poorly chosen words, but the confessors viewed their errors as something aberrant, and not due to internal flaws. Their sins were the result of a misstep rather than a sign of inner corruption. When Solomon Phips got into a public argument with John Fowle in 1688, he regretted that his "words and deeds" offended Fowle, acknowledged his poor behavior, and recognized

---

[68] For a description of "verbal order," see Gustafson, *Eloquence Is Power*, 25.
[69] Hunnewell, *Records of the First Church in Charlestown, 1632–1789*, iii.

that he needed the congregation's help. He could not admit his sinful nature; on the contrary, he blamed it on a "sinful demeanor."[70] Similarly, when David Winchill offered repentance for uttering unchristian words about Suffield minister John Younglove, he called his words "evil, sinful and offensive." He explained during his confession in front of his Westfield congregation that he "was Surprised with a Temptation e're I was aware…And [I] fell short of what the Rule & Duty requires."[71] Winchill was surprised by his aberrant behavior because he did not believe it was part of his nature – it was a "folly."[72] Conversely, women did not voice surprise over their sins, because they readily accepted their inherent sinfulness.[73] When Dorchester's only witch felt the noose around her neck in 1651, Alice Lake did not admit to being Satan's handmaiden. But she did believe she should be hung for her sinfulness, for her "harlotry," and for "concealing her sin and shame" by killing her unborn baby.[74] She lamented her sinful nature and shameful soul. It was not her action of infanticide that brought her to the scaffold, but instead her internal weakness that led her to murder.

It was important for men to maintain or restore their good reputations. In 1667 the Cambridge church had to confront John Gool for his "schismatical withdrawing from the church" and "impenitency" and for "neglecting to hear the church." The congregation agreed to restore him upon hearing his masculine confession that emphasized his "offense to his community," that he could not "justify" his actions, and that he respected the congregation's "duty" to discipline his waywardness.[75]

---

70 Hunnewell, *Records of the First Church in Charlestown, 1632–1789*, ix–x.

71 Taylor, *Church Records*, 185–7.

72 For a further discussion of men noting their particular sin and not their sinful natures, see Reis, *Damned Women*, 12–54; and Richard Godbeer, "'The Cry of Sodom': Discourse, Intercourse, and Desire in Colonial New England," *William and Mary Quarterly* 52 (April 1995): 259–86.

73 "Inner" and "outer" even in the seventeenth- and eighteenth-century ideas of anatomy were viewed as feminine and masculine. See Reis, *Damned Women*; Anthony Fletcher, *Gender, Sex, and Subordination in England, 1500–1800* (New Haven: Yale University Press, 1995); Martha L. Finch, *Dissenting Bodies: Corporealities in Early New England* (New York: Columbia University Press, 2010); and Richard Godbeer, "'The Cry of Sodom': Discourse, Intercourse, and Desire in Colonial New England." *The William and Mary Quarterly* 52, no. 2 (1995): 259–86.

74 Reis, *Damned Women*, 125; also in David Hall, ed., *Witch-Hunting in Seventeenth-Century New England: A Documentary History, 1638–1692* (Boston: Northeastern University Press, 1991), 28; and in Selement, *Keepers of the Vineyard*, 82.

75 Hunnewell, *Records of the First Church in Charlestown, 1632–1789*, v.

Gool agreed that the congregation was right to censure him and that by following the disciplinary procedures he could be reinstated as a member of the church. His confession allowed him to retain his church membership and his masculine reputation by focusing on duty, law, and public responsibility.

Women consistently employed debasing language in their confessions.[76] In 1712 young Abiel Williams, being "ensnared" by young John Sacket, confessed to fornication after her lying-in:

Oh the sorrow of my heart is such in that I have thus Sind against God, it wounds my Soule... The publick shame is great, but oh! The Dishonour of God is greater... help me with your prayers... that he would pardon my sin & pour his spirit upon me & would Secure me from overbearing temptations & enable me to resist all the assaults of the Adversary. That I might walk Humbly & without offence & come to an Holie Closing with all Gods Rules both in the inward & outward men.[77]

Williams could have easily blamed Sacket for forcing himself on her, or she could have attributed her sin to circumstance. However, she expressed her remorse over her own sinful and weak soul. Her language illustrates her self-contempt. She hurt her own soul and shamed herself by dishonoring God. Her weakness led to Sacket's sexual advances. She asked for prayers for her spirit, not help for her reputation. The Westfield congregation urged Williams to be more "watchful over herself and more humbly walk with God."[78] While the court fined them both, only Williams faced censure charges. No congregations ever described a male fornication censure with the same language as they did for a female, such as referring to their "shameful sin" or their "scandalous sin." When it came to fornication charges, it seemed more acceptable to fine a man's pocketbook in court rather than question his piety in church.[79]

Regardless of their transgressions, women lamented the dangers to their souls. In 1667 Elizabeth Healy confessed that Sam Reynolds had

---

[76] Willen, "Godly Women in Early Modern England"; Westerkamp, "Engendering Puritan Religious Culture in Old and New England," 105–77. See also Reis, *Damned Women*; Masson, "The Typology of the Female as a Model for the Regenerate"; and Westerkamp, "Engendering Puritan Religious Culture in Old and New England."

[77] Taylor, *Church Records*, 205–6.

[78] Taylor, *Church Records*, 205–6.

[79] See Dayton, *Women before the Bar*; also, St. George's study focuses on court records.

fathered her baby after getting her drunk. She offered a confession filled with remorse over her lack of piety:

It is my hearts desire to confess and bewail my sin before God and his people ... and by ye great and open sin I may be humbled before God for all my sins of disobedience & against the gospel ... but have furlowed my low hearts lusts and justly hath ... left me to the corrupting of my nature ... with yt great sin so far I know my own heart ... my great ignorance ... left me open to hordom ... it is a sinsir desire of my heart to beewal my sin ... and pray of Gods people that ... the remainder of my life might bee abundant by mor to his glory.

Healy clearly articulated what ministers preached from congregational doctrine: a person's corrupting nature left them open to sin if they did not constantly seek God's word. Healy believed she could have prevented her sin if she had been more pious. She may have disappointed her parents and betrayed the gospel, but she would reform if she improved spiritually.[80] Like her godly sisters, Healy understood the rewards of piety and its self-abasing nature.

With their confessions, women hoped to recover their souls from the temptations of sin. Charlestown's Experience Holiar married James Capen while they lived in Dorchester. Although she had already confessed to the sin of fornication in Dorchester, upon moving to Charlestown in 1689, she confessed a second time for her new congregation. She wrote that she fell "into that great & scandalous sin." Her confession also pointed to the "wounding of my precious soule" and the "filthyness and shame" for which she did "humbly begg of my offended God the pardon of my sin," and she prayed that she "may have grace to walk to Gods glory & my own Soules good."[81]

Women's social status also derived from their piety. In their confessions they scrutinized their spiritual weakness in order to ensure their place in the church. Gustafson explains that female verbal forms signified an agreement to perform the Puritan "semiotics of speech" of the humbled soul. Women achieved social recognition as godly women by conforming to this female "language community."[82] Women adopted Puritan doctrine, while men reinterpreted it.

---

[80] Elizabeth Healy, "Confession on Paternity 1667," ms., Misc. 1667–1669, Massachusetts Historical Society.
[81] Hunnewell, *Records of the First Church in Charlestown, 1632–1789*, x–xi.
[82] Gustafson, *Eloquence Is Power*, 16, 25.

In their confessions, men and women divided the covenant down gendered lines, which led to innovative practices of community. Rachel Ashley focused on her personal shame – that she wounded people who tried to help her and that she increased sin in her town with her sinful nature. Only through piety and individual religious experience could she be saved from such sin.[83] Conversely, Major Pike asked for help from his community to mend his ways.

Male confessors were much more concerned about their relationship with the community. John Gool let his brethren down, failed the covenants, and believed his brethren were justified in proceeding against him.[84] Fosdick's first words in his confession were how he broke the promise of the covenant to walk with God and his people – he failed his community.[85] Thomas Dewy could only ward off the temptation of sin with the help of his whole congregation.[86] He needed the community and could not fight off sin with his pious prayers alone.

By examining the language of confessions, we can see how Puritan congregations began to reinforce men's secular roles through patterns of church discipline. Language became an important way for Puritans to enforce gendered expectations for godly men and women and played a significant role in how Puritans developed different patterns of responsibility, identity, and duty in the church. Language developed a pattern that became a practice of community.

This study offers further corroboration for Elizabeth Reis's arguments that women more easily conformed to the expectations of their ministers and that in confessions men separated their natures from their actual sins.[87] Reis has a very compelling argument that because of the Puritan distinction between the body and the soul, men's inner self could have the feminized virtues espoused by the clergy without jeopardizing its outward masculinity.[88] This study builds on her premise by suggesting that in that fractured experience between inner and outer selves, laymen actually reconstructed daily lived religion in a deeply gendered way. Through their gendering of the requirements of confession, laymen protected and promoted a male verbal order that undermined the gender fluidity of the

---

[83] Taylor, *Church Records*, 468–69.
[84] Hunnewell, *Records of the First Church in Charlestown, 1632–1789*, v.
[85] Hunnewell, *Records of the First Church in Charlestown, 1632–1789*, iii.
[86] Taylor, *Church Records*, 183–85.
[87] Reis, *Damned Women*, 38–42. Reis focuses on confessions on witchcraft accusation but also analyzes conversion narratives.
[88] Reis, *Damned Women*, 101.

seventeenth century. Laymen reinforced ideas that male religiosity was based on external performance – public service and duty – and not on men's internal piety. Thus, men could express and affirm their religiosity in public spaces outside of church walls.

Despite his censures and warnings, Dorchester's Robert Spur worked hard to retain his church membership. An 1859 town history described Spur as a "person of some distinction," although it would be Robert Spur, Jr., and his son who would truly become distinguished as civic leaders.[89] Nevertheless, in 1698 the elder Robert Spur's assignment in the new seating chart for the meetinghouse suggests a level of respect, as he sat at the "Deacon's Seat the End Next to it, second best after Table."[90] He was an esteemed member of the laity, but descendants would find distinction through their civic service, as Robert Jr. became a selectman, constable, and justice. Grandson Robert Spur became a captain, also serving as selectman and constable. The Spur family exemplifies how Puritan men recreated their religious identity through the course of the seventeenth and early eighteenth centuries by transferring their religious duties onto the civil community.

---

[89] Committee of the Dorchester Antiquarian Society, *History of Dorchester*, 279, 302. There may be a few errors where the Spurs are concerned. On Robert Spur's passing in 1703, the history reads, "He had been a very prominent man in the town, and more liberal in his religious belief than most of his contemporaries." On his son's death in 1739, the entry reads, "He appears to have been quite a popular man in the town, and unusually liberal in his religious opinions. This later trait frequently brought him in contact with church authorities." Yet clearly his father was the Spur who the congregation repeatedly called into question. While both father and son could have had liberal religious opinions, the younger Spur became a civic leader and had no entries in the church ledger.

[90] Hope, *Records of the First Church of Dorchester*, 243.

A "Blubbering" War Hero and the Middle Ground of Masculinity

The Case of Captain John Underhill

The sound of rain echoed through Boston's First Church as parishioners sat in their pews watching tears stream down Captain John Underhill's face. At times his confession was inaudible through his sobbing. Parents surely tried to quiet their children, and the normal Sabbath whispered conversations likely fell silent so that everyone could decipher his words. Men must have squirmed uncomfortably as they watched this war hero break down. This was not what anyone expected when they trudged through the mud to their daylong services. A ruthless soldier with a reputation as a ladies' man was not the typical bewailing confessor. The emotional impact of his confession was felt throughout the meetinghouse as people choked up listening to him. John Winthrop described it as a "spectacle that caused many weeping eyes" and noted that the captain "spoke well" despite the "blubbering." When the pastor, John Wilson, called Underhill to the front of the congregation after services on September 3, 1640, the congregation may not have even recognized their famous captain. Gone were the fine wardrobe and grand stature they were accustomed to.[1] Underhill stood before them in old clothes and a foul, worn linen cap pulled close to his eyes – a piteous sight of a fallen, sinful man. Winthrop described him as "worn out with sorry" and said that his "strength was wasted" due to his "broken heart." Winthrop recorded the confession, noting that the Captain "did with many deep sighs and abundance of tears, lay open his wicked course, his adultery,

---

[1] It is worth mentioning that Captain Underhill's grandfather Thomas Underhill and great grandfather Hugh Underhill were keepers of the wardrobe for Leicester and Queen Elizabeth. Surely Captain Underhill understood the statements clothes made.

his hypocrisy, his persecution of God's people here, and especially his
pride...and contempt for the magistrates."[2] Not even Edward Taylor
could have written a better script (and over the years, he certainly tried).
In his confession, Underhill warned his brethren against the evils of vanity that caused his own fall and declared that "he discovered a broken
and melting heart, and...in the end he earnestly and humbly besought
the church to have compassion of him, and to deliver him out of the
hands of Satan."[3] Underhill's emotional performance did not end there.
In dramatic fashion, he walked down the aisle and collapsed on his knees
in front of Joseph Faber, the man he cuckolded, and begged forgiveness.
His near-perfect supplication was tainted by his description of his sexual
prowess: he preened himself, saying that Faber's wife admirably fought
off his advances for six months, noting that was an accomplishment no
other woman could have achieved. He blustered that it was only through
his dogged pursuit that she finally submitted and was then "wholly at his
will."[4] To his credit, Underhill's confession was so emotionally mesmer-
izing that no one seemed offended by that overtly sexual and prideful
boasting. His performance was so convincing that Faber later sent Underhill's wife a small gift, as a token of his forgiveness of her husband's transgressions with Faber's wife. After his confession, the church removed the
excommunication that had loomed over him for two years.

Captain John Underhill's attempt to regain his status in the church
reveals some of the complexities of masculinity in early New England.[5]
Migrants to New England in the seventeenth century brought with them
a relatively new gender construction, a result of the Reformation and

---

[2] Richard S. Dunn, James Savage, and Laetitia Yeandle, eds. *The Journal of John Winthrop, 1630–1649* (Cambridge: Belknap Press of Harvard University Press, 1996), 342.
See also Oberholzer, *Delinquent Saints*, 143. See Kamensky for her analysis of Underhill's
confession. Kamensky argues that the success of Underhill's confession lies in Winthrop's
note that he "spake well." This study argues that it was the particular feminized speech
and demeanor that ultimately made the difference.

[3] Dunn, Savage, and Yeandle, *Journal of John Winthrop*, 342.

[4] Dunn, Savage, and Yeandle, *Journal of John Winthrop*, 342.

[5] In the past decade, several historians have examined the ideas of manhood in this period.
See Ann M. Little, *Abraham in Arms: War and Gender in Colonial New England* (Phila-
delphia: University of Pennsylvania Press, 2007); Lombard, *Making Manhood*; Thomas
A. Foster, ed., *New Men: Manliness in Early America* (New York: New York University
Press, 2011); R. Todd Romero, *Making War and Minting Christians* (Boston: University
of Massachusetts Press, 2011); Fletcher, *Gender, Sex, and Subordination in England*;
Mark Breitenberg, *Anxious Masculinity in Early Modern England* (Cambridge: Cambridge University Press, 1996); Thomas Walter Laqueur, *Making Sex: Body and Gender
from the Greeks to Freud* (Cambridge: Harvard University Press, 1990).

the crisis of land enclosure that drastically altered men's ability to own land.[6] Traditional manhood was tied to the independence associated with owning property and the self-reliance associated with working such land. The economic crisis and enclosure movement forced the need for new definitions of manhood. In general, the Protestant movement called for a reformation of morals, values, behaviors, and responsibilities for men and women. This fluidity of new gender constructions brought opportunity and challenge. Historian R. Todd Romero explains that "manliness was at once essential to Christian living in colonial New England and a frequent source of anxiety."[7] In the first generation of founding a city on the hill, the gender terrain was being mapped by men and women alike. John Underhill provides an interesting case study of how one man tried to navigate this contested new world.[8]

Underhill had a tumultuous ten years in Boston. What started as a promising future ended in exile. Before the 1637 massacre at Mystic River during the Pequot War, he had gained civil appointments as a leader. But after the war he experienced rejection and left the colony in 1638 to travel to England, where he wrote about his experiences of the war. What he said about the Massachusetts Bay leadership while aboard the ship would get him banished from the colony and excommunicated from Boston First Church. After a failed attempt to regain his status, he briefly became governor in Dover in 1639 but was dismissed when Dover leaders learned of his sins in Boston. After the successful blubbering confession in the fall of 1640, he would essentially leave the Massachusetts Bay colony for good.

---

[6] John Gilbert McCurdy, "Gentlemen and Soldiers: Competing Visions of Manhood in Early Jamestown," in *New Men: Manliness in Early America*, ed. Thomas Foster (New York: New York University Press, 2011), 9–30. McCurdy discusses how manhood had been tied to mastery of the land and how the economic crisis and the Enclosure Movement severely undermined traditional ideas, sending manhood into crisis.

[7] Romero, *Making War and Minting Christians*, 31. Romero describes the anxiety over masculinity in early New England, 41. See also, Toby L. Ditz, "Contending Masculinities in Early America," in *New Men: Manliness in Early America*, ed. Thomas Foster (New York: New York University Press, 2011), 256–67.

[8] Mark Breitenberg contends that the term "anxious masculinity" is redundant: "Masculine subjectivity constructed and sustained by a patriarchal culture – infused with patriarchal assumptions about power, privilege, sexual desire, the body – inevitably engenders varying degrees of anxiety in its male members." He also writes, "I argue that masculine anxiety is a necessary and inevitable condition that operates on at least two significant levels: it reveals the fissures and contradictions of patriarchal systems, and, at the same time, it paradoxically enables and drives patriarchy's reproduction and continuation of itself." Breitenberg, *Anxious Masculinity in Early Modern England*, 1–2. See also Fletcher, *Gender, Sex, and Subordination in England*.

When he first arrived in Massachusetts in 1630, John Underhill believed he could establish himself as a leader. The Massachusetts Bay Company recruited him as a military expert. He then became an early member of the Boston Church, was appointed to the General Court, was chosen as a selectman in 1634, was one of the original members of the Ancient and Honorable Artillery Company, and was made a captain just prior to the expedition against the native Pequot. All of these appointments reified his sense of self – his strength, military prowess, talent, bravery, pride, and honor.[9]

Underhill achieved fame and glory during the Pequot War. English skirmishes with the tribe over land, property, and trading escalated as the English expanded into Pequot territory in the Connecticut River valley. Smallpox and tribal divisions over alliances had already weakened the Pequots. The war essentially started when the English sought retribution for the murder of English trader John Oldman in July 1636. With their Narragansett and Mohegan allies, and under the leadership of Captains John Mason and John Underhill, the English attacked the Pequot village at Mystic River. Underhill and his men surrounded the village, setting it on fire and killing approximately 700 people, mostly women and children. English soldiers then attacked anyone who tried to escape the flames. The slaughter was so bloody and foul that Indian allies questioned the methods of the English soldiers.[10] For his contributions to this massacre Underhill became a celebrated hero, and his plans for becoming a leading figure in the colony seemed secured. However, Underhill would soon discover that he had to contend with New World ideas of manhood that did not quite embrace his fierce, sexualized representation of masculinity (Figure 4.1).

COMPETING MASCULINITIES

Ministers and laymen had different expectations for manhood. Historian Ann Braude explains that the espoused Christian virtues differed from traditional ideas of manhood: "For men, ideals of masculinity often conflicted with Christian virtues rather than reinforcing them."[11] Through

---

[9] Breen, *Transgressing the Bounds*, 5, 64.

[10] For a history of the Pequot War, see Charles Orr, ed., *History of the Pequot War; the Contemporary Accounts of Mason, Underhill, Vincent and Gardener* (reprinted from the Collections of the Massachusetts Historical Society; Cleveland: The Helman-Taylor Company, 1897); Alfred A. Cave, *The Pequot War* (Amherst: University of Massachusetts Press, 1996); and Alan Axelrod, *Chronicle of the Indian Wars: From Colonial Times to Wounded Knee* (New York: Prentice Hall, 1993).

[11] Braude, "Women's History Is American Religious History," 87–107, 104.

FIGURE 4.1. Scene from the Pequot War. *Source:* Bettmann/Bettmann
Collection/Getty Images.

their control over church discipline, laymen confronted such contested
ideas, navigating a middle ground of masculinity. Laymen adopted a version of manhood that was sober and tempered, rationale and legalistic,
but not bound by the more feminized mandates of the clergy. While they
disapproved of Underhill's hypermasculine exploits with women and his
contentious dealings with magistrates, Boston's laymen certainly did not
expect or even want to see their war hero bawling over his corrupted soul.

Even with new ideas of masculinity being asserted in New
England, this was a society in great need of military men. Taming the
"wilderness" of land and subordinating native peoples summoned a
level of violence and physical excess associated with a hypermasculine
identity.[12] The military man had to be physically and mentally strong,
unemotional, violent, aggressive, and able to operate from a sense of
pride and honor.[13] Historian Ann Little explains that the early successful battles with Indians "intensified New England men's identification

---

[12] See Ditz, who argues that battles of empire and Native American groups meant that New
England was at constant war, necessitating a highly militarized group of men, 256.
[13] See Ditz, "Contending Masculinities in Early America," 256; and McCurdy, "Gentlemen
and Soldiers," 9–30; for an explanation of expectations of the New England soldier, see
John Ferling, "The New England Soldier: A Study in Changing Perceptions," *American
Quarterly* 33, no. 1 (1981): 26–45.

of war with manliness."[14] A "hegemonic masculinity" existed in the military, but the soldiers faced difficulties transitioning from military to civilian life.[15]

Puritans attempted to soften the edges of the soldier by redefining his duties in godly terms. They heralded a soldier who fought for faith and family, in whom violence was acceptable through a Christian rationale of a just or holy war.[16] In casting the conflict with indigenous peoples as ordained by God, the Puritans were able to justify the violence and bloodshed. They may also have believed that Indians consorted with the Devil.[17] In his famous account of the Pequot War, *Newes from America*, Underhill addressed the violence that some of his English countrymen must have called into question:

Why should you be so furious (as some have said) should not Christians have more mercy and compassion? But I would referre you to Davids warre, when a people is growne to such a height of bloud, and sinne against God and man, and all confederates in the action, there hee hath no respect to persons ... and the most terriblest of death that may bee: sometimes the Scripture declareth women and children must perish with their parents ... We had sufficient light from the word of God for our proceedings.[18]

Underhill not only justified the Pequot massacre as blessed by God, but he compared himself to David, the biblical hero who conquered Goliath and the Philistines. As a warrior, David led the defeat against the enemies of the Israelites and became king of Israel. It is an interesting comparison for Underhill to make. David was a handsome, talented, chivalric hero who gained acclaim, recognition, and power for his success as a soldier. Moreover, he had to defeat not only his enemies, but also battle those who were jealous of his abilities. The life of David is believed to foreshadow the life of Christ, who was considered to be a descendent of David. In his account, Underhill explained how God saved him several times as Indian arrows almost killed him. In heralding how only the

---

14 Little, *Abraham in Arms*, 28.

15 McCurdy, "Gentlemen and Soldiers," 10–11.

16 Timothy George, "War and Peace in the Puritan Tradition," *Church History* 53, 4 (1984), 492–503; Little, *Abraham in Arms*, 22; see also Romero, *Making War and Minting Christians*.

17 Little argues that Underhill had to justify his brutality in the Pequot War, 47.

18 John Underhill, *Newes from America; or, A New and Experimental Discoverie of New England; Containing, A True Relation of Their War-Like Proceedings These Two Yeares Last Past, with a Figure of the Indian Fort, or Palizado* (London: J. D. for Peter Cole, 1638), 35–36.

bravest of men became soldiers, he recalled David again: "I will not fear
that man can doe unto me, saith David, no more what troubles can doe,
but will trust in the Lord, who is my God."[19] Underhill compares himself
to a biblical hero, while describing the men of Boston as effeminate and
jealous of his prowess. His inflated ego underscores how much his pride
and honor were at stake.

Underhill may have wanted to remind his compatriots of the importance of holy warriors to save a people (or a colony). Underhill wrote his
account of the Pequot War in 1638, during his time in England after the
General Court banished him from Massachusetts for heresy. He certainly
used his account to validate his masculinity. In an interesting passage, he
justified English violence by explaining that the soldiers showed restraint.
He described how the Indians "jeered" at them, "daring" them to fight,
and howled that the English were "all like women."[20] Certainly calling
these heroic soldiers "women" was an affront that justified an aggressive
response. Ann Little explains that it was a "universally understood insult
if you called a man a 'woman.'"[21]

Underhill rationalized the hardship he endured as a soldier of Christ,
vowing that you "cannot know Christ without knowing the cross." In
the most overt reference to his troubles in Massachusetts Bay, he wrote,
"We meet with many crosses in the world, losses at home and abroad,
in Church and Commonwealth."[22] He painted himself as a godly soldier
unjustly persecuted. Comparing the Pequot War and his own sojourn
to scripture stories, Underhill sanctified the violence and the heroism of
his own hypermasculinity, suggesting that those in the New World who
doubted him may very well have been the real Pharisees. Captain John
Underhill clumsily tried to navigate the middle ground of masculinity,
and ultimately was not successful. Underhill's story is interesting because
he continually (and stubbornly) fought to preserve his definition of
manhood.

---

[19] Underhill, *Newes from America*, 31.
[20] Underhill, *Newes from America*, 14. For a discussion of the contest of gender between
English and Native Americans in New England, see Little, *Abraham in Arms*, 12–55. Little explains how "colonial warfare was often expressed as a contest between the Indian
and English notions of manhood ... both Indian and English men claimed to be disturbed
by the other's ideas of gender roles, most particularly in the proper performance of manhood," 13. Little also notes that the Puritans saw the victory over the Pequots as a vindication of English manhood, 28.
[21] Little, *Abraham in Arms*, 2 (and unfortunately still is).
[22] Underhill, *Newes from America*, 29.

TEMPERED MASCULINITY

Although it still reified patriarchy, the new masculinity in New England tempered some of the more violent, unruly aspects of traditional manhood in order to avoid excesses and remake men into rational, controlled, and responsible Protestants.[23] The creation of a godly social order required men to be disciplined, sober, and mature. A new emphasis on family meant that men were more involved in the domestic realm as fathers and husbands. New World circumstances created much more interdependence between men and women than existed in England. Born in 1652, Samuel Sewall epitomized this new, remade man.[24] Throughout his six-decade-long diary, we see examples of the balancing act required of the successful Puritan man. He was not afraid to challenge ministers or governors, yet he also was sure to brew his wife's groaning beer and wrote lovingly about her and his children.[25] He doted on his grandchildren, bringing them trinkets and cakes. He not only loved his wife, Hannah, but trusted her with their family finances. In 1704 he gave his wife money to manage: "Gave my wife the rest of my cash and tell her she shall now keep the Cash; if I want I will borrow of her. She has a better faculty than I at managing Affairs; I will assist her: and will endeavour to live upon my Salary. Will see what it will doe. The Lord give his Blessing."[26] Sewall was committed to being a responsible husband, father, and member of his church and community. He was also critical of men who "failed" in their manhood. When Mrs. Mercy Wade filed a complaint against her son-in-law, Jonathan Willis, for being an abusive husband to her daughter, Dorothy, Sewall reflects, "If persons would not be spirited by Love to their Wives, Children, Parents, Religion, twas a bad Omen fell below the heathen Romans." While his diary is filled with the many funerals he regularly attended, he refused to go to James Penniman's service because the man was a drunkard.[27] Sewall modeled a tempered masculinity celebrated by New Englanders and had little sympathy for men who did not.

---

[23] For a discussion of this new tempered manhood in early New England, see Lombard, *Making Manhood*; Lisa Wilson, *Ye Heart of a Man*; and Foster, *New Men*.

[24] On the ideal of the rational man, see Lombard, *Making Manhood*, 3–15.

[25] Groaning beer was a beer made for when a woman went into labor and served to her and her attendants. It was also for celebrating the end of her lying-in period after childbirth.

[26] Sewall, *Diary of Samuel Sewall*, 496.

[27] Sewall, *Diary of Samuel Sewall*, 691, 707.

This new tempered masculinity was a balancing act, not to feminize men, but to quell some of the excesses of the traditional English man. Historian Anne Lombard explains that the "New England definition of manhood was part of a seventeenth-century attempt to remake men into responsible and self-controlled members of society, and to eradicate certain violent, unruly variants of manhood traditionally found in England."[28] Historian Toby L. Ditz argued that there were several competing masculinities at play in the colonial period: "What is most striking about early America is the sheer variety of manhood ideals and their associated practices."[29] The sober, rational new man had to contend with the feminized Puritan ideology celebrated by the clergy, the hypermasculinity associated with military service, and the traditional aspects of manhood that carried over to the New World.

HYPERMASCULINITY

John Underhill adopted the tenants of hypermasculinity early in his life. As a child and young man in the Netherlands, his father trained him to be a soldier and sent him to the renowned military academy founded by Maurice of Nassau, Prince of Orange. Historian J. G. McCurdy explains that the military served as training ground for a "hegemonic masculinity" that valorized strength and aggression, while debasing any displays of emotion. The military offered a path to manhood that also permitted men to revel in all sorts of excesses: violence, adventure, and sexual conquest.[30] Conquering a new world required hypermasculine behavior: exploring, penetrating, defending, and attacking. Such men had to be strong, assertive, and in control. This was a manhood steeped in the triumph of conquest. New England needed men to build and protect their communities by "conquering" the wilderness and the Indians. The celebration of violence and sexual conquest was interwoven into the language of subduing the land. Connecticut's Roger Wolcott inked a poem about his emotions at first seeing the "virgin land":

[28] Lombard, *Making Manhood*, 12.

[29] Ditz, "Contending Masculinities in Early America," 256–67, 256. See also Breen, *Transgressing the Bounds*, who also writes that masculinity was a contested ground, 61.

[30] McCurdy, "Gentlemen and Soldiers," 10. Military masculinity stood in contrast to the new masculinity of sobriety and restraint propounded by the civil leaders and clergy in Massachusetts Bay. See Anne Marie Plane, "Indian and English Dreams: Colonial Hierarchy and Manly Restraint in Seventeenth-Century New England," in *New Men: Manliness in Early America*, ed. Thomas Foster (New York: New York University Press, 2011), 31–47.

> As when the wounded amorous doth spy
> His smiling fortune in his lady's eye,
> O how his veins and breast swell with a flood
> Of pleasing raptures that revive his blood!

In his final stanza, he wrote:

> This most delightful country to possess;
> And forward, with industrious speed, we press,
> Upon the virgin stream, who had, as yet,
> Never been violated with a ship.

Like Wolcott, poet Thomas Morton compared New England to "a fair virgin longing to be sped and meet her lover in a nuptial bed." He described how "English industry would fertilize her fruitful womb."[31] The conflation of colonization with sexual conquest valorized hypermasculinity. This language is the polar opposite of the feminized language used and espoused by the clergy.

Underhill's family reputation, military prowess, relentless ambition, pride, good looks, and womanizing made him a "man's man" by today's lexicon. Historian Louise Breen describes how men like Underhill represented the male honor culture of England, whereby men gained respect and distinction through their gallantry, military acumen, chivalry, and heroism.[32] Upon migrating to Massachusetts Bay with a military appointment, certainly Underhill expected that his skills and code of honor would earn him not only respect but a position of power within the colonial government.

Captain Underhill had little interest in taming his excesses and mastering the domestic realm. As Breen describes, Underhill thought most men in New England were "soft."[33] Underhill took great pride in his ability to conquer men in the battlefield and women in the bedroom, and boasted of both. An early twentieth-century historian, J. Franklin Jameson, called Underhill an "amusing reprobate" with "no core values."[34] Historian

---

[31] Roger Wolcott, "A Brief Account of the Agency of the Honorable John Winthrop, Esq. in the Court of King Charles the Second, Annon Dom. 1662," *Massachusetts Historical Society Collections* 4 (1795), 267; Thomas Morton, *The New English Canaan* (Boston: Prince Society, 1883), cited in Godbeer, *Sexual Revolution in Early America*, 154–55.

[32] Breen, *Transgressing the Bounds*, 11; see also Fletcher, *Gender, Sex, and Subordination in England*, 126–53.

[33] Breen, *Transgressing the Bounds*, 11.

[34] J. Franklin Jameson, ed., *Narratives of New Netherland, 1609–1664* (New York: Charles Scribner's Sons, 1908; reprint, New York: Barnes & Noble, 1967), 282, n. 2.

FIGURE 4.2. Captain John Underhill. *Source:* Courtesy of HathiTrust.

Lawrence Hauptman goes further, diagnosing Underhill as a sociopath with antisocial personality disorder who was unable to conform to social norms and was "truly disturbed."[35] New Englanders needed soldiers to do the dirty work of colonization, but they did not have a place for those who could not make the transition from the battlefield to the barnyard.[36] Underhill entered a gender terrain he did not understand, and he certainly did not respect. He would spend his lifetime fighting for the respect he thought he deserved (Figure 4.2).

[35] Lawrence M. Hauptman, "John Underhill: A Psychological Portrait of an Indian Fighter," *The Hudson Valley Regional Review* 9 (1992): 101–11.
[36] McCurdy explains that it was often difficult for soldiers to transition back to civilian life and the expectations of laboring on the land, 15.

NAVIGATING MASCULINITY

Underhill sought alliances that bolstered his sense of masculinity. He supported the Antinomians, which was a religious and political movement in Massachusetts Bay that believed most Boston ministers did not strictly adhere to the covenant of grace but instead preached a covenant of works. Antinomians believed in "free grace" preached by John Cotton. Its leaders included the minister John Wheelwright, magistrate and governor Henry Vane, and Anne Hutchinson. In addition to their theological contentions, they also challenged the Massachusetts Bay political leadership. Breen contends that Underhill was attracted to the Antinomians because he thought the culture of honor he subscribed to more closely aligned with their beliefs of a more heterogeneous and individualistic society.[37] He joined the Ancient and Honorable Artillery Company for similar reasons. Not only was this a military training group that respected Underhill's expertise, but the men also clashed with the orthodoxy. Breen contends, "The inclusion of Pequot War hero and incorrigible Antinomian John Underhill on the first roster at a time when the captain's future in the colony was in serious doubt testified to this great openness."[38] Both of these groups allowed space for competing masculinities (and femininities). However, neither of these groups gained the status necessary for legitimacy. Antinomian leaders were exiled and the movement discredited, and the Artillery Company never achieved any real power or authority, as their training days were known more for the amount of beer consumed than anything else.[39]

Several experiences that followed the Pequot War diminished Underhill's sense of power and respect. The Massachusetts Bay Company reorganized the militia, putting civilian leaders in charge of regiments, which meant professional soldiers were essentially paid for hire. Underhill was reduced to a salaried position, dependent on the colony for his livelihood. Being a dependent did not meet the standards for masculinity

[37] Breen, *Transgressing the Bounds*, 61–62; see also, Bozeman, *The Precisianist Strain*, 232. Bozeman also argues that the Antinomian movement offered military men a greater sense of power and honor. For more on the Antinomian movement, see David D. Hall, *The Antinomian Controversy, 1636–1638: A Documentary History* (Durham: Duke University Press, 1990); and Winship, *Making Heretics*.

[38] Breen, *Transgressing the Bound*, 5. In his autobiography, Shepard compares defeating the Pequots to ridding the colonies of the Antinomian dissenters (Adams, *Autobiography of Thomas Shepard*, 61–62).

[39] See Salinger, *Taverns and Drinking in Early America*.

for Underhill or even the new ideals of manhood in New England. Manhood was defined as being economically independent, usually through land ownership. Underhill might have rejected the New England definitions of manhood, but it had to be humiliating to not even meet this "soft" definition due to being a salaried employee of these effeminate men. Underhill tried to rectify the situation. In 1638, as a reward for his heroism against the Pequots, Underhill requested a grant of 300 acres in order to establish himself as a man of independence. But he was denied the land.

During the 1630s there were clashes in Massachusetts Bay over how to govern. As the ideas of the New England Way propounded by Governor John Winthrop prevailed, leaders began to confront some of the more problematic men and women, starting with the Antinomians. Not only did the colony banish the movement's leaders such as John Wheelwright and Anne Hutchinson, they also went after their supporters. Just months after his victory over the Pequots, Underhill was discharged from his post as captain after he wrote a letter of support for Wheelwright and Hutchinson. That was only the beginning of his troubles.

Angered over losing his post, Underhill's hubris would strike again when he openly condemned the government and made heretical statements about his own salvation. Clearly, officials needed to get him under control. In 1638 the General Court called Underhill to hear charges levied against him by a young woman who was a passenger aboard ship on his earlier voyage to England. While this "godly woman" confessed that Underhill seduced her, the court was more interested in his deck-side speeches in which he compared the leaders in New England to the Pharisee zealots or to Paul before his conversion. He also committed heresy by explaining how the spirit came to him while he was smoking tobacco one day and "set home an absolute promise of free grace with such assurance and joy" that he would never again doubt his salvation, even if he fell into sin again. At first, Underhill did not confirm or deny the charges but instead questioned the integrity of the witness. Underhill had actually written a retraction to the governor to present to the General Court; however, when pressed by the magistrates, he boasted that his apology was disingenuous and that he stood by his original shipboard commentaries. His motivation in baiting the magistrates is unclear. Antinomian leaders had already been banished. Was he trying to rally the cause? Did he expect supporters to materialize? Or did his own inflated ego blind him to the inevitable outcome? The very next day, the General Court called him forth and banished him from the colony. Underhill still made a speech the following day in the assembly, arguing against the ruling. He declared that he was confident he was saved by God and argued his actions were justified. John Cotton even tried to intervene and tell Underhill that he was breaking the law by ridiculing the ruling before privately appealing to the court.[40]

Underhill's fall from grace continued. Besides being banished by the court, the Boston First Church called him to appear to address accusations of sinful behavior with the wife of his neighbor, Joseph Faber. Underhill initially fought off the accusations with a thin excuse that he was trying to save her soul. He denied the affair, justifying his daily visits by explaining that Goodwife Faber was in "great trouble of mind and sore temptations." Underhill admitted that it may have had the appearance of impropriety; after all, they went to the extraordinary measure of locking the door.[41] But he explained that his intentions were pure; it was just her soul he was trying to comfort, and they merely locked the door to assure their holy prayers would not be interrupted. Neighbors had found them together behind the locked door on more than one occasion. Countering Underhill's description of a greatly troubled young woman, Winthrop described Goodwife Faber as "being young, and beautiful, and withal of a jovial spirit and behavior." The laity must have been very suspicious of Underhill's dubious account. No one corroborated his story that Goodwife Faber was in spiritual crisis and despair. Moreover, church elders explained that even when a parishioner was in need of spiritual guidance, they would never lock the door.[42] The church admonished him and awaited a confession.

Without a home, church, job, or reputation, Underhill decided to try his fortune with the banished Wheelwright in a new colony, Pascataquack (later named Dover). Massachusetts leaders felt it was their godly duty to inform Dover officials of their sinful new resident and began writing letters to the colony's leaders. They explained that the Boston officials still wanted Underhill to appear for his censure, and they warned the Dover leaders to be careful about "advancing" him to any position of leadership. In his journal, John Winthrop recorded what they detailed for the Dover leaders:

---

[40] Winthrop, *Winthrop's Journal*, September 1638.

[41] New England colonial society did not have the same levels of interest in privacy, and neighbors would often walk right into someone's home. Locking the door was unheard of at that time.

[42] Winthrop, *Winthrop's Journal*, September 1638.

Capt Underhill [was] thrust out for abusing the court with feigning a retraction both of his seditious practice and also of his corrupt opinions, and after denying it again, and for casting reproach upon our churches, etc. signifying withal that he was now found to have been an unclean person (for he was charged by a godly young woman to have solicited her Chastity under the pretense of Christian love, and to have confessed to her, that he had his will oftentimes of the cooper's wife, and all out of strength of love).[43]

Underhill refused to appear on the charges unless the court overturned his banishment. Certainly Wheelwright had ample reason to distrust Winthrop and other Boston leaders. According to Winthrop, Dover appointed John Underhill governor before even receiving the warnings from Massachusetts's officials.

In his indignation at yet another stain to his character, Underhill began his war of words, abroad and at home. According to Winthrop, Underhill wrote to John Cotton "full of high and threatening words" but simultaneously wrote a letter to Winthrop that sought reconciliation. A vociferous letter-writing campaign ensued. Underhill even tried to circumvent the censure of Boston's First Church by having a church at Dover write to them, asserting that he was a "worshipful man" and "honored governor." In his journal, Winthrop dismissed their assessment, explaining that the Dover church was founded by a few "loose men" and a weak minister.[44]

The leaders at Dover were becoming apprehensive about the escalating conflict over their governor and agreed to hold him accountable but asked that Massachusetts not send forces after him. This left Underhill little choice but to retract his virulent statements.[45] He had to try to make amends with Massachusetts, or it threatened his livelihood in Dover. As governor, he had the opportunity to craft his own masculine type of leadership that would celebrate his military acumen and sense of honor. Underhill had to do whatever was necessary to maintain his status in Dover.

He asked the magistrates to allow him to return to the colony in order to confess his sins to his congregation. Winthrop recorded on February 20, 1640, that Underhill "being struck with horror and remorse for his offences, both against the church and civil state, could have no rest till he had obtained a safe conduct to come give satisfaction."[46] The court granted him passage, and he publicly appeared after lecture day to give his confession.

[43] Winthrop, *Winthrop's Journal*, November 1638.
[44] Winthrop, *Winthrop's Journal*, March 1639.
[45] Winthrop, *Winthrop's Journal*, March 1639.
[46] Winthrop, *Winthrop's Journal*, February 20, 1640.

Underhill approached this confession to the congregation as a means to an end, to safeguard his standing in Dover. Underhill walked a fine line with this initial public confession. His performance sought to gain forgiveness for very serious sins without compromising his masculinity. He confessed to adultery and fornication and to "injuring the state." He even admitted that the courts were right to banish him. His male pride and ego prevented him from offering enough of a sincere confession to garner support among the laity. Winthrop explained that his confession was

mixed with such excuses and extenuations, as it did not give satisfaction of the truth of his repentance, so as it seemed to be done rather out of policy, and to pacify the sting of his conscience, than in sincerity. But, however, his offense being so foul and scandalous, the church presently cast him out; which censure he seemed to submit unto, and for the time he staid in Boston he was very much dejected.[47]

By Winthrop's estimation, Underhill's performance seemed to be a disingenuous political move that offered no real remorse. Although much of the male laity must have still considered Underhill a war hero, even they felt Underhill lacked the necessary sincerity. They officially excommunicated him on March 5, 1640, finding his behavior to be "so foul and scandalous" that they had no other choice. Winthrop noted that Underhill seemed dejected but "soon recovered his spirits" and showed no signs of a broken heart.[48] His personal ambition and sense of honor may have blinded him from seeing the way to navigate through, even when it was in his own best interests.

Dover officials now had to contend with the fact that their governor was an admitted adulterer; they could no longer ignore the issue. When Underhill was called to the Dover court, some magistrates announced they could not serve with a man of such ill repute. Underhill could see the writing on the wall and abruptly left the courtroom before they issued their decision. He thought the only way to save his position in Dover was to persuade the Boston church to rescind his excommunication. And so he returned again. But the church refused to hear a confession so soon after his initial failure, since he continued to show no signs of repentance. Dover then proceeded to remove him from his post as governor.

47 Winthrop, *Winthrop's Journal*, February 20, 1640.
48 Winthrop, *Winthrop's Journal*, February 1640.

PERFORMATIVE FEMINIZED SPEECH

Only after he was removed as governor did Underhill change tactics. He once again returned to Boston to confess, but this time he appeared in tattered clothes, delivering a confession filled with feminized language and flourishes of emotion. While his crying and debasing confession certainly crossed gender boundaries, so too did Underhill's physical mannerisms and clothing. In every aspect possible, Underhill presented a version of himself that was wholly opposite of his previous self-fashioning. He betrayed his own male pride by kneeling to beg forgiveness from a man well below his status and reputation. Men knelt before nobility or in prayer as a sign of humility, reverence, and obedience; to kneel before someone was a physical expression of one's inferiority in the presence of a superior. Underhill had cuckolded the cooper, emasculating him in the most intimate way possible, yet then attempted to reverse roles by approaching him in church on bended knees. Even Underhill's simple worn clothes betrayed his masculinity and status. Clothing was an important marker of identity – signifying social status, rank, character, and even one's piety.[49] Underhill put aside his military uniform associated with his hypermasculinity for clothes that clearly expressed a sense of inferiority and dependence. He needed to be restored to the church, and so in the public theater of confession he saw his only recourse was to offer such a highly feminized, demeaning, self-debasing confession that the congregation would have to accept it. This final performance was successful.

After the confession, Underhill went to court, where the magistrates pardoned him for everything except the adultery but decided that he would not have to face the death penalty for it. On October 7, 1640, the General Court stated:

Whereas Capt John Underhill hath come upon safe conduct into the court this present day and there openly and humbly acknowledged and bewayled his offences against God and this commonwealth, as hee had formerly done the like to the church of Boston, who have thereupon received him againe into the church, this court also, being charitably and well perswaded of the truth of his repentance, are willing to forgive his former offences so far as many concerne every of our private interest and are freely reconsiled to him in Christian love...this court

---

[49] See Finch, *Dissenting Bodies*, 107–9; see also, Thomas A. Foster, "New Men: Feminist Histories of Manliness in Early British America," in *New Men: Manliness in Early America*, ed. Thomas Foster (New York: New York University Press, 2011), 1–6. Foster discusses how it was a sign of masculinity to have control over one's public demeanor.

doth order that his sentence of banishment shall be suspended till the end of the next Court of Elections, and then the court will further consider his condition.[50]

Underhill formally regained his residency and church membership, but he would never regain his stature or call Massachusetts home.

UNDERHILL'S SOJOURN

This was not the end of Underhill's tribulations. After his confession in the fall of 1640, Underhill quickly shed his worn clothes. He attempted to settle in several different colonies. In 1642 Winthrop recorded that Underhill "finding no employment here that would maintain him and his family" sought to accept an offer from the Dutch.[51] His military expertise bought him short-term success in New Netherlands, but his hubris and his inability to moderate his behavior continued to be problematic. The Dutch initially celebrated the hero. Underhill displayed his prowess in more Indian battles by recreating the strategy of the Pequot War and massacring whole villages. However, his antics continued to cause problems off the battlefield. In March 1644 Underhill was accused of starting a barroom brawl and destroying property at Philip Gerristseen's tavern in New Amsterdam. During a private party hosted by Nicholas Coorn, Underhill allegedly knocked to "pieces all but three of the mugs which hung from the shelf" and then drew his "sword in this right hand and his scabbard in the left" and made "cuts and hackings in the posts and doors." After making "unnecessary remarks" and battling with the landlady, he threatened the partygoers, yelling, "Clear out of here or I shall strike at random." In a written statement, Coorn testified that in order to "prevent further and more serious mischief, yes, even bloodshed, we broke up our pleasant party." Three other guests also signed affidavits of Underhill's attack.[52] Underhill could never find the middle ground of masculinity and leave the violence on the battlefield. For him, such outbursts must have demonstrated his superiority in strength, agility, and power. He continued to believe that men were made in conquest, whether in the tavern, battlefield, or bedroom. The Dutch eventually banished him, as he turned on them as warfare loomed between the Dutch and

---

[50] Colonial Society of Massachusetts, Records of the Suffolk County Court. Vol. II, II vols. Boston: The Society, 1933, October 7, 1640, 40–41.

[51] Winthrop, *Winthrop's Journal*, May 1642, vol. II.

[52] Hauptman, "John Underhill," 107–8.

the English.[53] Seeking glory, Underhill resorted to the only success he had – on the battlefield. He thought perhaps that another military victory could reestablish his reputation in New England. Thus, he sided with his former comrades over the Dutch. Throughout the course of his life Underhill held offices in seven governments, was arrested four times, and was banished on three different occasions.[54] He ended up settling down for the remainder of his years in Long Island. When his first wife, Helena, died in 1658, he married Elizabeth Feakes, converted to Quakerism, and had five children with Elizabeth.[55] Underhill died in 1672, leaving behind a large estate and eight living children.[56]

Underhill is an example of the confusing, competing, and sometimes overlapping ideas of manhood in the seventeenth century. Underhill's masculine excesses were his downfall in a society that elevated a moderate, sober manhood. The records tell us stories of other men who adhered to a more traditional English masculinity who were not interested in trying to show restraint or control, as well as those of men who simply rejected the social mandates of the new masculinity, thus emboldened to behave badly.

MISCHIEVOUS MEN

Around the same time that John Underhill was embroiled in his battle over excommunication and banishment in Boston, another nonconforming man was attempting to deal with his censure problems as well. The latter offers an interesting example of how one notorious sinner navigated the disciplinary process. In 1639, Richard Wayte was censured for his first offense, stealing buckskin, for which he was excommunicated for refusing to confess. Months later he sought his congregation's forgiveness. He faced some pressure to offer up a penitent confession, because some of his brethren were skeptical, gossiping that he kept lewd company and

---

[53] For more on Underhill's time with the Dutch and in New York, see Daniel M. Mead, *A History of the Town of Greenwich, Fairfield County Connecticut* (New York: Baker & Godwin, Printers, 1857).

[54] See Louis Effingham deForest, *Captain John Underhill Gentleman, Soldier of Fortune* (New York: Ria Publishing Company, 1934), 89.

[55] Elizabeth's sister Hannah was a leader in the Quaker movement. Their mother, Elizabeth Fones, scandalized the colony when she married her third husband while legally still married to Robert Feakes. Fones's first husband was Henry Winthrop, her first cousin and son of Governor John Winthrop. See Mead, *A History of the Town of Greenwich*, 45–54.

[56] The Underhill Burying Ground is located in Oyster Bay. The Underhill Society was formed in the nineteenth century to trace the descendants of Captain Underhill.

was not truly repentant. His confession is interesting because it not only followed the formula of a John Cotton sermon, but he actually "lifted" portions of it.[57] Although unwilling to temper his behavior, Wayte was savvy enough to know that the feminized language plagiarized from a sermon would warrant forgiveness. It was a long confession, filled with the stages of a tortured soul, temptation, regret, prayer, remorse, and re-commitment to Christ and the community:

Thank I had some desire to see my sin and to loath my former abominable sins, this did still much more astonish me to consider that god should change my mind from these things, and to admire God's patience to so vile a sinner, than so full as I know my own wicket heart, God brought me to a willingness to submit myself to what he should please bring upon me. Then my heart was desirous to be affected at the dishonor put upon his Name and the offence given to his people and now I desire to submit myself to him and to lie down at his foot stool and at the feet of all his people, to submit to what they dispose of.[58]

He clearly recognized the distinctions between the feminized language of the clergy and the traditional masculine language used by his male peers and borrowed language from Cotton in order to deliver what he thought would satisfy the congregation after his particularly unruly behavior. The minister's language proved beneficial, and the excommunication was lift-ed (albeit briefly, for over the course of his life Wayte would be excom-municated two more times for drunkenness).

Edward Mills was the epitome of a man who refused to conform. If ever a man needed a serious examination of his soul, it was he.[59] A lying, cheating, gambling womanizer, Mills boasted frequently of his sex-ual conquests. In 1699 the recorder of the Boston Second Church found his sins to be "too abominable to be mentioned." His landlady testified that she had an adulterous affair with him. The congregation blamed the breakup of this woman's family on Mills's "lewd, vile and lascivious carriage" since she was known for her good character prior to meeting Mills. Instead of confessing, he left the colony. He returned later that year to take up a life of gambling and games, spending most evenings in taverns drinking and seducing women. The congregation expressed its

---

[57] James F. Cooper Jr., "The Confession and Trial of Richard Wayte, Boston, 1640," *William and Mary Quarterly* 44, no. 2 (1987): 310–32, 312.

[58] Cooper, "The Confession and Trial of Richard Wayte," 318.

[59] See Oberholzer, *Delinquent Saints*, 44–45, 144; Godbeer, *Sexual Revolution in Early America*, 98; Boston Second Church, Notebooks from 17th Century on Sermons (Cotton Mather, Increase Mather), Massachusetts Historical Society, 1699.

concern that his "family suffered under a scandalous misgovernment." Mills seemed to mock the disciplinary process by boasting of "his wickedness, even of no less than incestuous wickedness." He showed no interest in reforming his ways. He started several fights with neighbors and seemed to bask in his outrageous behavior, slandering "several young gentlewomen" as "infamous whores." The congregation sought a mere "shadow of repentance," any sign of his remorse. Instead, Mills sent the elders a letter – a "rude, venomous, and villainous paper" – arguing that they had no proof against him. The congregation concluded, "He was not only an abomination unto the Lord, but was also intolerable and abominable to all Civil Society."[60] Unlike Underhill, Mills did not need to seek respect or status, nor did he worry about his reputation. He rejected outright the confines of a tempered masculinity and disappeared from New England. While most men navigated the middle ground of masculinity with relative success, some men chose a different path – one straight out of town.

One hundred years after Underhill's death, poet John Greenleaf Whittier offered him the admiration he never got in life. Whittier, critical of feminine Puritan culture, reified the hypermasculinity and violence in Underhill's Indian campaigns.[61] His poem, "John Underhill," published in *Hazel Blossoms* in 1875, celebrated Underhill as a hero, a true Christian, and a real man. The poem credited him with saving the colonies through his bravery and lauded the scars he bore from his battles. Whittier was critical of the Massachusetts General Court, writing that Underhill "braved" their "wrath" by defending his religious principles:

> He shook from his feet as he rode away
> The dust of the Massachusetts Bay.
> The world might bless and the world might ban,
> What did it matter the perfect man.
> To whom the freedom of earth was given,
> Proof against sin, and sure of heaven?

---

[60] Boston Second Church, Book of Second Church Records from 1689–1717, Massachusetts Historical Society.

[61] For more on Whittier's critique of feminized Puritanism and his defense of Underhill's violent masculinity, see David T. Haberly, "Male Anxiety and Sacrificial Masculinity: The Case of Echeverría," *Hispanic Review* 73 (Summer 2005): 291–307; Peter J. Gomes, "'Heroes' and 'Villains' in the Creation of the American Past," *Proceedings of the Massachusetts Historical Society*, Third Series, 95 (1983): 1–16; and Louis C. Schaedler, "Whittier's Attitude towards Colonial Puritanism," *The New England Quarterly* 21, no. 3 (September 1948): 350–67.

Whittier chronicled how a righteous man was falsely condemned, but because of his true goodness, Underhill persevered in a godly path. In Whittier's vision, Underhill says:

> Now, as God appointeth, I keep my way,
> I shall not stumble, I shall not stray;
> He hath taken away my fig-leaf dress,
> I wear the robe of His righteousness;
> And the shafts of Satan no more avail
> Than Pequot arrows on Christian mail.

Whittier postured Underhill as a brave and valiant leader who withstood accusations, faced his sins, and bore his burden like a manly hero should: "His words were wise and his rule was good…And through the camps of the heathen ran / A wholesome fear of the valiant man." Whittier reclaimed Underhill as a hero for Boston, as one of their "fairest and bravest" in the land. Whittier's acclaim did not withstand the analyses of twenty-first-century historians, but it did foster the creation of the Underhill Society, which still continues to celebrate the captain and trace his descendants.

Masculinity, as well as femininity, is a fluid and constantly changing construct, as seventeenth-century Puritans, nineteenth-century poets, and twenty-first-century students can surely attest. These competing versions of masculinity reveal the ideals, concerns, and realities of each society. John Underhill fought his entire life for a masculinity that New Englanders found too rough for their well-ordered colony; and yet they depended on this very violence to safeguard their community. Ministers reified a masculinity that was highly feminized. New Englanders did not fully reconcile this gender paradox, but tried to forge a middle ground of masculinity – one that Underhill and men like him could not embrace. As to the soldiers and the scoundrels, they escaped the confines of the New England order and likely continued their scandalous ways.

5

"Unquiet Frame of Spirit"

Ann Hibbens, a Troublesome and Insubordinate Woman

With a noose tightened and taut around her neck, Mistress Hibbens's body hung limp from a tree in Boston Commons. Once officials were assured she had taken her last breath, they cut down her body and examined it for the telltale signs of witchery. They found no teats that the Devil would suckle, so they proceeded to her house in search of poppets or other tokens a witch would use to weave her magic.[1] They found none. The crowd that gathered after lecture day to witness the execution would have included an array of neighbors, friends, and foes. Ann Hibbens was the third witch executed in the Bay Colony, but certainly the first of such prominent social status.[2] It would have been high theater. More than a few onlookers likely gossiped about how the mighty had fallen or expressed their disdain for a woman many viewed as crabby, quarrelsome, turbulent, and generally unlikable.[3] As nineteenth-century historian William Hubbard explained, this was a woman with the *vox populi* against her.[4] Those gathered around the

---

[1] Thomas Hutchinson, *The History of the Colony of Massachusetts Bay: From the First Settlement Thereof in 1628, until its Incorporation with the Colony of Plimouth Province, Province of Main, etc., by the Charter of King William and Queen Mary in 1691.* Volume 1 (Boston: Thomas and John Fleet, 1764), 173; William Hubbard, *A General History of New England: From the Discovery to MDCLXXX.* Vol. 2nd Series, vols. 5–6. Massachusetts Historical Society Collections v. 15–16; Cat. Office (Boston: Massachusetts Historical Society, 1848), 574 (originally written in the 1670s).

[2] Alice Young, from Windsor, was executed in 1647, Margaret Jones, from Charleston, in 1648. See Hall, *Witch-Hunting in Seventeenth-Century New England*, 21–23.

[3] Hall, *Witch-Hunting*, 91.

[4] In other words, "popular sentiment"; Hubbard, *General History of New England*, 574.

killing tree surely recalled how the troublesome Ann first vexed the community more than a decade before her witchcraft trial. The trouble started as a seemingly small business dispute with a carpenter she had hired to do some work in her house and turned into a war of words that culminated in her excommunication for a whole array of heinous crimes.

A WOMAN IN BUSINESS

Church and court records are filled with disputes over business. Men often confronted other men (and occasionally women) about breaking contracts, fraud, sabotage, or slander regarding their businesses. Arguments over roads, mills, property lines, late payments, or shoddy work abound in the archives. For example, Robert Keayne never quite got over his censure for price fixing; he was still defensive in his last will and testament.[5] But in most instances men offered an oblique confession or paid a court fine and all was forgiven. In the case of the most stubborn of male offenders, such as Edward Mills or John Underhill, they faced excommunication or banishment. Ann Hibbens questioned the bill from her carpenter, and she swung from a tree.

Men who transgressed with hypermasculine behavior were not nearly the threat to society that women who behaved like men were. Hibbens asserted her right to negotiate a business deal and was unrelenting in believing she was correct. When her congregation censured her, she continued to defend her position. By not deferring to the male laity with a feminized confession, by proclaiming she had a legitimate voice in commerce and business, and by trying to speak up to clear her name, Ann became too dangerous to the social order. While seventeenth-century women had a degree of informal power and authority, Ann tested those limits. She maintained she was justified in challenging the carpenter; after all, she did win a lawsuit in the case.[6] Her story illuminates what happened to the women who crossed the prescribed boundaries of womanhood.

Hibbens initially began her life in the colonies with all the benefits church membership and high status could offer. Ann was married to William Hibbens, and as their titles "Mr. and Mrs." indicated, they were

---

[5] See Bailyn, *Apologia of Robert Keayne.*
[6] See John Demos, *The Enemy Within: 2,000 Years of Witch-Hunting in the Western World* (New York: Viking, 2008), 107–8.

among the financial and social elite. Shortly after arriving in Massachusetts Bay in 1638, both were made church members. A respected merchant, Mr. Hibbens was made a representative in 1640 and 1641. He frequently served as selectman and was also an assistant on the General Court from 1643 until his death in 1654. Months prior to his wife's censure, he was part of an official contingent sent to visit and report on the exiled Anne Hutchinson in Rhode Island.[7] Ann's husband and the couple's political, economic, and social status certainly offered a level of protection, yet her story shows how gender trumped class and how even her well-connected friends could not save her once she so flagrantly crossed the gender divide. Nineteenth-century historians recorded that minister John Norton tried to stop the execution and wealthy merchant Joshua Scottow defended Ann to his own peril (and later felt the pressure to apologize to the court for his behavior).[8] But neither of these prominent men could halt the popular ill will and hysteria against her. Ann made the fatal mistake of forgetting her place.[9]

In 1640 the Hibbenses hired a joiner (carpenter) to work on a chimney and a bedroom set. At some point, Mr. Hibbens agreed that Ann would supervise the project, which was not uncommon.[10] When the joiner, Crabtree, charged her more for the project than originally negotiated, she disputed the charge. She actually won the civil suit, but her behavior in court was so "abrasive" that the congregation took up the issue.[11] In private meetings with church elders, they suggested she hire other carpenters to evaluate the work and fees. Both sides brought in different carpenters, some of whom apparently agreed with Crabtree, and others with Hibbens. One of the carpenters, named Davis, accused her of lying about the placement of her bed and the chimney piece, and he said that

---

[7] Winsor, The Memorial History of Boston, 559–60, New England Historic Genealogical Society, ed. The New England Historical and Genealogical Register. Vol. VI (Boston: Thomas Prince, Printer and Publisher, 1852), 283.

[8] Winsor, The Memorial History of Boston, 141; Pool, 2, cited from Massachusetts Archives, cxxxv.1.

[9] For a study of commerce of the time, see Valeri, Heavenly Merchandize; Barry Levy, Town Born: The Political Economy of New England from Its Founding to the Revolution (Philadelphia: University of Pennsylvania Press, 2013); and John J. McCusker, The Economy of British America, 1607–1789 (Chapel Hill: University of North Carolina Press, 1991).

[10] Ulrich, Good Wives. As "deputy husband," the wife had informal power and authority to conduct business in her husband's absence, and this example illustrates the joint household economy in which women actively participated.

[11] Demos, The Enemy Within, 107–8.

while the bed was "fashionably done," she found fault with them, calling them "toys and gewgaws."[12] What seemed like a straightforward dispute about the quality of services turned into a long series of private meetings that resulted in the congregation charging Ann with the sin of lying.

AN OBSTINATE WOMAN

Tensions between the parties were already running high at the first censure meeting after Sabbath services on September 13, 1640. By the time Davis offered his testimony, he was more upset about how Ann had publicly characterized him than about the original lie for which she was being censured. Disgruntled that Davis defended the shoddy carpentry work, Ann accused him of being disreputable. Davis explained, "She said my sin was so great that if she should not speak the timber of the room would cry out for judgement against me." Mr. Hibbens tried to interject and explain that his wife had already apologized to Davis for this offense and that "Davis did receive satisfaction from my wife, and such satisfaction that he did bless God that he had so much humbled her spirit, she confessing her error with tears." Mr. Hibbens questioned how this situation could be brought up to the congregation if it was already resolved. "How seasonable it is, or according to rule, for our Brother to make mention of this publicly and to tell the church of it."[13] He seemed to have realized the scope of the censure charges and actively sought to quell the situation to protect his wife. What happened next fully illustrates the extent of the transgression: a woman tried to behave like a man, and no simple confession would suffice.

The male laity did not seem interested in Ann's lie, but focused instead on her demeanor and attitude, which was unequivocally not feminine enough for her church brethren. Responding to Mr. Hibbens's query, Brother Hutchinson suggested that one confession was not enough, considering Ann's "other heinous evils that lie upon her which she

---

[12] Beds were built into rooms during this era and would have been installed by the joiner. See Robert Keayne, Sermon Notes, R. Keayne III microfilm P-85 2 reels, Massachusetts Historical Society, 1624–1646; John Demos, ed., *Remarkable Providences, 1600–1760* (New York: G. Braziller, 1972).

[13] The records of the censure meetings were recorded in the journal of Robert Keayne, and partial excerpts are included in Demos, *Remarkable Providences*. It seems out of character that Ann would have been brought to tears in her apology, but it is significant that Mr. Hibbens felt the need to describe her "with tears" in order to soften her character and satisfy the expectations of the laity.

gives no satisfaction." It is unclear what "heinous evils" he referred to, but it was awfully strong language for a dispute over a home remodel. Another brother, Button, jumped into the fray, saying that Mrs. Hibbens was not penitent enough, that her first apology was "too constrained." Pastor John Wilson quickly concurred, adding that other witnesses had said she had contradicted herself when she talked about the incident. A Hibbens family friend, Mr. Colborn, came to her defense explaining that he had personally met with Ann and that she was more penitent than she appeared. But the pastor responded by issuing an additional complaint against her (the first among many new charges to appear in the course of the censure meetings): that she defamed Davis's reputation by questioning his professional assessment. Wilson argued that she was "divulging and publishing it all abroad to ministers, magistrates, neighbors and others to lay infamy, disgrace and reproach upon our brother."[14] In discussing the merits of her case, Ann dared to threaten the professional reputation of a man.

The charge of slandering a man's character and professional integrity stirred the ire of other men, who promptly accused Hibbens of further mischief. In growing frustration, one brother noticed Ann sitting in her pew and lashed out at her for not standing up in church before the elders. "I marvel she shows so much contempt for the church as to sit when the elders speak." Brother Button joined in: "It is a great offence to us that she shows so much disrespect to our elders that she dares not to attend to what was spoken." Here is the heart of the matter: this was a woman not submitting – not to men in the world of business nor now in church.

Even when Hibbens tried to claim a submissive role – that women should remain silent – she was chastised. One of her friends tried to mollify the situation by suggesting that perhaps Ann did not respond because she was not sure, as a woman, that she was allowed to speak in church. He suggested the congregation give her a week to come up with a response, which infuriated John Cotton: "Indeed Sister, when the Pastor shall speak...you therefore ought to humbly to stand upon your feet, and not to sit." Yet another sin was leveled against her as Brother Penn argued, "Her carriage hath been so broad and contemptuous and irreverent in the church, when the church is dealing with her that it is intolerable. Therefore, I think she ought first to be dealt with on this,

[14] In his journal record of these proceedings, Robert Keayne refers to each of the men speaking as "Brother."

and some admonishment ought to be passed upon her for this." Now the censure charges mounted: (1) lying about the business dispute, (2) ill carriage toward Davis, (3) damaging the reputation of Davis, (4) not penitent or submissive enough, (5) contemptuous behavior in church, and (6) disrespecting the pastor and elders.

The men continued to question her stubborn demeanor. Minister Wilson was not willing to stop the proceedings and let Mrs. Hibbens collect her thoughts, but rather reprimanded her further: "Sister Hibbens...Hath God convinced you or begun to melt your spirit for...contempt that you have shown...in your irreverent carriage and turning aside to talk...when the Elders are speaking to you? Do you see it to be a sin in you?" His unrelenting attack asserting that she failed to see her sinful ways continued. Another ally tried to step in to suggest that they halt the meeting to give Mrs. Hibbens time to regroup. It was only when Governor John Winthrop concurred that the hour was late and they should continue the censure the following week that Wilson deferred, but not without the warning, veiled in a prayer, "to give our sister a humbler heart and kindly melt and to lay down her pride and veil her pomp and any thoughts of herself" and that she would "take all shame and confusion to her own face, both of her lies that she hath spoken, and other offences given."[15]

TRANSGRESSING THE GENDER BOUNDARIES

Ann's predicament was untenable. She was supposed to speak but stay silent, explain but acquiesce, be truthful but admit she had lied. She would have a week to decide what to do. She could give the congregation what they demanded, which was a full, weeping confession to an array of sins and for her to throw herself on the mercy of the congregation. Indeed, she would need to offer a very feminized confession to garner their forgiveness. She surely had seen and heard such confessions from women before. Her other option was to continue to defend herself with reason and logic, although that had not served her especially well thus far.

Round two of the disciplinary meeting, set for the next Sabbath, was eagerly anticipated. The minister had to quiet the chatter coming from

15 Keayne, Sermon Notes.

the congregation in order to resume proceedings against Mrs. Hibbens. Some of the gossip during the intervening week had probably focused on Mr. Hibbens, as he had asked permission from the church elders to speak first. Mr. Hibbens started by apologizing for referring to people as "Mr." instead of "Brother" during the last meeting.

Because the title of Brother is such a phrase that I have found my heart many times enlarged when in the use of it. And therefore my Brethren telling me of it, with their advice and free consent of my own heart, I desire that the Brother to which I spake it would pardon it, and so I desire of all the rest of my Brethren.

There is an interesting class dynamic at work here: at least some of the chatter that week must have ridiculed the Hibbenses for their inflated social standing. "Brother" was a term of equal status, whereas "Mr." differentiated men by social and economic status. Was Mr. Hibbens trying to assuage the tensions that may have surfaced over a woman of high ranking criticizing men socially beneath her? If Mr. Hibbens had brought the claims forward against the carpenters, it would not have gone this far; even those women in the highest ranks of society could not behave like men.

If William Hibbens was hoping to set a tone of contrition, he failed. The minister, Wilson, turned William's admirable humility into a lesson for Ann: "Let it be an example to yourself from your husband to…take shame to your own face, and freely and openly readily confess." He chastised her further by offering up the example of Mary Magdalene, who "having sinned and given great offense she doth abase and humble herself." For disputing a carpentry bill, Ann was compared to Mary Magdalene, a purported prostitute. Mary Magdalene was a loose woman; Ann Hibbens was an uncontrollable one.

Ann Hibbens next offered a confession steeped in masculine language. She acknowledged that she should be humbled for her mistaken carriage – not that she intended to sin but that "there was such an appearance of evil as might give offence to others; and therefor I desired to be heartily sorry so as I may give satisfaction to such as was offended." Could it have ended here? Could the male laity have accepted this more masculine confession and let it all go? The records are filled with similar male confessions that merely acknowledge an error. Ann must have known what her brethren really wanted to hear, yet instead of offering a confession that was debasing and self-reflective, she stood her ground. When Brother Penn asked her to clarify what offense she was actually apologizing for, Mrs. Hibbens explained it was for her behavior in church the previous week and that she wanted to clarify the issue with Brother Davis, the carpenter:

I desire you all to take notice of my fall that you may stand, and to take heed of sleeping while you hear and of sleeping while you seem to hear, as it hath been my own fault. Take heed of the miscarriage of the congregation in now walking according to the rule and [in being ready] to make ourselves guilt of sin and receive false reports or believing true reports, and so to hate our brother in our heart. Because I know not how far the Lord hath withdrawn himself from me. And lest the Lord should not stand by me to assist me in giving satisfaction or in speaking to the satisfaction of the church [I desire] that the church could give me leave to express myself in writing to the church; so that it may be read.

Wilson was beside himself with anger when he asked her to clarify her statement: "Then the sum of your speech is this: that for the present God hath not yet convinced you of your sin in telling a lie, or of your accusation against the Brethren of a combination against you, or of the unrighteousness of your cause; and therefor you would clear it in your writings, that so you may speak less yourself?" Ann answered, "Yes, that is my meaning." The flustered men quickly consulted together, unsure how to respond to her audacity. They turned to their teacher, John Cotton, for his advice on how to proceed. He called the practice of writing "uncouth" and ordered her to speak, explaining that they did not want to drag this on for another week, because she had already taken up too much of their time.

Although the brethren demanded that Ann speak, they only wanted to hear particular words of submission. When she tried to defend herself by reviewing the original dispute with the carpenters, the brethren complained that she was wasting their time. The pastor accused Ann of "casting aspersion upon others rather than deal with her sin." Other men chimed in that they were tired of hearing her speak. When she explained that she was almost done, another brother demanded that she "cut short this impertinent discourse" and address her sin. Ann was in a double bind: they required her to stand up to speak but also wanted her to sit down and shut up.

Ann's refusal to concede stymied the congregation. The pastor then vented his own frustration, recapping how she stubbornly held to her side of the story and wasted the congregation's time. He argued that even if she was right, she should have let the matter go instead of stirring up trouble. She should have been a good woman and followed directions. Wilson elaborated:

Such hath been the unquiet frame of your spirits that you would take no warning nor hearken to our council and exhortation, but have still been stirring to the offense of many of the congregation whose names and credits you have defamed, and we are unsatisfied also.

He warned of further actions against her.

Charges escalated against the unwavering Ann as the male laity accused her of violating the most sacred responsibility of a woman – duty to her husband. Sergeant Savidge suggested to the congregation that through this whole sordid affair, Ann fundamentally undermined the authority of her husband. Worse than arguing with men in the community, Ann violated family government: "More offensive than any of her sins, she has one sin worthy of reproof: and that is transgressing the rule of the Apostle in usurping authority over him whom God hath made her head and husband and in taking the power and authority which God hath given to him out of his hands." Brother Savidge questioned her impudence at thinking she could handle the dispute better than her husband. Wilson agreed, commenting that other people noted the same, "in so much that some do think she doth but make a wisp of her husband." A new, more damaging charge emerged; by claiming authority over the remodel, Ann emasculated her husband. The very foundation of society, the centrality of family government, was at stake.[16] William interjected, trying to explain that he agreed to have her attend to the business "as she saw fit" and that Ann kept him apprised of the situation. He had agreed with Ann that the final price was too high. However, William then admitted he was satisfied with Brother Davis's assessment: "I was very willing to stand to that agreement he made, and did persuade my wife, and could have wished with all my heart that she had been willing to have done the same, and I have had some exercise of spirit with her, that she hath not done so." If William thought his explanation would show he had asserted husbandly authority, it backfired and proved to the congregation that he could not control Ann.[17]

---

[16] See Demos, *A Little Commonwealth*; and Norton, *Founding Mothers and Fathers*.

[17] It does not seem likely that William was trying to testify against his wife, as he stood by her throughout and left his entire estate to her. It is more likely that in the moment he did a poor job of defending his male authority over his wife.

The floodgate of complaints opened against Ann Hibbens. Other members then spoke up, arguing that "this woman" had a "measure of hardness," that she was "uncharitable," and that they should not believe anything she said. Ann tried to interject, explaining that she sought counsel when the problem first occurred, soliciting other estimates as suggested and paying the amended price even though she thought it was too high. Her argument and rationale fell on deaf ears. Reason and logic were male domains, and what the men of the congregation wanted from Ann was not an explanation, but submission. The more she tried to reason or explain her actions, the more she enraged the brethren. Finally, Wilson put a stop to the accusations, citing the late hour and asking the laymen to decide their course of action against Ann Hibbens. Brother Penn suggested excommunicating her for her continuous lies and other "notorious crimes." The pastor suggested admonishing her and that perhaps they needed more evidence before issuing their harshest penalty.

DEFIANT WOMEN

The final bombshell was all Ann's. Before they voted on her admonishment, Mrs. Hibbens asked to speak: "I desire that you would not do so, though I shall be willing to submit to this censure as an ordinance of Christ, yet I pray God not to lay the blood of this act to the charge." In questioning the laymen's censure, all hell broke loose. Wilson quickly retorted, "To whose charge? Then it seems that you lay the blame upon the whole church." His final words were indignant:

Therefore, for your contempt of pride and spirit and for exalting yourself against your guide and head – your husband I mean – when you should have submitted yourself; and because you have rejected the advice of Brethren and Sisters and the council and exhortation of your Elders, when they persuaded, advised and earnestly exhorted you to be quiet and sit down satisfied...yet such has been the pride and unquiet frame of your spirit that, contrary to all these councils and exhortations and pains that have been taken with you, you have been stirring and uttering words tending to the disgrace and defamation of your Brethren, as if they had combined together to deal unjustly, when by covenant you ought to have a better opinion of them; therefore for these and many other of your grievous sins against His church, and for the pulling down of the pride and height of your spirit, and for the mortification of your lusts and covetous distempers, and in order that you would speedily seek to God that He would make you sensible of your sins and come to a holy confession of them and humiliation for them before the Lord and His church. Or else, if you shall delay to give the church satisfaction and out of pride and obstinacy of your heart shall refuse to do so, it will make the church more speedy in calling you to further account for such things as remain, and proceeding more speedily to cut you off by the great sentence of excommunication, and delivering you up to Satan for the further destruction of your unmortified flesh.

Wilson's fiery rhetoric and accusations revealed the extent of the community's animosity toward Ann. She would not capitulate, she did not acquiesce to men she disagreed with, and she believed she had the right to dispute such men. Wilson warned her to examine her soul and return with a more penitent and submissive heart if she wanted to avoid excommunication.

As Ann considered her options, surely she knew the fate of other women who had upset the social order. Ann and her husband had arrived in Boston just after the trial and banishment of Anne Hutchinson.[18] They knew her story. The two women shared certain characteristics: they were from well-respected families, were church members, and had husbands who did not control them. And both women challenged the male hierarchy and paid a price. When Hutchinson's nightly Bible meetings began to attract a large following of women and men, she fell under suspicion. It was common for women to gather together to discuss the Bible, but the fact that men were listening to Anne expound on the text was dangerous. When she challenged ministers for preaching a covenant of works instead of a covenant of grace, she was brought to trial. She was accused of a host of crimes, including dishonoring her parents, causing mothers to be neglectful of their families, and heresy. During the trial, she famously battled wits with Governor John Winthrop. She was articulate, smart, and well versed in the Bible. She, too, refused to submit. As the trial reached its second day, it seemed that she would win. However, Hutchinson revealed that she was guided by the voice of the Holy Spirit, which was blasphemy for Puritans. With Hutchinson's claim of revelation, the jury had its evidence to banish her from the colony and excommunicate her from the church, which they

---

[18] For discussions on the impact of Hutchinson, see Westerkamp, "Anne Hutchinson"; Westerkamp, "Puritan Patriarchy and the Problem of Revelation," *Journal of Interdisciplinary History* XXIII (Winter 1993): 571–95; Timothy Hall, *Anne Hutchinson: Puritan Prophet* (New York: Longman, 2010); Michael P. Winship, *The Times and Trial of Anne Hutchinson: Puritans Divided* (Lawrence: University Press of Kansas, 2005); and Eve LaPlante, *American Jezebel: The Uncommon Life of Anne Hutchinson, the Woman Who Defied the Puritans* (San Francisco: Harper San Francisco, 2004).

did in March 1638. Anne Hutchinson was part of the Puritan faction labeled "Antinomian," which believed that divine grace was a personal and internal experience of God between the individual and Christ.[19] This opposed the contention of most clergy and secular leaders that while good works did not earn one's way to heaven, they were the outward signs of the sanctified. Free grace theology challenged the secular and religious leaders in Massachusetts Bay. And while men such as minister John Wheelwright were banished in this crisis, Anne Hutchinson's experience was more about her gender than her theology. During the course of the trial, it was apparent that what bothered John Winthrop the most was that she dared to challenge her male superiors. The story of her downfall became a warning for others – and likely to Ann Hibbens as she pondered her next move.[20]

AN EVIL EXAMPLE TO OTHER WOMEN

The intervening months did little to change the tide of the community's sentiments, or Ann's disposition. Since the first two censure meetings had gone well into the night, officials decided to call for a special session of the entire congregation rather than hold another meeting after Sabbath services. The pastor immediately lamented that "we see that the Lord hath not yet broken her spirit"; other men discussed how she "cast aspersions" on the entire congregation and suggested that a second admonition would do no good. Brothers reminded the congregation that she had "exalted her own wit and will and way about [her husband]." Brother Captain Gibbons observed that "I do not know what sin she is not guilty of" and that she was "impenitent" and "obstinate." Another brother compared her to the biblical Miriam, who rose up and betrayed Moses. Others worried that if they did not excommunicate her, God could punish them for neglecting their duty.

---

[19] For more on the Antinomian crisis or "free grace" controversy, see Hall, *The Antinomian Controversy*; Bozeman, *The Precisianist Strain*; Winship, *Making Heretics*; and Breen, *Transgressing the Bounds*.

[20] In his nineteenth-century history of Massachusetts, William Hubbard describes Anne Hutchinson as a "gentlewoman of nimble wit, voluble tongue, eminent knowledge in the Scriptures, of great charity, and notable helpfulness" (283). He is also critical of the condemnation of Hibbens. For recent scholarship comparing Hutchinson and Hibbens, see Breen, *Transgressing the Bounds*; Reis, *Damned Women*; Kamensky, *Governing the Tongue*; and Karlsen, *Devil in the Shape of a Woman*.

Desperate now, William asked for more patience and leniency so he could work on his dear wife. He countered with a biblical example of his own, the story of Ephraim and Israel, which held that though God was provoked with Israel, he pitied them and promised to spare them. William begged his brethren to do the same for his wife: "So if the church would show their bowels of pity in sparing and respiting her censure for a time, the Lord may so bow the heart of my wife that she may give the church full satisfaction, which would be the rising of my soul." Brother Oliver replied to William's plea by explaining that excommunication would be the "best pity the church" could show her.

Wilson then delivered her excommunication, recounting her "gross sins and offenses" and her "uncharitable thoughts" in "raising up an evil report of [her] Brethren." He accused her of spreading lies about these good men. He even accused her of acting like God in judging the men, recounting the litany of complaints that "out of a covetous and greedy desire" she had withheld due payment to the workman and refused to submit to the advice of her husband and church elders. "With a restless and discontented spirit you have...vented your slander and evil reports...And for your stopping your ears and hardening your heart against the former admonition...you have turned with the dog to his vomit."[21]

Wilson continued, expressing the greater fear that Ann set an "evil example" for other wives by usurping her husband's authority, causing him grief, and acting like she knew better than he did. "You have continued to harden yourself in a way of disobedience, to the evil example and unquietness of the family. You have not only done so, but expressed it to be your judgement that husbands just hearken to their wives and be guided by them in all things."[22] Pious women could too easily be led astray by corrupt women, a fear also expressed during Anne Hutchinson's trial. Making an example of Hutchinson and Hibbens might prevent other women from such uppity notions.

The lengthy meeting ended with final words from Mr. Hibbens in which he "humbly" pleaded that in both "public and private" everyone "earnestly" pray for his wife to return to the fold. He knew how deeply felt their animosity was for his wife. Was he not perhaps subtly calling

---

[21] This is an interesting comment comparing Hibbens to a dog, a pejorative term generally reserved for men, as it referred to economic weakness or dependence. See St. George, "'Heated' Speech and Literacy in Seventeenth-Century New England," 295–97.

[22] Keayne, Sermon Notes.

out his fellow brothers and sisters for not having Christian love in their hearts for Ann? Did he think his credibility could eventually restore his wife's?

THE WIDOW IS A WITCH

For the next decade, Ann does not appear in the records. There was no indication that Ann ever tried to confess and have her excommunication removed. Her husband continued to serve in esteemed positions for the colony. However, once the shield and protection of her husband ended with his death in 1654, new and more deadly charges surfaced. Not liked, perhaps hated, there were undoubtedly insinuations that she was a witch. Her tongue, her attitude, her argumentativeness all added fuel to the innuendo. But while her husband lived, such claims were only whispered among neighbors, remaining in the shadows. Upon his death, rumors became accusations, and she was brought before the court and charged with witchcraft. While the details of the charges were not included in the court record, the story seems to be that Ann saw a group of people gathered in conversation down the road, and as she approached them, she accused them of gossiping about her. She was right. But they suggested that the only way Ann could have heard them from such a great distance was if she had special mind-reading powers.[23]

To go from a troublesome, unquiet, crabby, argumentative woman to a witch was not a big leap in the seventeenth century.[24] While we know

---

[23] Erikson, *Wayward Puritans*, 154; Hutchinson, *The History of the Colony of Massachusetts Bay*, 173.

[24] There is tremendous scholarship on New England witches. For document collections, see Demos, ed., *Remarkable Providences*, and Hall, ed., *Witch-Hunting*. For analysis, see also John Putnam Demos, *Entertaining Satan: Witchcraft and the Culture of Early New England* (New York: Oxford University Press, 1982); Demos, *Enemy Within*; Richard Weisman, *Witchcraft, Magic and Religion in Seventeenth-Century Massachusetts* (Amherst: University of Massachusetts Press, 1984); Reis, *Damned Women*; and Karlsen, *Devil in the Shape of a Woman*. On the Salem outbreak, see the document collections Paul Boyer and Stephen Nissenbaum, eds., *The Salem Witchcraft Papers: Verbatim Transcripts of the Legal Documents of the Salem Witchcraft Outbreak of 1692* (New York: DeCapo Press, 1977); Boyer and Nissenbaum, eds., *Salem Village Witchcraft: A Documentary Record of Local Conflict in Colonial New England* (Boston: Northeastern University Press, 1993); and Richard Godbeer, *The Salem Witch Hunt: A Brief History with Documents* (New York: Bedford St. Martins, 2011). For analysis, see Mary Beth Norton, *In the Devil's Snare: The Salem Witchcraft Crisis of 1692* (New York: Alfred A. Knopf, 2002).

Puritan women had more opportunities and informal power than previous gender systems allowed, there were lines that were dangerous to cross. As historian Carol F. Karlsen explains, "The story of witchcraft is primarily the story of women ... witchcraft confronts us with ideas about women, with fears about women, with the place of women in society, and with women themselves."[25] In her study, Karlsen acknowledges that Hibbens's case stood out at the time because of her high social status (Figure 5.1).[26]

The stereotype of a witch was that of a poor old hag who lived on the margins of society, a woman with seemingly no power. Karlsen's research reveals a different portrait of a witch – one based much more in the fear of female power. As Karlsen outlines, Hibbens fulfilled a lot of the requisites for women accused of witchcraft in seventeenth-century New England. The typical witch was a woman over the age of forty; and women over the age of sixty without husbands were at an even higher risk of accusations of witchcraft. Karlsen's work reveals an "economic basis of witchcraft," arguing that fears over "inheriting or potentially inheriting women" drove many accusations. Widows without male heirs were dangerous. William and Ann had no children together, but Ann did have three sons in London from her first marriage. "It was not unusual for women in families without male heirs to be accused of witchcraft shortly after the deaths of their fathers, husbands, brothers or sons."[27] William Hibbens left everything to Ann, and her own will detailed the sizable estate. Without a male heir, Ann controlled all of that wealth. Women without male heirs were the exception to the rule of feme covert, in which fathers and husbands legally controlled women and their property. Combined with her decades-long reputation as an "unquiet woman," the death of her husband exposed her too much: "If her husband could not subdue her, and the church could not break her, how much more dangerous she must have appeared by 1656, when she was an economically independent woman."[28] Hibbens's abrasiveness and willingness to stand up to male power in Boston also made it easier to accuse her of consorting with the Devil.[29]

[25] Karlsen, *Devil in the Shape of a Woman*, xiii.
[26] Karlsen, *Devil in the Shape of a Woman*, 2.
[27] Karlsen, *Devil in the Shape of a Woman*, 104.
[28] Karlsen, *Devil in the Shape of a Woman*, 152.
[29] See Reis, *Damned Women*, 2. Reis explains that while women had more opportunities than previously, they were also considered more easily tempted by the Devil, and there was a "sense of women's inherent wickedness."

FIGURE 5.1. Seventeenth-century witch trial. *Source:* Print Collector/Hulton Archive/Getty Images.

In spite of the popular clamor against her, some members of the higher class tried to intervene. The magistrates did not accept the verdict of the deputies' jury trial and ordered that she be tried before the General Court. They delivered a guilty verdict in the high court as well, and sentenced her to execution.

Nineteenth-century chronicles were much more sympathetic to Mrs. Hibbens than her peers, and offered some vindication of her memory.[30] William Poole conjectures that the reason Cotton Mather did not write about Hibbens's case in his famous book on witchcraft, *Remarkable Providences,* was that "notable" men believed she was unjustly condemned.[31] Several nineteenth-century historians, including William Hubbard, use a letter as evidence that some of her contemporaries regretted her execution. Written by Mr. Beach, a minister in Jamaica, to Increase Mather in 1684, the letter retold the story of a dinner party with ministers Norton and Wilson and Elder Penn (Wilson and Penn were active in the excommunication of Hibbens). Mr. Beach wrote that Norton had said that Hibbens was "hanged for a witch only for having more wit than her neighbors."[32] Hubbard suggested it was the popular uproar that could not be stopped and compared Ann to Joan of Arc, "which some counted a saint and some a witch." The Jamaican minister explained to his audience that "many times persons of hard favor and turbulent passions are apt to be condemned by the common people for witches" (Figure 5.2).[33]

---

[30] There was a seventeenth-century chronicler who expressed sympathy for Ann Hibbens. Thomas Lechford, a British lawyer critical of Puritans, visited New England and wrote an account of his travels describing the customs and manners of the colonists. When he described their church disciplinary practices, he contended that they were moderate, except for a particular case he recalled: "I have known a Gentlewoman excommunicated, for some indiscreet words with some business maintained, saying a brother, and others, she feared, did conspire to arbitrate the price of joyners work of a chamber ... I fear she is not yet absolved." See Thomas Lechford, *Plain Dealing: Or, Nevves from New-England: A Short View of New-England's Present Government, Both Ecclesiasticall and Civil, Compared with the Anciently-Received and Established Government* (London: Printed by W. E. & I. G. for Nath: Butter, at the Signe of the Pyde Bull neere S. Austins Gate, 1642).

[31] William F. Poole, *Witchcraft in Boston,* reproduced in Winsor, The Memorial History of Boston, 133.

[32] Hutchinson, *The History of the Colony of Massachusetts Bay,* 173; Winsor, The Memorial History of Boston, 283. See also Weisman, *Witchcraft, Magic and Religion,* 87.

[33] Hubbard, *General History of New England,* 574. Thomas Hutchinson also discussed the "popular clamour" against Hibbens, noting that this was one of the last cases in which popular clamor overruled the magistrates. See also Weisman, *Witchcraft, Magic and Religion,* 106.

FIGURE 5.2. The execution of Ann Hibbens. *Source:* Public domain;
Frank Thayer Merril – Lynn and Surroundings, by Clarence. W. Hobbs, Lynn,
Mass.: Lewis & Winship Publishers, 1886: 52. Artist: F. T. Merrill.

Ann spent the weeks between the verdict and her execution in jail. With deliberation and attention to detail, she finalized her will, appointing several prominent men as executors. She divided her assets between her three sons, making careful arrangements for overseers to administer her will and sell her land and houses. She paid particular attention to the care of her two chests and desk, and their contents. She noted outstanding debts owed to her and forgave some of them. She made provisions in case any of her sons died, the sons were delayed in coming to claim their inheritance, or fire or another disaster destroyed her estate. She asked to be buried next to her husband. Through her last will, she demonstrated reason, logic, and acumen in her business affairs. Her will tells us one last story as well. In a codicil, she bequeathed her son Jonathan an additional money for his "pains and charge in coming to see me." Her son arrived from England in time to see his mom and for them to say their good-byes. It was a heartfelt enough time together that Ann spent part of her final hours making one last addition to her will. She wrote, "My further mind and will is out of my sense of the more than ordinary affection and pains of my son Jonathan, in times of my distress, I give him as further legacy ten pounds."[34] Luckily for Ann, she spent her final hours with a loved one. Her son was likely among the crowd in Boston Commons on that June day and watched as his mother was hanged for witchcraft.

---

[34] New England Historic Genealogical Society, *The New England Historical*, 283.

Conclusion

Three Generations in the Wilderness: Gendered Puritanism and Separate Spheres

Before Jonathan Edwards became one of the most famous orators of the revivalist period, he was a young man smitten by the virtues of his beloved. In his diary he wrote about his bride to be, Sarah Peirrepont, and lovingly described her as a woman of piety: "There are certain seasons in which this great being in some way or other invisibly comes to her and fills her mind with exceeding sweet delights, and that she hardly cares for anything except to meditate on him." Edwards admired her inner spirituality and her conviction that she would one day be with God. He wrote that she was "assured that he loved her too well to let her remain at a distance from him always." Edwards praised her for rejecting worldly interests:

Therefore, if you present all the world before her with the richest of its treasures, she disregards it and cares nothing of it and is unmindful of any pain or affliction. She has a strange sweetness in her mind and a singular purity in her affections, is most just and conscientious in her conduct, and you could not persuade her to do anything wrong or sinful if you would give her all the world, lest she should offend the Great being.

Edwards complimented Peirrepont's "sweetness, calmness, and universal benevolence of mind." He praised her inner peace that her faith provided. "She will sometimes go about from place to place singing sweetly and seems to be always full of joy and pleasure, and no one knows for what." Edwards also recognized that his fiancée had an individual connection to God: "She loves to be alone walking in the field and groves and seems to have someone invisible always conversing with her." Edwards's 1723 love letter about his fiancée also served as praise for the model Christian woman.[1]

By the early eighteenth century, Puritan women had developed a sense of religious self as their path to godliness. In 1712 Mary Quinsey gave a confession of faith to her Braintree congregation. She offered her obedience and loyalty and desired "to be sensible how evil and bitter ye thing sin is," praying that "I hope I can truly say I am sick of sin and desire to loath and abhor myself." She committed her body and soul to God, "humbly hoping... in his mercy and favor and giving up my self absolutely to him and being resolved through his grace to depend upon him and upon him alone for all supplies of grace."[2] Like Peirrepont and other Puritan sisters, Quinsey viewed her faith as something deeply personal between her and God.

Quinsey and Pierrepont exemplify the generational shifts that disciplinary practices forged – a change that gendered Puritanism and defined different roles for godly men and women. Exploring church censures over three generations contributes to the scholarship on the rise of the individual, the debate of religious declension, and the gendering of Puritanism, all of which contributed to the creation of the modern gender ideology of separate spheres.

Scholars chronicle the rise of the individual through men's involvement in the public sphere: economic self-interest, voting status, control of property. However, within Puritanism, it was women who viewed themselves as individuals. Censure practices reinforced the process of introspection and self-awareness in women. The continual emphasis on personal piety, self-abasement, and internal examination – as evident in their confessions and daily practices – required women to utilize a verbal form that validated their identity as individuals in a relationship with God.[3] Women were integral in the creation of a religious self.

The reform theology of Puritanism emphasized the individual soul in relation to God. Sacvan Bercovitch explains that reform ideology rested on "the principle of sola fides: which removes the center of authority from ecclesiastical institutions and relocates it in the elect soul." Writing

---

[1] John A. Stoughton, "*Windsor Farmes*": *A Glimpse of an Old Parish, Together with the Deciphered Inscriptions from a Few Foundation Stones of a Much Abused Theology* (Hartford: Clark & Smith, book and job printers, 1883), 82–83. Jonathan Edwards was the son of minister Timothy Edwards.
[2] Mary Quinsey, Confession of Faith 1713, ms., Quincy Family Papers, Massachusetts Historical Society.
[3] For a discussion of verbal forms, see Gustafson, *Eloquence Is Power*, xvi, 32.

about the Puritan view of the self, Bercovitch asserts that "Protestant-ism shift[ed] the grounds of private identity from the institution to the individual."[4] In censure practices, as laymen reinforced women's internal piety, they also validated the female sense of self.

The links between the "Colonial Goodwife," "Liberty's Daughter," and "the Republican Mother" derive from women's religious ethos.[5] Because disciplinary practices demanded that women see themselves as pious indi-viduals, they fostered the idea that women had value and important moral authority to offer their world. This created the path for Mary Quinsey's great great niece, Abigail Adams, to call for a greater public role for women after the American Revolution. She wrote to her husband in March, 1776, "If particular care and attention is not paid to the Ladies, we are deter-mined to foment a Rebellion and will not hold ourselves bound by any Laws in which we have no voice or Representation." Abigail Adams could utilize the language of individual freedom and rights because for over one hundred thirty years New England women saw themselves as individuals. Historian Leslie Lindenauer contends that women's impetus for action in the eighteenth century stemmed from their seventeenth-century religious roots as "soldiers of Christ." Their belief that they should play a public role also stems from their ability to see themselves as individuals, as spiritually autonomous beings who could act on their faith. The seventeenth-century goodwife passed on to her daughter and granddaughter a religious men-tality that refashioned their godly mission.[6]

Over three generations, the public power of the church diminished, which has led scholars to argue that religion was on the decline. Indeed, third-generation Puritans themselves lamented the perceived rise in corrup-tion and fall in church membership, while revering the first generation

4 Bercovitch, *Puritan Origins of the American Self*, 10–11. See also Bozeman, *The Preci-sianist Strain*, 106; and Erikson, *Wayward Puritans*, 53.
5 The concept of Liberty's Daughters helps explain the role women played in the Revolu-tion, in economic boycotts, and in patriotic fervor and how women would use republican rhetoric after the Revolution to advocate for their interests. See Mary Beth Norton, *Lib-erty's Daughters: The Revolutionary Experience of American Women, 1750–1800* (New York: HarperCollins, 1980). For a discussion on republican motherhood, see Linda K. Kerber, "The Republican Mother," in *Women's America: Refocusing the Past*, ed. Linda K. Kerber and Jane Sherron De Hart (New York: Oxford University Press, 1995), 89–95. The term applied to the need for women steeped in republican ideals to raise virtuous democratic sons to lead the country. Kerber explains how women seized on the idea that they were moral arbiters in their families to advocate for causes and issues, including women's education. Women pushed the boundaries of this separate-sphere ideology to legitimize their participation in public life.
6 Lindenauer, *Piety and Power*, xvi.

as a "golden age" of morality.[7] However, as David Hall points out, each generation of ministers criticized the spiritual fervor of its flock. John Cotton worried that the first generation lacked the necessary zeal. In the second generation, Increase Mather scolded people for wanting church membership for its privileges rather than for its spirit. Third-generation minister Cotton Mather actually preached for conversions because he was so worried about membership.[8] Historian Mary Maples Dunn argues against the declension theory, explaining that religion was not on the decline but that there was a loss of public ministerial power and male piety.[9] Ann Braude contends that since society viewed women as less powerful, their majority in the church weakened the status of the church.[10] She argues that declension addresses the issue of male focus rather than the loss of religiosity. Braude explains that "because women are viewed as the less powerful half of society, their numerical dominance is interpreted as a decline in power for a religious institution."[11] Some historians have referred to this as a feminization of the church. However, Braude contends that "it is the temporary gender equity characterizing some first generation Puritan churches, not the development of a predominantly female laity that departs from American norms."[12] Religion did not decline in the eighteenth century. Women continued to seek membership and involvement. Although official church membership for men waned, men entered the public sphere infused with a religious sensibility that stressed civic duty. The church moved into the private realm, but men stayed in the public world because their mission focused on civic responsibility. Historian Mark Valeri emphasizes the influence of religion on men's secular and commercial decisions in the public sphere.[13] Other forces certainly contributed to pulling men

---

[7] M. Michelle Jarrett Morris argues that the first generation experienced their share of sin and immorality but that the third generation didn't feel they lived up to their grandparents' generation; see *Under Household Government*, 241.

[8] Hall, *The Faithful Shepard*, 250.

[9] Dunn, "Saints and Sisters," 582–601. See also Braude, "Women's History Is American Religious History," 92.

[10] Braude, "Women's History Is American Religious History," 97.

[11] Braude, "Women's History Is American Religious History," 93–96.

[12] Braude, "Women's History Is American Religious History," 87.

[13] Valeri, *Heavenly Merchandize*, 6. See also Grasso, *A Speaking Aristocracy*. Grasso explores the ways in which religion impacted public discourse in the eighteenth century. For a discussion of how by the nineteenth century Christian manhood was redefined to be about service, and fears that religious men were not masculine, see Evelyn A. Kirkley, "Is It Manly to Be a Christian? The Debate in Victorian and Modern America," in *Redeeming Men: Religion and Masculinities*, ed. W. Merle Longwood, Steven B. Boyd, and Mark W. Muesse (Louisville: Westminster John Knox Press, 1996).

into the secular world – such as increased trade, shifts in public power, the political climate, and commercial enterprise[14] – but it was Puritan censure practices that pushed men into worldly matters by continually stressing their covenanted responsibility to the community over their personal piety.

The gendered split between piety and duty that occurred over three generations of disciplinary practices also affected Puritan theology. During the first two generations, Puritan covenants and ministers emphasized both an individual and a communal responsibility. Bercovitch explains that the founding generation sought "the congruence of private and public salvation." They wanted sainthood for the individual and national election for the community.[15] Puritans had to watch over their towns to ensure the godly way in business, government, and family life. The communal aspect of the covenant emphasized civic duty, external behavior, and public accountability.

In the gendering of Puritanism over three generations, church disciplinary practices contributed to the emergence of the modern gender ideology of separate spheres.[16] Popularized in the nineteenth century, the ideology dictated that men occupy the "public" sphere of work, politics, and law, while women were relegated to a "private" sphere of home, religion, and family. This theory reified the public space as powerful and reduced the feminized space as dependent and submissive. In the nineteenth century, popular literature described a "cult of true womanhood" wherein women fulfilled their biological destiny in the domestic space. Feminist scholars of the nineteenth century explored the ways in which women capitalized on their moral authority in the domestic sphere to participate in the many reform movements of the period, thus challenging the notion that the ideology removed women from power. Historians

---

[14] See Dayton, *Women before the Bar*.

[15] Bercovitch, *Puritan Origins of the American Self*, 48, 90.

[16] For a discussion of separate spheres and its changing historiography, which places the development of the ideology in the nineteenth century, see Nancy Cott, *The Bonds of Womanhood: "Woman's Sphere" in New England, 1780–1835* (New Haven: Yale University Press, 1977); Rosalind Rosenberg, *Beyond Separate Spheres: Intellectual Roots of Modern Feminism* (New Haven: Yale University Press, 1982); and Caroll Smith-Rosenberg, *Disorderly Conduct: Visions of Gender in Victorian America* (New York: Oxford University Press, 1986). Other historians argue for the early eighteenth century, due to the influence of secularization and the market economy. See Ulrich, *Good Wives*; Dayton, *Women before the Bar*; Norton, *Founding Mothers and Fathers*; and Mary Beth Norton, *Separated by Their Sex: Women in Public and Private in the Colonial Atlantic World 1640–1760* (Ithaca: Cornell University Press, 2011).

of the colonial period identified the early eighteenth century as the time when this concept first emerged, finding that by the mid-eighteenth century, it had become "normative."[17] Most of the focus on the development of modern gender ideology has centered on the rise of market and secular forces. However, as the stories we have read demonstrate, church disciplinary practices also contributed to the creation of the separate spheres ideology, by pushing men toward the civic responsibilities of the public space while reifying women for their spirituality, which was relegated to the private sphere.

As many historians have described, during the first generation, not only did the concepts of "public" and "private" differ in meaning compared to their usage in future generations, but gender roles were fluid. In *Good Wives: Image and Reality in the Lives of Women in Northern New England, 1650–1750*, Laurel Thatcher Ulrich explores the many roles women assumed in the seventeenth century, illustrating the fluidity of gender and the types of power and influence women possessed. Historian Lisa Wilson describes the period as much more "interdependent," with women and men navigating household, civic, and religious responsibilities.[18] Mary Beth Norton argues that status mattered more than gender in the seventeenth century and that women did exercise authority outside the home. She explains that "prescriptive directions for men and women were similar."[19]

The Puritan mission in New England had the potential to fundamentally alter traditional gender roles. The emphasis on spiritual equality and the expectations for men and women to fulfill the covenant could have undermined the gender hierarchy and ideology. But in reinforcing different parts of the covenant for men and women, church disciplinary practices gendered Puritanism, ultimately leading to a "public/private" split between men and women, government and church.

In the first two generations, Puritan ministers expected their followers to uphold both aspects of the covenant. In their call for individual piety, ministers challenged traditional gender construction by asking both men and women to embrace the feminized religious practices. Ministers described the soul as feminine and required a feminized language to express one's religiosity. Yet in disciplinary actions that laymen controlled, men did not adopt such feminization, instead choosing to emphasize masculinized public duty rather than personal piety.

---

[17] Norton, *Separated by Their Sex*, xiv.
[18] Wilson, *Ye Heart of a Man*, 2.
[19] Norton, *Separated by Their Sex*, xii.

First-generation ministers believed that duty to the community was critical to the Puritan mission of creating a "city on a hill." Richard Mather described how watchfulness and duty were "commanded and required of God." They wanted to create a society of visible saints, to be an example for all of England. Such an "errand" required pious men and women to create a godly society. Neglect of such duty would bring God's judgment down upon everyone.[20] Mather wrote to his brethren in England describing the holy endeavor in New England:

Light of truth doth here ... clearly shine forth ... liberty and purity the Ordinances of Christ Jesus are here administered, by what magistrates civil justice is here dispensed, and the common-wealth governed, how holiness and righteousness is countenanced and encouraged, and all known impiety and iniquity prosecuted ... both in church and commonwealth.[21]

Mather heralded both aspects of the covenant: individual piety and communal responsibility. He praised the efforts to create a holy commonwealth. David Hall explains that "Cotton and other ministers came [to New England] prepared to demand a certain kind of state and social role."[22]

The second generation of Puritan ministers began to shift to a greater emphasis on personal piety. Within this generation, male lay influence increased, as did church censures. Hall argues that "magistrates and laymen did not feel as deferential to the ministers."[23] Censures increased because the Half-Way Covenant brought more people under the control of church discipline and because the second generation emphasized discipline out of their fear that they did not live up to their fathers. Robert Middlekauff contends, "By the end of the decade of the 1670s ... ministers continued to summon the people as a body to reformation ... But private concerns demanded recognition too that perhaps if appeals to the group failed, approaches to men in their private capacity would not."[24] While they continued to lecture on public duty and personal piety, the ministers began to emphasize piety as the path to reformation. During these decades, female church members began to outnumber men.

By the third generation, ministers developed an intense focus on piety as women outnumbered men three to two in church membership. By

---

[20] Mather, *Apology of the Churches in New England for Church Covenant*, 7.
[21] Richard Mather, *An Heart-Melting Exhortation Together with a Cordiall Consolation* (London: I. Rothwell, 1650), 6.
[22] Hall, *The Faithful Shepard*, 119.
[23] Hall, *The Faithful Shepard*, 136.
[24] Middlekauff, *The Mathers*, 114.

1692, Richard Mather's son, Cotton Mather, was "arguing for a renewal of the covenant, looked not toward the state, but voluntary groups and individuals."[25] Middlekauff explains that Cotton Mather was not concerned with social change in New England, but rather about an individual's preparation for the Second Coming. "In Cotton Mather terms, the truly introspective man would examine the fruits of faith or the signs of the process of conversion...[T]he critical feature of self-awareness was not to leave any faculty of the soul unexamined."[26] He believed the future of New England depended upon working on the souls of people.[27]

By the early eighteenth century, ministers were describing the attributes of humility, obedience, modesty, meekness, and purity as specifically female, and not universally Christian.[28] Cotton Mather's son, Samuel, urged his congregation in Windsor to do the necessary "heart work." He did not discourse on the covenant, but instead upon an individual struggle of piety. "Our hearts are so deep that we cannot see to the bottom of them; there we may see one deceit under another, and another still under that...so that we have need to be much in searching our hearts." He urged people to "labour to find out this Evil in your selves, and mourn under it."[29] The feminized Puritan theology of the first generation became a female space by the eighteenth century.

In this split between the private and public worlds of faith and government, ministers lost some of their power to control moral transgressions. In 1724 Reverend Timothy Edwards, the first minister of East Windsor, found himself in a difficult situation. His niece, Abigail, married John Moore, Jr., a man of reputed bad character. Abigail's parents and Edwards were greatly alarmed and appeared before a council of ministers to find out what they could do. The ministers ruled, "By the best light we have from the word of God and according to the concurrent Judgement of Learned Judicious and approved divines, we judge that the father hath a right or power to make void such contracts." The church agreed with Edwards, but civil authorities did not. In prior generations, it may have been easier to have the court invalidate a legal contract because of quandaries over moral character. The Edwards family even had Abigail write a letter to the court explaining that she was afraid Moore would

---

[25] Hall, *The Faithful Shepard*, 136.
[26] Middlekauff, *The Mathers*, 230.
[27] Mather, *Magnalia*, 655.
[28] Norton, *Separated by Their Sex*, 177.
[29] Samuel Mather, *Discourse Concerning the Difficulty and Necessity of Renouncing Our Own Righteousness* (Boston: J. Draper, 1707), 76.

kill her if she turned down his proposal and that she did not have the conscience or power to get married without her parents' permission. She asked the court to "set her at liberty," thus restoring the order of family government. Desperate, the Edwards family even invited seven men from the community to testify to Moore's character.[30] However, the court's priorities had changed. They honored the contract of the marriage over the words of the repenting Abigail, the disreputable behavior of Moore, and the precedence of honoring godly family government. Ministers no longer influenced civil affairs but could only wield authority within the walls of the meetinghouse. After this incident with his niece, when one of Edwards's parishioners married a woman without her parents' permission, Edwards refused to allow him to own the covenant without a confession. Edwards charged the young man, Joseph Diggens, with breaking the fifth and eighth commandments. Maintaining that his actions and behavior were within the law, Diggens counter-charged Edwards with abusing his authority. Edwards must have lamented that the church no longer had a civil arm protecting the godly social order.

Ministers mourned what they saw as the secularization of the courts and other forms of public life. When Samuel Mather wrote "Discourse Concerning the Difficulty Necessary of Renouncing our Own Righteousness" in 1698 (published in 1707), he dedicated it to the people of Windsor in "the service of their souls." He lamented, "We do not walk with god as our Fathers did, and hence we are continually from year to year, under his rebukes one way or other." Puritan laymen censure practices contributed to the male exodus to the public sphere of commerce and civic life. Yet they did so with a strong sense of religious conviction – which is why later it was easy for Revolution-era men to infuse their political goals with a religious message, because since deboarding the Arabella in 1630, men tied their religious identity to their civic duty.

Arriving on the shores of New England with a gender system in flux, the laymen who controlled the disciplinary process defined a masculinity and a femininity that did not adhere to Puritan theology or traditional English models. Laymen navigated a middle ground of masculinity, not requiring men to use a feminized public language of confession or expression of personal piety yet also not accepting the hypermasculine identity of the past. They reified a femininity that made the woman the normative Puritan, one who examined her soul and internal nature, thus creating a sense of status as a church member. While these gender constructs never

---

[30] Stoughton, *Windsor Farmes*, 71–72.

met the radical potential realized by other Protestant groups such as the Quakers, in which women gained formal power, they did create new realities for men and women. Even though women gained informal power through their sense of religious self and fostered respect as godly women and church members, disciplinary practices created gendered boundaries that diminished women's power over time. While both men and women transgressed the boundaries of gender, the consequences for nonconformity were greater for women. John Underhill encountered humiliation; Ann Hibbens faced execution.

Many things changed over the course of three generations, but New Englanders still believed that God answered their prayers when they walked an orderly path. However, how Puritans maintained that godly path changed. The Puritanism that prescribed the same rules and modes of worship for both men and women, holding the potential for religious equality, developed into a religion with defined and distinct roles and expectations for men and women.

The stories of these men and women still have lessons to teach us today. In his most recent study, *A Reforming People: Puritanism and the Transformation of Public Life in New England*, David Hall argues that twenty-first-century Americans are in dire need of learning some lessons from the Puritans. He contrasts the reform-mindedness of seventeenth-century Puritans – who he argues valued equity, community, and fairness – with our "out-of-control" capitalist self-interest. He wants Americans to learn how Puritans were able to mediate greed and self-interests by creating institutions and practices that valued the common good.[31] So, too, do the foregoing stories of the Puritan men and women provide some much-needed gender lessons. The potential of the Protestant reform movement to change gender constructs was not realized in Puritan New England because deeply rooted ideas of gender resisted the pressures of change. While there has been incredible progress over the past three hundred years, gender rules continue to circumscribe women's and men's lives.

As we see in contemporary America, gender ideology still frequently compromises equality and opportunity. In popular culture, mass media, the workforce, and politics, we see how power structures continue to privilege men. However, patriarchy limits both men and women to confined roles. Today we see a new version of hetero-hypermasculinity

---

[31] David Hall, *A Reforming People: Puritanism and the Transformation of Public Life in New England* (New York: Alfred A. Knopf, 2011), 190.

with language that tells our boys at an early age not to show emotion, to be strong, to be powerful, and to dominate women. Boys who do not fit this "bro code" identity are harassed and bullied.[32] Men's liberation to express a more fluid gender identity, career path, or self-presentation is tied to the liberation of women as well. As gay rights have made incredible progress over the last decade, with same-sex marriage legalized across the country, we also see a backlash at the state level to limit civil rights for gay, lesbian, and trans people. The cultural response is expressed on social media and in the rise of extreme, far-right rhetoric that has been given a platform since the 2016 presidential election.

While young girls have more opportunity than ever, the media continues to extol beauty as what really matters, and dictates that happiness depends on their sex appeal.[33] A new, "enlightened" sexism diminishes female power by co-opting the language of feminism for consumerism, as women are bombarded with advertisements proclaiming that they can express their strength through the beauty products, shoes, and clothes they buy.[34] Sexism has continued to allow the objectification of women, and such dehumanization leads to a greater propensity of violence against women. Sadly, it is no surprise that the most dangerous time in a woman's life is the four years she spends in college, when one in five women will experience sexual assault.[35] The successful backlash campaign against the women's movement that started in the 1980s continues to label "feminism" in negative ways – even among college women.[36] Hillary Clinton's historic run for the White House was fraught with sexist attacks, and women

---

[32] See Barbara Ehrenreich, *The Hearts of Men: American Dreams and the Flight from Commitment* (New York: Anchor Press, 1983); Michael Kimmel, *Guyland: The Perilous World Where Boys Become Men* (New York: Harper, 2009); and Michael Kimmel, *Angry White Men: American Masculinity at the End of an Era* (New York: Norton Books, 2nd ed., 2017).

[33] See Naomi Wolf, *The Beauty Myth: How Images of Beauty Are Used against Women* (New York: Harper, reprinted 2002).

[34] See Susan Douglass, *Where the Girls Are: Growing Up Female with the Mass Media* (New York: Three Rivers Press, 1995); and Douglass, *The Rise of Enlightened Sexism: How Pop Culture Took Us from Girl Power to Girls Gone Wild* (New York: St. Martin's Griffin, 2010).

[35] Kirby Dick and Amy Ziering, *The Hunting Ground: The Inside Story of Sexual Assault on American College Campuses* (New York: Hot Books, 2016).

[36] See Susan Faludi, *Backlash: The Undeclared War against Women* (New York: Crown Books, 1991). In response to the 2016 presidential election, with the rise of the national women's movement and the Women's March on Washington, there are signs that young women are embracing the word *feminism*.

leaders continue to face misogynistic assaults on their character, abilities, and appearance.[37]

As these stories from the past so clearly show us, words definitely matter. Language reinforces hierarchy, status, power, and worth. The words Puritans expected men and women to utilize in their confessions reinforced their roles and identities. The words we use today to talk about men and women reverberate into ideas with profound impact. When right-wing talk radio host Rush Limbaugh gets laughs for calling Hillary Clinton a hag, when pundits are allowed to call women sluts for demanding birth control, or when the media talks about female leaders as being "too aggressive" or "too emotional," it is a way of diminishing women's power.

Puritans offer us important examples of how language and our daily practices construct and reinforce identities, which influence power, authority, status, and voice. The "errand into the wilderness" did not create a utopia, nor did it achieve its goal of modeling for England how a society should be run. And indeed, it was not actually a "wilderness" but home to thousands of native peoples. Navigating a new gender terrain was a kind of wilderness, though, with its own threats, fears, tribulations, and potential. It is tempting to consider the what-ifs during this "experiment." What if a more traditional gender order had not vanquished the radical nature of a feminized faith? What if Puritan women had had authority in church affairs? What if a separate sphere ideology had not denied women public power? However, it is much more useful to take these lessons from the past to create a tomorrow that is more just. We need to learn from the stories that our runaway lovers, great hen squabblers, rogues, uppity women, saints, and sinners reveal through their lived experiences. Gender is a social construct, and it can change again. We can change it.

---

[37] See Jennifer L. Lawless, *It Still Takes a Candidate: Why Women Don't Run for Office* (New York: Cambridge University Press, 2010); Shawn J. Parry-Giles, *Hillary Clinton in the News: Gender and Authenticity in American Politics* (Champaign: University of Illinois Press, 2014); Susan J. Carroll, *Gender and Elections: Shaping the Future of American Politics* (New York: Cambridge University Press, 2014); Kristina Horn Sheeler and Karrin Vasby Anderson, *Woman President: Confronting Postfeminist Political Culture* (College Station: Texas A&M University Press, 2013); and Mary Douglas Vavrus, *Postfeminist News: Political Women in Media Culture* (New York: State University of New York Press, 2002).

Bibliography

PRIMARY SOURCES

Abington First Church. *Church Records of the First Church of Abington, 1714–1749.* Boston: Congregational Library & Archives.

Abstract and Index of the Records of the Inferior Court of Pleas (Suffolk County Court) Held at Boston, 1680–1698. Boston: The Historical Records Survey, 1940.

Boston Second Church. Book of Second Church Records from 1689–1717. Massachusetts Historical Society, 1690.

Notebooks from 17th Century on Sermons (Cotton Mather, Increase Mather). Massachusetts Historical Society, 1699.

Printed Sermons by Mather and Others. Massachusetts Historical Society, 1689.

Records of the Second Church, vol. III, 1675–1685. Massachusetts Historical Society.

The Cambridge and Saybrook Platforms of Church Discipline with the Confession of Faith of the New England Churches, Adopted in 1680. Boston: T. R. Marvin, 1829.

Congregational Order: The Ancient Platforms of the Congregational Churches of New England, with a Digest of Rules and Usages in Connecticut, and an Appendix Containing Notices of Congregational Bodies in Other States. Hartford: Edwin Hunt, 1845.

Connecticut Archives Crimes and Misdemeanors 1662/1663–1789, Index. Hartford: Connecticut State Library, 1913.

Dorchester Antiquarian and Historical Society Papers, 1641–1904. Massachusetts Historical Society.

Dorchester First Church. "Old Parish Song." Massachusetts Historical Society: Dorchester. First Parish Church Records, 1832.

"Will of Elizabeth Clap." Massachusetts Historical Society: Dorchester. First Parish Church. Records, II. C. Loose Property and Real Estate Records, 1715–1950, 1752.

Dorchester First Parish Church. "300th Anniversary Celebration in Dorchester." Massachusetts Historical Society: Dorchester. First Parish Church Records, 1636–1981, I.A. Loose Church Records, 1680–1981, 1929.

"Bounded Church Records, Book 1, 1636–1729." Dorchester Historical Society: Massachusetts Historical Society, 1636–1729.

"History Copied from Orcutt's, 'Good Old Dorchester'." Massachusetts Historical Society: Dorchester First Parish Church Records, 1881–1908.

"Letter About Old Burying Ground." Massachusetts Historical Society: Dorchester. First Church Records, 1936–1981, 1926.

Massachusetts Historical Society: Dorchester First Parish Church Records, 1636–1981. I.A. Loose Church Records, 1680–1981.

Dorchester First Parish Church Records. Massachusetts Historical Society, 1636–1981.

Dorchester Massachusetts Tercentenary Committee, ed. *Dorchester in the Old Bay Colony: 1630 Old and New 1930.* Dorchester: Chapple Publishing Company, Ltd., 1930.

East Hartford. First Congregational Church and Ecclesiastical Society. Records, 1699–1913. East Hartford First Church. Connecticut State Library.

East Hartford. First Congregational Church Society. Records, 1699–1795, vol. I. First Congregational Church Records. Connecticut State Library.

Fairfield. First Congregational Church. Records, 1694–1806. Connecticut State Library.

First Church of Christ Cambridge. Accounts of the First Church of Christ, Cambridge, 1668–1705. Massachusetts Historical Society, 1668–1705.

First Church of Christ in Bradford. Church Records. Congregational Library & Archives, Boston.

The First Church of Christ in Windsor, Connecticut, 1630–1905: The Two Hundred and Seventy-Fifth Anniversary November 19 to 26, 1905, Addresses and Sermons. Hartford: Hartford Printing, 1906.

First Church of Christ Simsbury, Connecticut, ed. *Simsbury First Church Records, 1682–1929.* Simsbury: First Church of Christ, 2004.

First Church of Danvers. Church Records. Congregational Library & Archives, Boston, 1672–1845.

First Congregational Church in Marblehead. Records of the Church. Congregational Library & Archives, Boston, MA.

First Congregational Church, Windsor. Family History Library, 1636–1832.

Form of Church Covenant. Misc. Collection: Massachusetts Historical Society, 1650.

Hingham Church Records. Copy of Early Ministers' Records. Massachusetts Historical Society, 1806–1862.

History of the First Church in Boston. Boston: Hall & Whiting, 1881.

James Hawke Account Book. Massachusetts Historical Society: Hingham First Church Records, 1679–1685.

John Norton's Sermons. Massachusetts Historical Society: Hingham Church Records, 1678–1716.

The Manifesto Church Record of the Church in Brattle Square Boston 1699–1872. Boston: The Benevolent Fraternity of Churches, 1902.

Plymouth Church Records, 1620–1859. New York: John Wilson & Son, 1920.

Record Commissioners of the City of Boston. *Dorchester Town Records*. Boston: Rockwell and Churchill City Printers, 1883.

Records of the Church of Christ at Cambridge in New England, 1632–1830. *Comprising the Ministerial Records of Baptisms, Marriages, Deaths, Admission to Covenant and Communion, Dismissals and Church Proceedings*, edited by Stephen Paschall Sharples. Cambridge, 1906.

Records of the East Parish Congregational Society, Barnstable, Massachusetts. Congregational Library & Archives, Boston, MA.

Records of the First Church at Dorchester in New England, 1636–1734. Boston: George H. Ellis, 1981.

Records of the First Church in Charlestown, Massachusetts, 1632–1789. Boston: David Clapp and Son, 1880.

Records of the First Church of Christ in East Windsor, Connecticut. Family History Library: 0004183 microfilm, 1695–1853.

Records of the First Church of Wareham, Massachusetts, 1739–1891. Baltimore: Clearfield Company, 1993.

A Report of the Record Commissioners of the City of Boston, Containing Boston Births from A.D. 1700 to A.D. 1800. Boston: Rockwell & Churchill, City Printers, 1894.

A Report of the Record Commissioners of the City of Boston Containing Dorchester Births, Marriages and Deaths to the End of 1825. Boston: Rockwell & Churchill, City Printers, 1891.

Salisbury First Church. Massachusetts Historical Society, 1687–1750.

Warrant for Fornication Case, Hingham. Massachusetts Historical Society: Misc. Bound, 1695–1698, 1697.

Warrant for Trial of Fornication. Massachusetts Historical Society, 1697.

Warrant to the Constables of Boston. Misc. Bound, 1695–1698: Massachusetts Historical Society, 1697.

West Parish of Barnstable, Massachusetts. Massachusetts Historical Society: photostat, 1668–1807.

West Roxbury First Church. Massachusetts Historical Society: West Roxbury, MA, 1712–1773.

Adams, Charles Francis. *Some Phases of Sexual Morality and Church Discipline in Colonial New England*. Boston: Massachusetts Historical Society, 1891.

Adams, Nehemiah, ed. *The Autobiography of Thomas Shepard, the Celebrated Minister of Cambridge, N.E.* Boston: Pierce and Parker, 1832.

Adams, William. An Account of His Experiences Transcribed from His Own Handwriting. William Adams Folder, 1659. Massachusetts Historical Society, Boston.

Alpert, Helle M. "Robert Keayne: Notes of Sermons by John Cotton and Proceedings of the First Church of Boston from 23 November 1639 to 1 June 1640." PhD diss., Tufts University, 1974.

Baker, Daniel Weld. *Historical Sketch of the Dorchester First Parish*. Boston: Turner & Co., 1916.

Barber, John W. *Historical Collections Relating to the History and Antiquities of Every Town in Massachusetts*. Baltimore: Clearfield, 1838; 1844, reprinted 1995.

Notebook. P-397 microfilm, 1715–1719. Massachusetts Historical Society, Boston.

Notebook of Religious Exercises. P-397 J. Barnard, 1701–1770. Massachusetts Historical Society, Boston.

Beecher, Henry Ward. *New Star Papers; or, View and Experiences of Religious Subjects*. New York: Derby & Jackson, 1859.

Blake, James. *Annals of the Town of Dorchester, 1750*. Boston: David Clapp, Jr., 1864.

Bradley, Samuel. *The Causes of the Innocent Pleaded*. London: Samuel Bradley, 1664.

Bragg, Robert. Robert Bragg Sermons. Massachusetts Historical Society, Boston, 1653.

Brattle, William. Sermons Delivered in Cambridge by Rev. Brattle. W. Brattle II, 1696–1715. Massachusetts Historical Society, Boston.

Brown, Richard. Sermons Notes. Hunting & Gibbs, 1696–1697. Massachusetts Historical Society, Boston.

Browne, Abraham. Volume of Reminiscences. A. Browne, 1653–1668. Massachusetts Historical Society, Boston.

Calvin, John. *Calvin's Ecclesiastical Advice*. Louisville: John Knox Press, 1991.

Clap, Captain Roger. *Memoirs of Captain Roger Clap*. Boston: Greenleaf's Printing Office for Samuel Whiting, 1731.

Clap, Nathaniel. "Epitome of Samuel Mathers, Figures or Types of the Old Testament," by Mr. Samuel Mather, 1684. Massachusetts Historical Society, Boston, 1687.

Miscellaneous Letters and Memos. N. Clap, 1687–1716. Massachusetts Historical Society, Boston.

Clap, Noah. Selling Church Buildings. Dorchester (Mass.) Church Records, 1636–1981. Massachusetts Historical Society, Boston, 1805.

Colonial Society of Massachusetts. Records of the Suffolk County Court, 1671–1680, vol. I, 2 vols. Boston: The Society, 1933.

Records of the Suffolk County Court, vol. II, 2 vols. Boston: The Society, 1933.

Seventeenth-Century New England. Boston: The Society, distributed by the University Press of Virginia, 1984, June 18 and 19, 1982.

Committee of the Dorchester Antiquarian and Historical Society. *History of the Town of Dorchester*. Boston: Ebenezer Clapp, Jr., 1859.

Connecticut Historical Society. *Records of the Particular Court of Connecticut, 1639–1663*. Hartford: Connecticut Historical Society, 1928.

Some Early Records and Documents of and Relating to the Town of Windsor Connecticut, 1639–1703. Hartford: Connecticut Historical Society, 1930.

Cotton, John. *The Keyes to the Kingdom of Heaven and Power Thereof*. London: M. Simmons, 1644.

Danforth, John. *Holy Striving against Sinful Strife*. London: Eleazer Philips, 1712.

Danforth, Samuel. Samuel Danforth Sermon. S. Danforth II. Massachusetts Historical Society, Boston, 1687.

Davenport, John. *The Saints Anchor Hold, in All Storms and Tempests Preached in Sundry Sermons*. London: WL for Geo. Hurlock, 1661.

Dorchester Antiquarian and Historical Society Papers. Letter about the First Settlers of Dorchester for the Newly Formed Antiquarian Society. Folder 1843. Dorchester Antiquarian and Historical Society, Dorchester.

Dunster, Henry. Notebook. P-84 microfilm, 1628–1654. Massachusetts Historical Society, Boston.

Ebenezer, Clapp, Jr. About Stoughton (for Naming School), Includes Biography and Will of William, Dorchester Antiquarian and Historical Society Papers. Massachusetts Historical Society, Boston, 1856.

Letter to Rev. James Flint about Flint Descendants. Bound vol. I, 1844. Dorchester Antiquarian and Historical Society, Dorchester.

Edwards, Timothy. Sermon at Suffield, October 29, 1695. Windsor Farmes by John Stoughton. Family History Library, Salt Lake City, 1695.

Eliot, John. Letter to Brother, "to Live in Faith." Massachusetts Historical Society, Boston, 1664.

Letter to Brother Regarding the Life of Faith. Misc. 1662–1666. Massachusetts Historical Society, Boston, 1664.

Notes on Sermon, "Fast at Roxbury." J. Eliot Sermon II. Massachusetts Historical Society, Boston, 1648.

Emerson, Everett H., ed. *Gods Mercie Mixed with His Justice; or His Peoples Deliverance in Times of Danger by John Cotton (1641)*. Gainesville: Scholars Facsimile Reprints, 1977.

Endicott, Frederic. *The Record of Birth, Marriages, and Deaths (Preceeded by the Records of the South Precinct of Dorchester from 1715–1727)*. Canton: Bense, 1896.

Eversull, Harry Kelso. *The Evolution of an Old New England Church: Being the History of the Old Stone Church in East Haven, Connecticut*. East Haven: unknown, 1924, p. 46.

Flint, Josiah. Notes on Sermons, ms. J. Flint Papers, 1669–1672. Massachusetts Historical Society, Boston.

Flynt, Henry. Sermons. P-116 microfilm, 1700–1760. Massachusetts Historical Society, Boston.

Genealogy of the Withington Family. Withington Family Papers, MsN.-214. Massachusetts Historical Society, Boston.

Gerrish, Joseph. *Diary*. J. Gerrish Papers, 1697–1719. Massachusetts Historical Society, Boston.

Gibbs, Henry. Henry Gibbs Sermon Notes and Accounts. H. Gibbs, 1697–1711. Massachusetts Historical Society, Boston.

Gladden, Charles Sanford. *An Index to the Vital Records of Dorchester, Massachusetts through 1825*. Boulder: Empire Reproduction and Print Company, 1970.

Gookin, Nathaniel. *Sermon Notes*. Boston: Massachusetts Historical Society, 1683.

Grant, Matthew. *Matthew Grant Diary*. Hartford: Connecticut State Library.

Some Early Records and Documents of and Relating to the Town of Windsor, Connecticut, 1639–1703. Hartford: Connecticut Historical Society, 1930.

Hale, John. *A Modest Enquiry into the Nature of Witchcraft: And How Persons Guilty of That Crime May Be Convicted: And the Means Used for Their Discovery Discussed, Both Negatively and Affirmatively, According to Scripture and Experience / by John Hale, Pastor*. Boston: B. Green, and J. Allen, for Benjamin Eliot under the Town House, 1702.

Hale, William. *A Series of Precedents and Proceedings in Criminal Causes, Extending from the Year 1475 to 1640; Extracted from the Act-Books of the Ecclesiastical Courts in the Diocese of London, Illustrative of the Discipline of the Church of England.* London: Francis & John Rivington, 1847.

Hanson, Robert Brand, ed. *Churches of Dedham, Massachusetts: Admissions, Dismissions, Adult Baptisms, and Proceedings under the Halfway Covenants, 1638–1844.* Bowie: Heritage Books, 1990.

——— ed. *The Deacon's Book: Records of the First Church, Dedham, Massachusetts, 1677–1737.* Bowie: Heritage Books, 1990.

Healy, Elizabeth. "Confession on Paternity 1667." Misc. 1667–1669. Massachusetts Historical Society, 1667.

Hobart, Peter. *Sermon Notes.* Massachusetts Historical Society: P-385 microfilm, 1671–1673.

——— Peter Hobart Diary and Record Book, 1635–1780. Vol. 121: New England Historic and Genealogical Society, 1967.

Holbrook, Jay Mack, ed. *Connecticut Colonists, Windor 1635–1703.* Oxford: Holbrook Research Institute, 1986.

Holbrook, John. *Massachusetts Vital Records: Dorchester, 1631–1868.* Oxford: Holbrook Research Institute, 1986.

Hooker, Thomas. *A Survey of the Summe of Church-Discipline.* London: Printed by A. M. for John Bellamy, 1648.

Hope, Charles H. *Records of the First Church of Dorchester, Massachusetts, 1636–1734.* Boston: George H. Ellis, 1981.

Jameson, J. Franklin, ed. *Narratives of New Netherland, 1609–1664.* New York: Charles Scribner's Sons, 1908; reprint, New York: Barnes & Noble, 1967.

Keayne, Robert. Sermon Notes. R. Keayne III (microfilm P-85, 2 reels). Massachusetts Historical Society, 1624–1646.

Lechford, Thomas. *Plain Dealing: Or, Nevves from New-England: A Short View of New-Englands Present Government, Both Ecclesiasticall and Civil, Compared with the Anciently-Received and Established Gove.* London: W. E. & I. G. for Nath: Butter, at the Signe of the Pyde Bull neere S. Austins Gate, 1642.

Marshall, John. John Marshall Diary, 1689–1711; Bulk: 1697–1711. Massachusetts Historical Society, P-363, reel 6.22 (microfilm); Ms. N-1626.

Mather, Cotton. *Addresses to Old Men, and Young Men and Little Children.* Boston: Printed by R. Pierce, for Nicholas Buttolph, at the corner shop, next to Gutteridge's Coffee-House, 1690.

——— *Proposals Assented to at Boston Council of Delegates.* Upham Family Papers: Massachusetts Historical Society, 1705.

——— *Ratio Discipline Fratrum Nov-Anglicorum.* Boston, 1726.

——— *Ornaments for the Daughters of Zion.* New York: Scholars Facsimiles and Reprints, 1741; reprinted 1950.

——— *Magnalia Christi Americana, or the Ecclesiastical History of New England*, vol. I, 2 vols. Hartford: Silas Andrus & Son, 1855.

Mather, Increase. *Jeremiads*, edited by Sacvan Bercovitch. New York: AMS Press, Inc., 1984.

Mather, Richard. *Essay on What the Visible Church Is and the Government of It.* Mather Family Papers, 1613–1819: American Antiquarian Society.

An Apology of the Churches in New-England for Church Covenant. London: T. P. & M. S. for Benjamin Allen, 1643.

A Modest & Brotherly Answer to Mr. Charles Herde His Book against the Independency of Churches. London: Henry Overton in Popes-head alley, 1644.

An Heart-Melting Exhortation Together with a Cordiall Consolation. London: A.M. for I. Rothwell, 1650.

The Summe of Certain Sermons upon Genes: 15.6. Cambridge: Sam Green, 1652.

The Last Will and Testament of Richard Mather. Dorchester Antiquarian and Historical Society. Massachusetts Historical Society, 1664.

Mather, Samuel. *A Dead Faith Anatomized: A Discourse on the Nature, and the Danger, with the Deadly Symptoms of a Death Faith in Those Who Profess the Faith of Christ.* Boston: Bartholomew Green & John Allen, 1697.

Discourse Concerning the Difficulty and Necessity of Renouncing Our Own Righteousness. Boston: J. Draper, 1707.

Morton, T. *The New English Canaan.* Boston: Prince Society, 1883.

New England Historic Genealogical Society, ed. *The New England Historical and Genealogical Register,* vol. VI. Boston: Thomas Prince, Printer and Publisher, 1852.

Orr, Charles, ed. *History of the Pequot War; the Contemporary Accounts of Mason, Underhill, Vincent and Gardener.* (Reprinted from the Collections of the Massachusetts Historical Society). Cleveland: The Helman-Taylor Company, 1897.

Oxenbridge, John. "Conversion of the Gentiles," Msc. SBd-56. Massachusetts Historical Society, 1670.

Phillips, Samuel. *Sermons.* Massachusetts Historical Society: S. Phillips, 1659–1678.

Pierce, Richard D., ed. *The Records of the First Church in Salem, Massachusetts, 1629–1736.* Salem: Essex Institute, 1974.

Pierce, Samuel. Samuel Pierce Papers, 1644–1820. Massachusetts Historical Society.

Pynchon, William. *William Pynchon and the Church of Windsor, 1640.* Massachusetts Historical Society: W. Pynchon, 1640–1647.

Quinsey, Mary. Confession of Faith. Quincy Family Papers. Massachusetts Historical Society, 1712/13.

Saltonstall, Gurdon. *Notes of Sermons Preached by Saltonstall & Others.* Massachusetts Historical Society: G. Saltonstall, 1703–1707.

Sewall, Joseph. Joseph Sewall Family Papers (1703–1716), microfilm P-363. Massachusetts Historical Society, 1703–1716.

Sewall, Samuel. *Diary in Travis Almanac.* Massachusetts Historical Society: S. Sewall, microfilm P-363, 1716.

The Diary of Samuel Sewall, 1674–1729, vols. I, II, edited by M. Halsey Thomas. New York: Farrar, Straus, and Giroux, 1973.

Shepard, Thomas. Diary of Thomas Shepard. Ms S-62, Massachusetts Historical Society, 1641.

Confessions of Thomas Shepard, edited by George Selement and Bruce C. Wooley. Boston: Colonial Society of Massachusetts, 1981.

Shurtleff, Nathaniel B., ed. *Records of the Governor and Company of the Massachusetts Bay in New England*, vol. IV Part 1. Boston: W. White, printer to the commonwealth, 1853–1854.

Spence, Joseph. *Spence's "Anecdotes, Observations, and Characters of Books and Men" a Selection, Edited, with an Introduction and Notes, by John Underhill.* PN165.S64: London: W. Scott, 1890.

Stone, Samuel. *Whole Body of Divinity in a Catecheticall Way Handled by Mr. Samuel Stone, Teacher of the Church in Hartford.* Massachusetts Historical Society: S. Stone, 1697.

Taylor, Edward. *Edward Taylor's "Church Records" and Related Sermons.* Vol. I of *The Unpublished Writings of Edward Taylor*, edited by Thomas M. Davis and Virginia L. Davis. Boston: Twayne Publishers, 1981.

Thacher, Peter. *Peter Thacher Diaries.* Massachusetts Historical Society: P. Thacher Diaries; vol. I microfilm, 1679–1699.

Papers of Rev. Thacher of Milton. Massachusetts Historical Society: P. Thacher, 1686–1727.

Sermon of Peter Thacher, Weymouth, Massachusetts. Massachusetts Historical Society: Ms S-96, 1711.

Thaddeus Mason Harris Papers, 1631–1868. 1 vol. and 1 folder. Massachusetts Historical Society.

Underhill, John. *Newes from America; or, a New and Experimental Discoverie of New England; Containing, a True Relation of Their War-Like Proceedings These Two Yeares Last Past, with a Figure of the Indian Fort, or Palizado.* London: J. D. for Peter Cole, 1638.

Unknown. "Relation Experience." Dorchester First Church Records. Massachusetts Historical Society.

Wadsworth, Benjamin. *Diary and Account Book.* Massachusetts Historical Society: B. Wadsworth, 1693–1737.

The Well-Ordered Family: Or, Relative Duties. Boston: Printed by B. Green, for Nicholas Buttolph, at his shop in Corn-Hill, 1712.

Invitations to the Gospel Feast or Free Offers of Salvation through Christ. Boston: B. Green for Benj. Eliot, 1715.

A Guide for the Doubting and Cordial for Fainting Saint. Boston: S. Kneeland, 1720.

Wigglesworth, Michael. *God's Controversy with New England: Written in the Time of the Great Drought.* Massachusetts Historical Society: Ms S-157, 1662.

The Day of Doom; or, a Poetical Description of the Great and Last Judgement with Other Poems. New York: American News Company, 1867.

Willard, Samuel. Sermons and Notes. Massachusetts Historical Society: S. Willard, 1658–1700.

Windsor, First Congregational Church South. Family History Library: 0005723 microfilm, 1694–1836.

Winthrop, John. *Winthrop's Journal, "History of New England," 1630–1649*, edited by James Kendall Hosmer. New York: Scribner's Sons, 1908.

"A Model of Christian Charity." In *Major Problems in American Colonial History: Documents and Essays*, edited by Karen Ordahl Kupperman. Lexington: D. C. Heath, 1993.

Whiting, John. Letter to Increase Mather, published in vol. VIII, Massachusetts Historical Society Collections.

Wolcott, Roger. "A Brief Account of the Agency of the Honorable John Winthrop, Esq. in the Court of King Charles the Second, Annon Dom. 1662." Massachusetts Historical Society Collections 4 (1795).

Worchester Antiquarian and Historical Society. *History of the Town of Dorchester, Massachusetts*. Boston: Ebenezer Clapp, 1859.

SECONDARY SOURCES

Anderson, Virginia DeJohn. *New England's Generation: The Great Migration and the Formation of Society and Culture in the Seventeenth Century*. Cambridge: Cambridge University Press, 1991.

Andrews, Charles McLean. *The River Towns of Connecticut: A Study of Wethersfield, Hartford, and Windsor*. Baltimore: Baltimore Publication Agency of the Johns Hopkins University, 1889.

Archer, Richard. *Fissures in the Rock: New England in the Seventeenth Century*. Hanover: University Press of New England, 2001.

Axelrod, Alan. *Chronicle of the Indian Wars: From Colonial Times to Wounded Knee*. New York: Prentice Hall, 1993.

Bailyn, Bernard. "The Apologia of Robert Keayne." *The William and Mary Quarterly* 7, no. 4 (1950): 568–87.

ed. *The Apologia of Robert Keayne: The Self-Portrait of a Puritan Merchant*. Boston: Colonial Society of Massachusetts, 1964.

The Ideological Origins of the American Revolution. New York: Belknap Press, 1968, 1992.

Barry, John M. *Roger Williams and the Creation of the American Soul: Church, State, and the Birth of Liberty*. New York: Viking, 2012.

Baskerville, Stephen. "The Family in Puritan Political Theology." *Journal of Family History* 18 (1993): 157–177.

Bellany, Alastair. "Mistress Turner's Deadly Sins: Sartorial Transgression, Court Scandal, and Politics in Early Stuart England." *Huntington Library Quarterly* 58, no. 2 (1995): 179–210.

Bercovitch, Sacvan, ed. *The American Puritan Imagination: Essays in Revaluation*. New York: Cambridge University Press, 1974.

The Puritan Origins of the American Self. New Haven: Yale University Press, 1975.

The American Jeremiad. Madison: University of Wisconsin Press, 1978.

Bloch, Ruth. *Visionary Republic: Millennial Themes in American Thought, 1750–1800*. Cambridge: University of Cambridge, 1986.

Bonfanti, Leo. *Massachusetts Bay Colony to 1645*. Wakefield: Massachusetts Pride Publications, 1980.

Bonomi, Patricia A. *Under the Cope of Heaven: Religion, Society and Politics in Colonial America*. New York: Oxford University Press, 1986.

Boyer, Paul, and Stephen Nissenbaum, eds. *The Salem Witchcraft Papers: Verbatim Transcripts of the Legal Documents of the Salem Witchcraft Outbreak of 1692*. New York: DeCapo Press, 1977.

Salem Village Witchcraft: A Documentary Record of Local Conflict in Colonial New England. Boston: Northeastern University Press, 1993.

Boyer, Paul S., and Stephen Nissenbaum. *Salem Possessed: The Social Origins of Witchcraft.* Cambridge: Harvard University Press, 1974.

Bozeman, Theodore Dwight. *To Live Ancient Lives: The Primitivist Dimension in Puritanism.* Institute of Early American History and Culture, Williamsburg. Chapel Hill: University of North Carolina Press, 1988.

The Precisianist Strain: Disciplinary Religion and Antinomian Backlash in Puritanism to 1638. Chapel Hill: University of North Carolina, 2004.

Braude, Ann. "Women's History Is American Religious History." In *Retelling U.S. Religious History,* edited by Thomas A. Tweed, 87–107. Berkeley: University of California Press, 1997.

Bray, Alan. "To Be a Man in Early Modern Society: The Curious Case of Michael Wigglesworth." *History Workshop Journal* 41 (Spring 1996): 155–65.

Breen, Louise A. *Transgressing the Bounds: Subversive Enterprises among the Puritan Elite in Massachusetts, 1630–1692.* Oxford: Oxford University Press, 2001.

Breen, T. H. *The Character of the Good Ruler: A Study of Puritan Political Ideas in New England, 1630–1730.* New Haven: Yale University Press, 1970.

Breitenberg, Mark. *Anxious Masculinity in Early Modern England.* Cambridge: Cambridge University Press, 1996.

Brown, Anne Speerschneider. "'Bound Up in a Bundle of Life': The Social Meaning of Religious Practice in Northeastern Massachusetts, 1700–1776." PhD diss., Boston University, 1995.

Brown, David C. "The Keys of the Kingdom: Excommunication in Colonial Massachusetts." *The New England Quarterly* 76, no. 4 (1994): 531–66.

Brown, Kathleen. *Good Wives, Nasty Wenches, and Anxious Patriarchs.* Chapel Hill: University of North Carolina Press, 1996.

Burg, B. R. *Richard Mather of Dorchester.* Lexington: University of Kentucky Press, 1976.

Richard Mather. Boston: Twayne Publishers, 1982.

Burnett, Amy Nelson. "Church Discipline and Moral Reformations in the Thought of Martin Bucer." *Sixteenth Century Journal* XXII (Fall, 1991): 439–56.

Burr, George Lincoln. *Narratives of the Witchcraft Cases, 1648–1706 / Edited by George Lincoln Burr.* New York: Barnes and Noble, 1975, c1914.

Bushman, Richard L. *From Puritan to Yankee: Character and Social Order in Connecticut, 1690–1765.* Cambridge: Harvard University Press, 1967.

Butler, Jon. *Awash in a Sea of Faith: Christianizing the American People.* Cambridge: Harvard University Press, 1992.

Becoming America: The Revolution before 1776. Cambridge: Harvard University Press, 2000.

Bynum, Caroline Walker. "Women's Stories, Women's Symbols: A Critique of Victor Turner's Theory of Liminality." In *Essays on Gender and the Human Body in Medieval Religion.* New York: Zone Books, 1991, 1996.

Caldwell, Patricia. *The Puritan Conversion Narrative: The Beginnings of American Expression.* New York: Cambridge University Press, 1983.

Capps, Donald. "Erikson's Theory of Religious Ritual: The Case of the Excommunication of Ann Hibbens." *Journal for the Scientific Study of Religion* 18, no. 4 (1979): 337–49.

Carroll, Lorrayne. "'My Outward Man': The Curious Case of Hannah Swarton." *Early American Literature* 31 (Winter 1996): 45–73.

Carroll, Susan J. *Gender and Elections: Shaping the Future of American Politics.* New York: Cambridge University Press, 2014.

Cave, Alfred A. *The Pequot War.* Amherst: University of Massachusetts Press, 1996.

Cohen, Charles Lloyd. *God's Caress: The Psychology of Puritan Religious Experience.* New York: Oxford University Press, 1986.

Cohen, Daniel A. "In Defense of the Gallows: Justifications of Capital Punishment in New England Execution Sermons, 1674–1825." *American Quarterly* 40 (June 1988): 147–65.

Conroy, David W. *In Public Houses: Drink and the Revolution of Authority in Colonial Massachusetts.* Chapel Hill: University of North Carolina Press, 1995.

Cooper, James F., Jr. "The Confession and Trial of Richard Wayte, Boston, 1640." *The William and Mary Quarterly* 44, no. 2 (1987): 310–32.

Cott, Nancy F. *The Bonds of Womanhood: "Woman's Sphere" in New England, 1780–1835.* New Haven: Yale University Press, 1977.

Cott, Nancy F., Jeanne Boydston, Ann Braude, Lori D. Ginzberg, and Molly Ladd-Taylor, eds. *Root of Bitterness: Documents of the Social History of American Women.* Boston: Northeastern University Press, 1996 (1972).

Crane, Elaine Forman. *Witches, Wife Beaters, and Whores: Common Law and Common Folk in Early America.* Ithaca: Cornell University Press, 2011.

Crowder, Richard Henry. *No Featherbed to Heaven: A Biography of Michael Wigglesworth, 1631–1705.* East Lansing: Michigan State University Press, 1962.

Dabhoiwala, Faramerz. *The Origins of Sex: A History of the First Sexual Revolution.* New York: Penguin Books, 2013.

Daniels, Bruce C. "The Imaginary Puritan: Literature, Intellectual Labor, and the Origins of Personal Life." *American Spectator* 35 (Spring 1984): 171–73.

The Connecticut Town: Growth and Development, 1635–1790. Middletown: Wesleyan University Press, 1979.

Davies, Kathleen M. "The Sacred Condition of Equality: How Original Were Puritan Doctrines of Marriage?" *Social History* 2, no. 5 (1977): 563–79.

Davis, Natalie Zemon. *Fiction in the Archives: Pardon Tales and Their Tellers in Sixteenth-Century France.* Stanford: Stanford University Press, 1987.

Dayton, Cornelia Hughes. "Taking the Trade: Abortion and Gender Relations in an Eighteenth-Century New England Village." *William and Mary Quarterly* 3d ser. 48 (January 1991): 19–49.

Women before the Bar: Gender, Law and Society in Connecticut, 1639–1789. Chapel Hill: University of North Carolina Press, 1995.

deForest, Louis Effingham. *Captain John Underhill Gentleman, Soldier of Fortune.* New York: DeForest Publishing Company, 1934.

Demos, John. *A Little Commonwealth: Family Life in Plymouth Colony.* New York: Oxford University Press, 1970.

ed. *Remarkable Providences, 1600–1760*. New York: G. Braziller, 1972.

The Enemy Within: 2,000 Years of Witch-Hunting in the Western World. New York: Viking, 2008.

Demos, John Putnam. *Entertaining Satan: Witchcraft and the Culture of Early New England*. New York: Oxford University Press, 1982.

Dick, Kirby, and Amy Ziering. *The Hunting Ground: The Inside Story of Sexual Assault on American College Campuses*. New York: Hot Books, 2016.

Ditz, Toby L. "Contending Masculinities in Early America." In *New Men: Manliness in Early America*, edited by Thomas A. Foster, 256–67. New York: New York University Press, 2011.

Dorsey, Gary. *Congregation: The Journey Back to the Church*. New York: Viking, 1995.

Douglas, Ann. *The Feminization of American Culture*. New York: Alfred A. Knopf, 1977.

Douglass, E. Jane Dempsey. *Women, Freedom, Calvin*. Philadelphia: Westminster Press, 1985.

Douglass, Susan. *Where the Girls Are: Growing Up Female with the Mass Media*. New York: Three Rivers Press, 1995.

The Rise of Enlightened Sexism: How Pop Culture Took Us from Girl Power to Girls Gone Wild. New York: St. Martin's Griffin, 2010.

Drake, Samuel G. *Annals of Witchcraft in New England and Elsewhere in the United States*. Boston: New England Historic Genealogical Society, 1869.

Dunn, Mary Maples. "Saints and Sisters: Congregational and Quaker Women in the Early Colonial Period." *American Quarterly* 30, no. 5, Special Issue: Women and Religion (1978): 582–601.

Women and Religion, edited by Janet Wilson James. Philadelphia: University of Pennsylvania, 1978.

Dunn, Richard S., James Savage, and Laetitia Yeandle, eds. *The Journal of John Winthrop, 1630–1649*. Cambridge: Belknap Press of Harvard University Press, 1996.

Ehrenreich, Barbara. *The Hearts of Men: American Dreams and the Flight from Commitment*. New York: Anchor Press, 1983.

Erikson, Kai T. *Wayward Puritans: A Study in the Sociology of Deviance*. New York: Wiley, 1966.

Faludi, Susan. *Backlash: The Undeclared War against Women*. New York: Crown Books, 1991.

Felt, Joseph B. *The Customs of New England*. Boston: Press of T. R. Marvin, 1853.

The Ecclesiastical History of New England: Comprising Not Only Religious, but Also Moral, and Other Relations, vol. II. BR530.F32 1855: Boston: Congregational Library Association, 1855–62, 1855.

Ferling, John. "The New England Soldier: A Study in Changing Perceptions." *American Quarterly* 33, no. 1 (1981): 26–45.

Finch, Martha L. *Dissenting Bodies: Corporealities in Early New England*. New York: Columbia University Press, 2010.

Fitzgerald, Monica D. "'Safely Delivered': Social Childbirth and Female Authority in Colonial New England." Master's thesis, California State University, Hayward, 1996.

Fletcher, Anthony. *Gender, Sex, and Subordination in England, 1500–1800.* New Haven: Yale University Press, 1995.

Forbes, Allyn Bailey, ed. *Records of the Suffolk County Court, 1671–1680,* vol. I, 2 vols. Boston: Colonial Society of Massachusetts, 1933.

Foster, Stephen. *The Long Argument: English Puritanism and the Shaping of New England Culture, 1570–1700.* Chapel Hill: Published for the Institute of Early American History and Culture, Williamsburg, VA, by the University of North Carolina Press, 1991.

Foster, Thomas A. *Sex and the Eighteenth-Century Man: Massachusetts and the History of Sexuality in America.* Boston: Beacon Press, 2006.

"New Men: Feminist Histories of Manliness in Early British America." In *New Men: Manliness in Early America,* edited by Thomas A. Foster, 1–6. New York: New York University Press, 2011.

ed. *New Men: Manliness in Early America.* New York: New York University Press, 2011.

Frost, Josephine C., ed. *Underhill Genealogy,* vol. I. New York: Myron C. Taylor in the interests of the Underhill Society of America, 1932.

Garvin, Harry R. *Women, Literature, Criticism.* London: Bucknell University Press, 1978.

George, Robert St. "'Heated' Speech and Literacy in Seventeenth-Century New England." In *Seventeenth-Century New England,* edited by David D. Hall, 275–317. Boston: The Colonial Society of Massachusetts Distributed by The University Press of Virginia, 1984.

George, Timothy. "War and Peace in the Puritan Tradition." *Church History* 53, no. 4 (1984): 492–503.

Gilligan, Carol. *In a Different Voice: Psychological Theory and Women's Development.* Cambridge: Harvard University Press, 1982.

Glenn, Myra C. "Troubled Manhood in the Early Republic: The Life and Autobiography of Sailor Horace Lane." *Journal of the Early Republic* 26, no. 1 (2006): 59–93.

Godbeer, Richard. *Sexual Revolution in Early America.* Baltimore: Johns Hopkins University Press, 2002.

"'The Cry of Sodom': Discourse, Intercourse, and Desire in Colonial New England." *William and Mary Quarterly* 52 (April 1995): 259–86.

The Salem Witch Hunt: A Brief History with Documents. New York: Bedford St. Martins, 2011.

Gomes, Peter J. "'Heroes' and 'Villains' in the Creation of the American Past." *Proceedings of the Massachusetts Historical Society,* Third Series, 95 (1983): 1–16. Boston: Massachusetts Historical Society.

Graham, Judith S. *Puritan Family Life: The Diary of Samuel Sewall.* Boston: Northeastern University Press, 2000.

Graham, Michael F. *The Uses of Reform: 'Godly Discipline' and Popular Behavior in Scotland and Beyond, 1560–1610.* New York: E. J. Brill, 1996.

Grasso, Christopher. *A Speaking Aristocracy: Transforming Public Discourse in Eighteenth-Century Connecticut.* Williamsburg: Omohundro Institute of Early American History and Culture, 1999.

Greven, Philip. *The Protestant Temperament: Patterns of Child-Rearing, Religious Experience, and the Self in Early America*. New York: Alfred A. Knopf, 1977.

Gudorf, Christine E. "The Social Construction of Sexuality." In *God Forbid: Religion and Sex in American Public Life*, edited by Kathleen M. Sands, 42–59. Oxford: Oxford University Press, 2000.

Gustafson, Sandra M. *Eloquence Is Power: Oratory and Performance in Early America*. Chapel Hill: Published for the Omohundro Institute of Early American History and Culture by the University of North Carolina Press, 2000.

"Morality and Citizenship in the Early Republic." *American Literary History* 15, no. 1 (2003): 172–87.

Haberly, David T. "Male Anxiety and Sacrificial Masculinity: The Case of Echeverría." *Hispanic Review* 73 (Summer 2005): 291–307.

Hacker, David J., and Daniel Scott Smith. "Cultural Demography: New England Deaths and the Puritan Perception of Risk." *Journal of Interdisciplinary History* XXVI (Winter 1996): 367–92.

Hall, David D. *Puritanism in Seventeenth-Century Massachusetts*. New York: Hold, Rinehart, and Winston, 1968.

The Faithful Shepherd: A History of the New England Ministry in the Seventeenth Century. Williamsburg: Institute of Early American History, University of North Carolina Press, 1972.

ed. *Saints and Revolutionaries: Essays on Early American History*. New York: W. W. Norton Books, 1984.

Worlds of Wonder, Days of Judgment: A Popular Religious Belief in Early New England. New York: Alfred A. Knopf: Distributed by Random House, 1989.

ed. *The Antinomian Controversy, 1636–1638: A Documentary History*. Durham: Duke University Press, 1990.

ed. *Witch-Hunting in Seventeenth-Century New England: A Documentary History, 1638–1692*. Boston: Northeastern University Press, 1991.

ed. *Lived Religion in America: Toward a History of Practice*. Princeton: Princeton University Press, 1997.

"Narrating Puritanism." In *New Directions in American Religious History*, edited by D. G. Hart and Harry S. Stout. New York: Oxford University Press, 1997.

A Reforming People: Puritanism and the Transformation of Public Life in New England. New York: Alfred A. Knopf, 2011.

Hall, David, and Alan Taylor. "Reassessing the Local History of New England." In *New England: A Bibliography of Its History*, edited by Roger Parks. Hanover: University Press of New England, 1989.

Hall, Timothy D. *Anne Hutchinson: Puritan Prophet*. New York: Longman, 2010.

Hambrick-Stowe, Charles E. *The Practice of Piety: Puritan Devotional Disciplines in Seventeenth-Century New England*. Chapel Hill: Institute of Early American History and Culture, Williamsburg, VA by the University of North Carolina Press, 1982.

Hansen, Ann Natalie. *The Dorchester Group: Puritanism and the Revolution*. Columbus: At the Sign of the Clock, 1987.

Harris, Gerald. "The Beginnings of Church Discipline: 1 Corinthians 5." *New Testament Studies* 37 (1991): 1–21.

Harrison, Wes. "The Role of Women in Anabaptist Thought and Practice: The Hutterite Experience of the Sixteenth and Seventeenth Centuries." *Sixteenth Century Journal* XXIII, no. 1 (1992): 49–69.

Hauptman, Lawrence M. "John Underhill: A Psychological Portrait of an Indian Fighter." *The Hudson Valley Regional Review* 9 (1992): 101–11.

Hazen, Azel Washburn. *A Brief History of the First Church of Christ in Middleton Connecticut for Two Centuries and a Half, 1688–1918.* Middletown: Azel Washburn Hazen, 1920.

Heimert, Alan. *Religion and the American Mind: From the Great Awakening to the Revolution.* Cambridge: Harvard University Press, 1966.

Herndon, Ruth Wallis. *Unwelcome Americans: Living in the Margins in Early New England.* Philadelphia: University of Pennsylvania Press, 2001.

Hobart, Benjamin. *History of the Town of Abington, Plymouth Colony, Massachusetts from Its First Settlement.* Abington: T. H. Carter & Sons, 1866.

Hoffman, Ronald, Mechal Sobel, and Fredricks J. Teute, eds. *Through a Glass Darkly: Reflections on Personal Identity in Early America.* Chapel Hill: University of North Carolina Press, 1997.

Holifield, E. Brooks. *The Covenant Sealed: The Development of Puritan Sacramental Theology in Old and New England, 1570–1720.* New Haven: Yale University Press, 1974.

"Peace, Conflict, and Ritual in Puritan Congregations." *Journal of Interdisciplinary History* XXIII (Winter 1993): 551–70.

Howard, Daniel. *A New History of Old Windsor Connecticut.* Windsor Locks: The Journal Press, 1935.

Hubbard, William. *A General History of New England: From the Discovery to MDCLXXX.* Boston: Massachusetts Historical Society, 1848.

Hutchinson, Thomas. *The History of the Colony of Massachusetts Bay: From the First Settlement Thereof in 1628, until Its Incorporation with the Colony of Plimouth Province, Province of Main, etc., by the Charter of King William and Queen Mary in 1691.* Vol. 1. Boston: Thomas and John Fleet, 1764.

Hutchinson, Thomas. *Anne Hutchinson in Massachusetts/from Governor Hutchinson's History of Massachusetts Bay.* Boston: Directors of the Old South Work, 1907.

Ingram, Martin. *Church, Courts, Sex, and Marriage in England, 1570–1640.* New York: Cambridge University Press, 1987.

Isaac, Rhys. *The Transformation of Virginia, 1740–1790.* Chapel Hill: Omohundro Institute of Early American History and Culture, University of North Carolina Press, 1999.

James, Janet Wilson, ed. *Women in American Religion.* Philadelphia: University of Pennsylvania Press, 1978.

Jones, Mary Jeanne Anderson. *Congregational Commonwealth Connecticut, 1636–1662.* Middletown: Wesleyan University Press, 1968.

Jones, Phyllis M., and Nicholas R. Jones, eds. *Salvation in New England: Selections from the Sermons of the First Preachers.* London: University of Texas Press, 1977.

Juster, Susan. *Disorderly Women: Sexual Politics and Evangelism in Revolutionary New England*. London: Cornell University Press, 1994.

Kamensky, Jane. *Governing the Tongue: The Politics of Speech in Early New England*. New York: Oxford University Press, 1999.

Karlsen, Carol F. *The Devil in the Shape of a Woman: Witchcraft in Colonial New England*. New York: W. W. Norton Books, 1987.

Kerber, Linda K. "The Republican Mother." In *Women's America: Refocusing the Past*, 4th ed., edited by Linda K. Kerber and Jane Sherron De Hart, 89–95. New York: Oxford University Press, 1982 (1995).

Kerber, Linda K., and Jane Sherron DeHart, eds. *Women's America: Refocusing the Past*. New York: Oxford University Press, 1995.

Kimmel, Michael. *Guyland: The Perilous World Where Boys Become Men*. New York: Harper, 2009.

Angry White Men: American Masculinity at the End of an Era, 2nd ed. New York: W. W. Norton Books, 2017.

Kirkley, Evelyn A. "Is It Manly to Be a Christian? The Debate in Victorian and Modern America." In *Redeeming Men: Religion and Masculinities*, edited by W. Merle Longwood, Steven B. Boyd, and Mark W. Muesse. Louisville: Westminster John Knox Press, 1996.

Koehler, Lyle. *A Search for Power: The "Weaker Sex" in Seventeenth-Century New England*. Urbana: University of Illinois Press, 1980.

Kuhns, Maude Pinney. *The "Mary and John": A Story of the Founding of Dorchester, Massachusetts, 1630*. Rutland: Charles E. Tuttle, 1943.

Lake, Peter. "Feminine Piety and Personal Potency: The 'Emancipation' of Mrs. Jane Ratcliffe." *The Seventeenth Century* ii (1987): 143–65.

Lang, Amy Schrager. *Prophetic Woman: Anne Hutchinson and the Problem of Dissent in the Literature of New England*. Berkeley: University of California Press, 1987.

LaPlante, Eve. *American Jezebel: The Uncommon Life of Anne Hutchinson, the Woman Who Defied the Puritans*. San Francisco: Harper San Francisco, 2004.

Salem Witch Judge: The Life and Repentance of Samuel Sewall. New York: HarperCollins, 2007.

Laqueur, Thomas Walter. *Making Sex: Body and Gender from the Greeks to Freud*. Cambridge: Harvard University Press, 1990.

Lasser, Carol. "Gender, Ideology, and Class in the Early Republic." *Journal of the Early Republic* 10, no. 3 (1990): 331–37.

Lawless, Jennifer L. *It Still Takes a Candidate: Why Women Don't Run for Office*. New York: Cambridge University Press, 2010.

Lepore, Jill. *The Name of War: King Philip's War and the Origins of American Identity*. New York: Alfred A. Knopf, 1998.

Levy, Barry. *Quakers and the American Family: British Settlement in the Delaware Valley*. New York: Oxford University Press, 1988.

Town Born: The Political Economy of New England from Its Founding to the Revolution. Philadelphia: University of Pennsylvania Press, 2013.

Lindenauer, Leslie J. *Piety and Power: Gender and Religious Culture in the American Colonies, 1630–1700*. New York: Routledge, 2002.

Lindholdt, Paul J. "Crimes of Gender in Puritan America." *American Quarterly* 40 (December 1988): 563–63.

Lindman, Janet Moore. "Acting the Manly Christian: White Evangelical Masculinity in Revolutionary Virginia." *The William and Mary Quarterly* 57, no. 2 (2000): 393–416.

Little, Ann M. "Men on Top? The Farmer, the Minister, and Marriage in Early New England." *Pennsylvania History: A Journal of Mid-Atlantic Studies* 65, Empire, Society, and Labor Essays in Honor of Richard S. Dunn (Summer 1997): 123–50.

Abraham in Arms: War and Gender in Colonial New England. Philadelphia: University of Pennsylvania Press, 2007.

Lockridge, Kenneth. *A New England Town: The First Hundred Years, Dedham, Massachusetts, 1636–1736*. New York: W. W. Norton Books, 1970.

Literacy in Colonial New England: An Enquiry into the Social Context of Literacy in the Early Modern West. New York: W. W. Norton Books, 1974.

On the Sources of Patriarchal Rage: The Commonplace Books of William Byrd and Thomas Jefferson and the Gendering Power in the Eighteenth Century. New York: New York University Press, 1992.

Lombard, Anne S. *Making Manhood: Growing Up Male in Colonial New England*. Cambridge: Harvard University Press, 2003.

Lyttle, David. *Studies in Religion in Early American Literature: Edwards, Poe, Channing, Emerson, Some Minor Transcendentalists, Hawthorne, and Thoreau*. New York: University Press of America, 1983.

Mack, Phyllis. *Visionary Women: Ecstatic Prophecy in Seventeenth-Century England*. Berkeley: University of California Press, 1992.

MacLean, Ian. *The Renaissance Notion of Woman: A Study in the Fortunes of Scholasticism and Medical Science in European Intellectual Life*. New York: Cambridge University Press, 1980.

Madden, Etta. "Resurrecting Life through Rhetorical Ritual: A Buried Value of the Puritan Funeral Sermon." *Early American Literature* 26 (February 1991): 232–50.

Masson, Margaret W. "The Typology of the Female as a Model for the Regenerate: Puritan Preaching, 1690–1730." *Signs* 2, no. 2 (1976): 304–15.

McCurdy, John Gilbert. "Gentlemen and Soldiers: Competing Visions of Manhood in Early Jamestown." In *New Men: Manliness in Early America*, edited by Thomas A. Foster, 9–30. New York: New York University Press, 2011.

McCusker, John J. *The Economy of British America, 1607–1789*. Chapel Hill: University of North Carolina Press, 1991.

McElrath, Joseph R., and Allen P. Robb, eds. *The Complete Works of Anne Bradstreet*. Boston: Twayne Publishers, 1981.

McGiffert, Michael, ed. *God's Plot: Puritan Spirituality in Thomas Shepard's Cambridge*. Amherst: University of Massachusetts Press, 1994.

McLouglin, William G. *New England Dissent, 1630–1833: The Baptists and the Separation of Church and State*. Cambridge: Harvard University Press, 1971.

McManus, Edward J. *Law and Liberty in Early New England*. Amherst: University of Massachusetts Press, 1993.

Mead, Daniel M. *A History of the Town of Greenwich, Fairfield County Connecticut.* New York: Baker & Godwin, Printers, 1857.

Mentzer, Raymond A. *Sins and the Calvinists: Morals, Control, and the Consistory in the Reformed Tradition.* Kirksville: Sixteenth-Century Journal Publishers, Inc., 1994.

Merchant, Carolyn. *The Death of Nature: Women, Ecology and the Scientific Revolution.* San Francisco: Harper & Row, 1980.

Meyer, Freeman. *Connecticut Congregationalism in the Revolutionary Era.* Hartford: American Revolution Bicentennial Commission of Connecticut, 1977.

Meyers, Debra. *Common Whores, Vertuous Women, and Loveing Wives.* Bloomington: Indiana University Press, 2003.

Middlekauff, Robert. *The Mathers: Three Generations of Puritan Intellectuals, 1596–1728.* New York: Oxford University Press, 1999 (1971).

Miller, Joshua. "Direct Democracy and the Puritan Theory of Membership." *Journal of Politics* 53 (February 1991): 57–74.

Miller, Perry. *The New England Mind: The Seventeenth Century.* Cambridge: Harvard University Press, 1939.

Minkema, Kenneth P. "A Great Awakening Conversion: The Relation of Samuel Belcher." *The William and Mary Quarterly* 44, no. 1 (1987): 121–27.

"The Devil Will Roar in Me Anon": The Possession of Martha Roberson, Boston, 1741." In *Spellbound: Women and Witchcraft in America*, edited by Elizabeth Reis. New York: SR Books, 1998.

Moran, Gerald Francis. *The Puritan Saint: Religious Experience, Church Membership, and Piety in Connecticut, 1636–1776.* Newark: Rutgers University, 1973.

"'Sisters in Christ': Women and the Church in Seventeenth-Century New England." In *Women in American Religion*, edited by Janet Wilson James. New York: Harper & Row, 1976.

Moran, Gerald F., and Maris A. Vinovskis. *Religion, Family and the Life Course: Explorations in the Social History of Early America.* New York: Harper & Row, 1992.

Morgan, Edmund Sears. "The Case against Anne Hutchinson." *The New England Quarterly* 10, no. 4 (1937): 635–47.

The Puritan Family: Religion and Domestic Relations in Seventeenth-Century New England. New York: Harper & Row, 1944 (1966).

ed. *The Diary of Michael Wigglesworth, 1653–1657.* New York: Harper & Row, 1946.

The Puritan Dilemma: The Story of John Winthrop, edited by Oscar Handlin. Boston: Little, Brown, 1958.

Visible Saints: The History of a Puritan Idea. Ithaca: Cornell University Press, 1963; 1965.

Roger Williams: The Church and State. New York: Harcourt, Brace & World, 1967.

Morris, M. Michelle Jarrett. *Under Household Government: Sex and Family in Puritan Massachusetts.* Cambridge: Harvard University Press, 2013.

Moxey, Keith. *Peasants, Warriors, and Wives: Popular Imagery in the Reformation.* Chicago: University of Chicago Press, 1989.

Muir, Edward, and Guido Ruggiero. *Sex and Gender in Historical Perspective.* Baltimore: Johns Hopkins University Press, 1990.

Neem, Johann N. "Creating Social Capital in the Early American Republic: The View from Connecticut." *The Journal of Interdisciplinary History* 39, no. 4 (2009): 471–95.

Nelson, William E. *Dispute and Conflict Resolution in Plymouth County, Massachusetts, 1725–1825.* Chapel Hill: University of North Carolina Press, 1981.

Norton, Mary Beth. *Liberty's Daughters: The Revolutionary Experience of American Women, 1750–1800.* New York: HarperCollins, 1980.

Founding Mothers and Fathers: Gendered Power and the Founding of Early American Society. New York: Alfred A. Knopf, 1996.

In the Devil's Snare: The Salem Witchcraft Crisis of 1692. New York: Alfred A. Knopf, 2002.

Separated by Their Sex: Women in Public and Private in the Colonial Atlantic World. Ithaca: Cornell University Press, 2011.

Oberholzer, Emil, Jr. *Delinquent Saints: Disciplinary Action in the Early Congregational Churches of Massachusetts.* New York: Columbia University Press, 1956.

Ortner, Sherry B. *Making Gender: The Politics and Erotics of Culture.* Boston: Beacon Press, 1996.

Ortner, Sherry B., and Harriet Whitehead, eds. *Sexual Meanings, the Cultural Construction of Gender and Sexuality.* New York: Cambridge University Press, 1981.

Parks, Roger, ed. *New England: A Bibliography of Its History*, edited by historiographic essay by David D. Hall and Alan Taylor, Committee for a New England Bibliography. Hanover: University Press of New England, 1989.

Parry-Giles, Shawn J. *Hillary Clinton in the News: Gender and Authenticity in American Politics.* Champaign: University of Illinois Press, 2014.

Piercy, Josephine K. *The Tenth Muse by Anne Bradstreet.* Gainesville: Scholars Facisimile, 1965.

Plane, Ann Marie. "Indian and English Dreams: Colonial Hierarchy and Manly Restraint in Seventeenth-Century New England." In *New Men: Manliness in Early America*, edited by Thomas A. Foster, 31–47. New York: New York University Press, 2011.

Poole, William F., Justin Winsor, and Paul Royster. "The Case of Ann Hibbins, Executed for Witchcraft at Boston." 1656. *Joshua Scottow Papers.*

Porterfield, Amanda. *Female Piety in Puritan New England: The Emergence of Religious Humanism.* New York: Oxford University Press, 1992.

The Power of Religion: A Comparative Introduction. New York: Oxford University Press, 1998.

Potter, Mary. "Gender Equality and Gender Hierarchy in Calvin's Theory." *Signs* 11, no. 4 (1986): 735–39.

Reis, Elizabeth. "The Devil, the Body, and the Feminine Soul in Puritan New England." *Journal of American History* 82, June (1995): 15–36.

Damned Women: Sinners and Witches in Puritan New England. Ithaca: Cornell University Press, 1997.

Reuther, Rosemary Radford. "Church, Feminism, and Family." In *God Forbid: Religion and Sex in American Public Life*, edited by Kathleen M. Sands, 93–103. Oxford: Oxford University Press, 2000.

Robey, Richard C., ed. *Increase Mather vs. Soloman Stoddard*. New York: Arno Press, 1972.

Romero, R. Todd. *Making War and Minting Christians*. Boston: University of Massachusetts Press, 2011.

Rorabaugh, W. T. "The Political Duel in the Early Republic." *Journal of the Early Republic* 15, no. 1 (1995): 1–23.

Rosenberg, Rosalind. *Beyond Separate Spheres: Intellectual Roots of Modern Feminism*. New Haven: Yale University Press, 1982.

Rose-Troup, Frances. *John White, the Patriarch of Dorchester and the Founder of Massachusetts, 1575–1648, with an Account of the Early Settlement in Massachusetts, 1620–1630*. New York: Putnam and Sons, 1930.

The Massachusetts Bay Company and Its Predecessors. Bowie: Heritage Books, 1998.

Ross, Richard J. "The Legal Past of Early New England: Notes for the Study of Law, Legal Culture, and Intellectual History." *William and Mary Quarterly* 50 (January 1993): 28–41.

Salinger, Sharon. *Taverns and Drinking in Early America*. Baltimore: Johns Hopkins University Press, 2002.

Salisbury, Neal, ed. *The Sovereignty and Goodness of God, Together with the Faithfulness of His Promises Displayed: Being a Narrative of the Captivity and Restoration of Mrs. Mary Rowlandson*. Boston: Bedford Books, 1996.

Sands, Kathleen M., ed. *God Forbid: Religion and Sex in American Public Life*, edited by Harry S. Stout, Religion in America Series. Oxford: Oxford University Press, 2000.

Saunders, Ralph Helperin. "You Be Our Eyes and Ears: Doing Community Policing in Dorchester." PhD diss., University of Arizona, 1997.

Schaedler, Louis C. "Whittier's Attitude towards Colonial Puritanism." *The New England Quarterly* 21, no. 3 (September 1948): 350–67.

Schenck, Elizabeth Hubbell. *The History of Fairfield, from the Settlement of the Town in 1639 to 1818*. New York: self-pub., 1889.

Schocket, Andrew M. "Thinking About Elites in the Early Republic." *Journal of the Early Republic* 25, no. 4 (2005): 547–55.

Scholten, Catherine M. *Childbearing in American Society: 1650–1850*. New York: New York University, 1985.

Scott, Joan. "Gender: A Useful Category of Historical Analysis." *American Historical Review* 91, no. 5 (1986): 1053–1075.

Selement, George. *Keepers of the Vineyard: The Puritan Ministry and Collective Culture in Colonial New England*. Lanham: University Press of America, 1984.

"The Meeting of Elite and Popular Minds at Cambridge, New England, 1638–1645." *William and Mary Quarterly* 41, no. I (1984): 32–48.

Seligman, Adam. "Inner-Worldly Individualism and the Institutionalization of Puritanism in Late Seventeenth-Century New England." *British Journal of Sociology* 41 (December 1990): 537–57.

Sheeler, Kristina Horn, and Karrin Vasby Anderson. *Woman President: Confronting Postfeminist Political Culture.* College Station: Texas A&M University Press, 2013.

Sheils, Richard D. "The Feminization of American Congregationalism, 1730–1835." *American Quarterly* 33, no. 1 (1981): 42–62.

Shelley, Henry C. *John Underhill: Captain of New England and New Netherland.* New York: D. Appleton, 1932.

Smith-Rosenberg, Caroll. *Disorderly Conduct: Visions of Gender in Victorian America.* New York: Oxford University Press, 1986.

Snyder, Terri L. "Refiguring Women in Early American History." *The William and Mary Quarterly* 69, no. 3 (2012): 421–50.

Springer, Marlene. *What Manner of Woman: Essays of England and American Life and Literature.* New York: New York University Press, 1977.

St. George, Robert Blair. "'Heated' Speech and Literacy in Seventeenth-Century New England." In *Seventeenth Century New England,* ed. David D. Hall. Boston: Colonial Society of Massachusetts, distributed by the University Press of Virginia, 1984.

Conversing by Signs: Poetics of Implication in Colonial New England. Chapel Hill: University of North Carolina Press, 1998.

Stabler, Lois K., and Laurel Thatcher Ulrich. "'Girling of It' in Eighteenth-Century New Hampshire." In *The Dublin Seminar for New England Folklife Annual Proceedings; Families and Children,* edited by Peter Benes. Boston: Boston University Press, 1985.

Stanford, Donald E., ed. *The Poems of Edward Taylor.* New Haven: Yale University Press, 1960.

Stiles, Henry R. *The History and Genealogies of Ancient Windsor, Connecticut, 1635–1891.* Volume I History. Hartford: Press of the Case, Lockwood & Brainard Company, 1891.

Families of Ancient Windsor, Connecticut: Consisting of Volume II of the History and Genealogies of Ancient Windsor, Connecticut; Including East Windsor, South Windsor, Bloomfield, Windsor Locks, and Ellington, 1635–1891. Baltimore: Reprinted for Clearfield Co. by Genealogical Publishing Company, 1999.

Stone, Lawrence. *The Family, Sex, and Marriage in England, 1500–1800.* New York: Harper & Row, 1977.

Stoughton, John A. *"Windsor Farmes": A Glimpse of an Old Parish, Together with the Deciphered Inscriptions from a Few Foundation Stones of a Much Abused Theology.* Hartford: Clark & Smith, book and job printers, 1883.

Stout, Harry S. *The New England Soul: Preaching and Religious Culture in Colonial New England.* New York: Oxford University Press, 1986.

Thomas, Keith. *Religion and the Decline of Magic.* New York: Scribner, 1971.

Thompson, Roger. *Sex in Middlesex: Popular Mores in a Massachusetts County, 1649–1699.* Amherst: University of Massachusetts Press, 1986.

Tobin, Lad. "A Radically Different Voice: Gender and Language in the Trials of Anne Hutchinson." *Early American Literature* 25 (Fall 1990): 353–70.

Todd, Margo. "Humanists, Puritans, and the Spiritualized Household." *Church History* 49 (March 1980).

Trumbull, J. Hammond, ed. *Public Records of the Colony of Connecticut*. Hartford: Brown & Parsons, 1850.

Turner, Victor. *The Ritual Process: Structure and Anti-Structure*. Chicago: Aldine Publishing Company, 1969.

Ulrich, Laurel Thatcher. *Good Wives: Image and Reality in the Lives of Women in Northern New England, 1650–1750*. New York: Vintage Books, 1980.

———. "Daughters of Liberty: Religious Women in Revolutionary New England." In *Women in the Age of the American Revolution*, edited by Ronald Hoffman and Peter J. Albert. Charlottesville: University of Virginia Press, 1989.

———. *A Midwife's Tale: The Life of Martha Ballard, Based on Her Diary, 1785–1812*. New York: Vintage, 1991.

Underhill, David Harris. *The Underhill Burying Ground, an Account of a Parcel of Land Situate at Locust Valley, Long Island, New York, Deeded by the Matinecock Indians, February Twentieth, Sixteen Hundred and Sixty Seven, to Captain John Underhill for Meritorious Service and Know*. F129.L76 U5. New York: Printed by the Hine Publishing Company, 1826 [i.e. 1926].

Valeri, Mark. *Heavenly Merchandize: How Religion Shaped Commerce in Puritan America*. Princeton: Princeton University Press, 2010.

VanBurkleo, Sandra F. "'Instruments of Seduction': A Tale of Two Women." *OAH Magazine of History* 9, no. 2 (1995): 8–18.

Vavrus, Mary Douglas. *Postfeminist News: Political Women in Media Culture*. New York: State University of New York Press, 2002.

Walker, George Leon. *History of the First Church in Hartford, 1633–1883*. Hartford: Brown & Gross, 1884.

Watkins, Owen C. *The Puritan Experience*. London: Routledge and K. Paul, 1972.

Weisman, Richard. *Witchcraft, Magic and Religion in 17th-Century Massachusetts*. Amherst: University of Massachusetts Press, 1984.

Welter, Barbara. "The Cult of True Womanhood: 1820–1860." *American Quarterly* 18, Part 1 (1966): 151–74.

Wertz, Richard W., and Dorothy C. Wertz. *Lying-In: A History of Childbirth in America*. New York: The Free Press, 1977.

Westerkamp, Marilyn J. "Engendering Puritan Religious Culture in Old and New England." *Pennsylvania History* 64, Special Supplement (Summer 1977): 105–27.

———. *Triumph of the Laity: Scots-Irish Piety and the Great Awakening, 1625–1760*. New York: Oxford University Press, 1988.

———. "Anne Hutchinson, Sectarian Mysticism, and the Puritan Order." *Church History* 59 (December 1990): 482–96.

———. "Puritan Patriarchy and the Problem of Revelation." *Journal of Interdisciplinary History* XXIII (Winter 1993): 571–95.

———. *Women and Religion in Early America, 1600–1850*. New York: Oxford University Press, 1999.

Wiesner-Hanks, Merry. *Christianity and Sexuality in the Early Modern World: Regulating Desire, Reforming Practice*. Christianity and Society in the Modern World, edited by Hugh McLeod. New York: Routledge, 2010.

Wiethaus, Ulrike. "Christian Piety and the Legacy of Medieval Masculinity." In *Redeeming Men: Religion and Masculinities*, edited by W. Merle Longwood,

Mark W. Muesse, and Steven B. Boyd. Louisville: Westminster John Knox Press, 1996.

Wilberforce, Robert Isaac. *Church Courts and Church Discipline.* London: John Murray, 1843.

Willen, Diane. "Godly Women in Early Modern England: Puritanism and Gender." *Journal of Ecclesiastical History* 43 (October 1992): 561–81.

Williams, Selmar R. *Divine Rebel: The Life of Anne Marbury Hutchinson.* New York: Holt, Rinehard and Winston, 1981.

Wilson, Lisa. *Ye Heart of a Man.* New Haven: Yale University Press, 1999.

Winship, Michael P. *Making Heretics: Militant Protestantism and Free Grace in Massachusetts, 1636–1641.* Princeton: Princeton University Press, 2002.

The Times and Trial of Anne Hutchinson: Puritans Divided. Lawrence: University Press of Kansas, 2005.

Winsor, Justin, ed. *The Memorial History of Boston, Including Suffolk County, Massachusetts, 1630–1880,* vol. I. Boston: Ticknor and Company, 1880.

Early Boston. F64.5.W59; 1850–1892. Massachusetts Historical Society, 1881.

Wolf, Naomi. *The Beauty Myth: How Images of Beauty Are Used against Women.* New York: Harper, reprinted 2002.

Wood, Gordon S. *The Radicalism of the American Revolution.* New York: Vintage Books, 1991.

Zurawski, Carol. *Seventeenth-Century Survey of Dorchester,* edited by David R. Starbuck. Boston: Boston University, 1979.

Zurawski, Carol, and Lynn Whitney. "Seventeenth Century Survey of Dorchester." PhD diss., Boston University, 1979.

Index